WOLF

Two American Teenagers
and Mexico's Most
Dangerous Drug Cartel

BOYS

DAN SLATER

Simon & Schuster
NEW YORK LONDON TORONTO SYDNEY NEW DELHI

Simon & Schuster
1230 Avenue of the Americas
New York, NY 10020

First Simon & Schuster hardcover edition September 2016

SIMON & SCHUSTER and colophon are registered trademarks
of Simon & Schuster, Inc.

For information about special discounts for bulk purchases,
please contact Simon & Schuster Special Sales at 1-866-506-1949
or business@simonandschuster.com.

The Simon & Schuster Speakers Bureau can bring authors to your
live event. For more information or to book an event, contact the
Simon & Schuster Speakers Bureau at 1-866-248-3049 or visit our
website at www.simonspeakers.com.

Interior design by Lewelin Polanco

Manufactured in the United States of America

10 9 8 7 6 5 4 3 2 1

Library of Congress Cataloging-in-Publication Data is available.

ISBN 978-1-5011-2654-3
ISBN 978-1-5011-2662-8 (ebook)

CONTENTS

7861

CONTENTS

WOLF BOYS

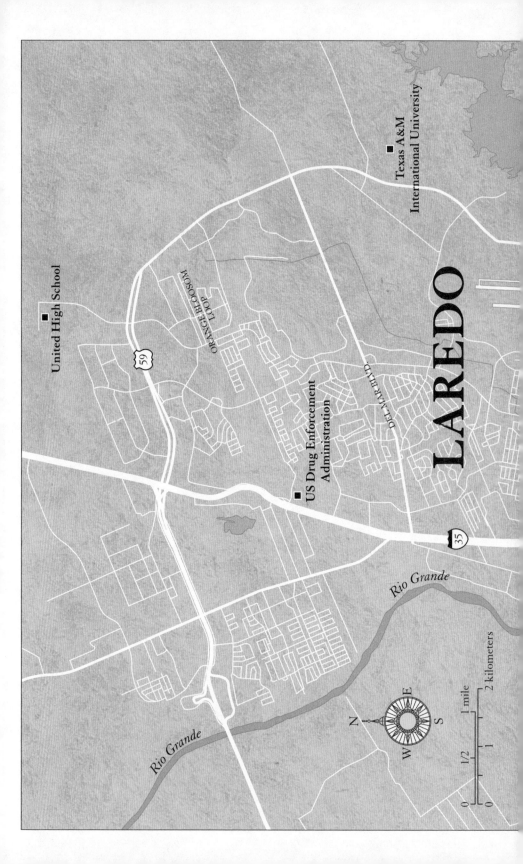

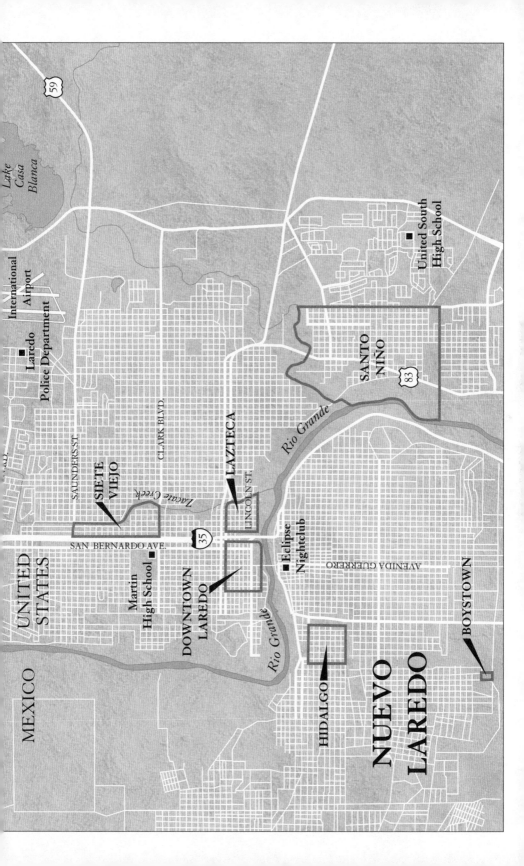

PROLOGUE

As dusk settled over South Texas, Gabriel Cardona stood in the kitchen of the safe house and offered a last-minute tutorial. "You walk up to him and just *poom!*" he told his newest recruit. "*En la cabezota*. But with both hands. In the crown, *poom!* You'll fuck him up. Otherwise, *poom! poom! poom! poom!* Four in the chest. And then *en la cabezota,* to make sure."

The recruit nodded, and scattered to his preparations.

Four days had passed without a successful action. Other than one bungled job, in which they nearly killed the wrong guy, they'd been hanging out in the rented house, a charming brick rambler on Orange Blossom Loop, eating fast food, mowing the lawn, shopping for housewares at Wal-Mart, and talking to girls on their wiretapped cell phones. They were young and vigorous, fiery in their belief of success. Now they were getting ready to kill again.

"It's time to take care of business!" Gabriel yelled, clapping encouragement like a high school football coach on Friday night. He'd come quite a way from the ramshackle house across town on Lincoln Street—three blocks north of the international border between Mexico and Laredo, Texas—where his mother raised him and his three brothers on less than $20,000 a year. Gone were the days of borrowing mom's Escort, of dressing in jeans and generic white T-shirts. His closet was now stuffed with brand names like Hugo Boss, Ralph Lauren, Versace, and Kenneth Cole. He still cut his hair at Nydia's Salon. That would never change. But now he drove new cars—a Jetta, a Ram, a Mercedes SUV. His silver Benz was being customized; it would be ready any day.

He paced the kitchen, threw away a greasy fast-food bag, and washed the dishes left in the sink.

Success, the young man was finding, came with its own stress: the hangers-on, the wannabes, the phony homies, the unwanted attention from a certain detective. The *competition*. Richard, his new lieutenant, was growing more subversive by the day. Uncle Raul, his mother's brother, a perennial troublemaker, kept hitting the clubs across the border and mouthing off, relying on his nephew's reputation to keep him out of trouble. Uncle Raul would not last long if he kept that up. And then there was Christina, she of the pretty face and the not-too-wide hips, who felt abandoned while her boy worked constantly, always on the run.

It was six months from his twentieth birthday, and Gabriel Cardona was being primed for a managerial position in a global enterprise. A bilingual businessman, savvy in two cultures, he could work both sides of the border with ease. A born leader, handsome and serious, he had caramel skin, full lips, and the dark, brooding eyes of a sad Catholic saint—the type that lined the walls of his mother's home in fading lithographs. The deity, fellow decider of fates, had cut him strong and wiry. Angel of the Lord, lord of the hood. A thug. The *chuco* that even preppy girls competed over.

He'd made some mistakes. But any man of action did. He'd

proven himself a *firme vato,* a loyal soldier with balls of steel. In the shit-nothing town of Laredo, Texas, where Company membership was the pinnacle of achievement, this status meant everything. His boss, Comandante Cuarenta—or simply "Forty"—precisely the most feared drug lord in Mexico, liked him. Liked him so much that he wanted to protect him. Recently, Forty instructed Gabriel to exclude himself from jobs, to hang back and direct via cell phone but not participate unless necessary. Liked him so much, in fact, that Gabriel had been bailed out of jail, not once, but three times in the last eight months, at a cost of several hundred thousand dollars.

The law kept letting him out. The Company kept paying for it. What clearer validation could there be?

A year earlier, when Forty began sending him on jobs in Texas— as in the *States*—Gabriel was reluctant, caught between the futureless fringe of his birth country and the narco-state where success accrued to the ruthless warrior. Doing missions in a place where authorities frowned on homicide was not an appealing prospect. But it was Forty asking. That a boy from Lazteca received orders directly from *El Comandante,* even for suicide missions, was immense.

Gabriel had long imagined a moment such as this, one of great responsibility, an opportunity to advance in a way his community admired. For months he'd been breakfasting on "roches," a heavy tranquilizer, and Red Bull. And risk, well, it was the toll of immortality. Look no further than Forty himself. Stoic. Serious. Never asked you to do something he wouldn't. Loyal to friends. Enemy to enemies. A good man, *for and about the idea.* Gabriel was part of something, and a true Wolf Boy never said no.

That evening, the cars had been cleaned, the weapons loaded. Everything was ready. This was it. The beginning of something. He could see a future. As the battle with the Sinaloans, the rival cartel, drove up costs and pinched smuggling profits, the border's underworld economy cycled down. The transport business would come and go. But enforcement was steady work. He would stack money. He would be transferred to deep Mexico, where he would run his own city. If he could cook his nemesis, La Barbie, a Sinaloan, then third-in-command was not out of the question. The other boys looked up to him. Richard would fall in line. Christina would calm down. She was mad. But earlier that evening they had returned from Applebee's, where they had had a constructive conversation. When he dropped her off, she told him to hug her. "Tighter," she said.

He moved about now with quicker steps, rolling a fist in a palm, rubbing the scars beneath his buzzed hair where shotgun fragments remained from old battles. If Gabriel could cement his reputation as a leader, if the past year could ever make sense, it would have to come now, at the battle's most crucial point, under a flood of spotlights, before hundreds of men who would either anoint him the next *mero mero,* the true shit, or throw him to the hungry tigers like one more disposable spic.

Forty said 2006 was the last year of war. Forty said Mexico's next president was on lock, paid for, and the country would be theirs. *Todo va a ser de La Compañía.* Everything will belong to the Company.

But there was a commotion outside the house, then a slamming. A stun grenade came through the front door. The concussive blast disturbed the fluid in Gabriel's ears. He wobbled. A bright flash bleached the photoreceptors in his eyes, blinding him for three seconds. *One. Two. Three.*

He was facedown on the carpet, hands cuffed behind him. He thought he might die. He thought he might escape.

The world of possibility was vast.

PART I

The Straight Hard Workers

Praise belonged to those most daring in the quest for rare and exotic things, for their physical and mental toughness, their stamina, their fighting prowess in face of sudden ambush, their audacity in the face of the unknown.

—*AZTECS,* INGA CLENDINNEN

1

You're Not from Here

Robert Garcia was twenty-nine the first time he questioned success. Every accomplishment, it seemed, came with some deficit or drawback or innocence-eroding knowledge. You earned a scholarship but didn't feel college. You won the battle but lost the bonus. You fell in love, and faced a dishonorable discharge. The autumn of 1997 should've been the brightest season in Robert's promising career, but it arrived with sorrow. The yin and the yang, he called it.

Two decades earlier, as a child of Norma and Robert Sr., Robert emigrated from Piedras Negras, Mexico, to the Texas border town of Eagle Pass—an international journey of one mile. Robert Sr., needing to support his family, had been working in the States as an illegal immigrant; once he demonstrated an income and showed that he was spending money in Texas, he gained a green card for the family, meaning that Norma, Robert Sr., Robert, and Robert's younger sister, Blanca, could come to the States as "resident aliens," not U.S.

citizens. After they arrived, Norma gave birth to another daughter, Diana, and another son, Jesse.

Robert, the oldest, started third grade in an American school. After school and on weekends, he and Robert Sr. picked cucumbers, onions, and cantaloupes on local farms. In spring and summer, Norma, a seamstress for Dickie's, the work-wear manufacturer, stayed in Eagle Pass with the girls and Jesse while Robert and his father followed fellow migrants to Oregon and Montana for the sugar beet season. There, Robert attended migrant programs at local schools. Dark-skinned but ethnically ambiguous, he found northern communities mostly welcoming, with their food festivals and roadside stands where Indians sold tourist stuff. The verdant landscapes were a reprieve from the dusty flatiron of South Texas. America was a beautiful place.

Back in Eagle Pass, land was cheap. There were no codes. People could build what they wanted. The Garcia family lived in a two-room hut while they built the home they'd live in forever. It was piecework. They saved up, then tiled the bathroom; saved more, then bought a tub. In winter they heated the place with *brazas,* coal fires in barrels, and in the mornings Robert went to school smelling like smoke.

When would the house be finished? No one asked. Work drew them together.

As other immigrants settled nearby, Robert Sr. built a one-man concession stand where he sold snacks and sodas to neighborhood kids. Robert Sr. brought his family to the States for a better way of life, but in his mind he would always be Mexican. He was proud to live next to other immigrants in Eagle Pass. By the time Reagan took office, their patch of dirt was becoming a bona fide suburb, sprouting neat rows of handmade houses. When neighbors needed assistance with an addition or a plumbing issue, they turned to "the Roberts" for help.

Robert Sr. treated his oldest boy like a man, and Robert's siblings respected him as a kind of second father. Trim, bony, and bespectacled, he walked taller than his five feet, eight inches. In high school, he enrolled in ROTC and played bass clarinet in the marching band. He finished high school a semester early, took a fast-food job at Long John Silver's, and deliberated over whether he should capitalize on a college scholarship in design, or go in a different direction.

At seventeen he seemed to know himself: hyperactive, confident. He had a talent for improvisation. He was respectful in a rank-conscious way, but didn't care what others said or advised. Introverted and impatient, he had his own way of doing things. He learned as much from his father as he did in school. He also felt the lure of service, a patriotic duty toward the adopted country that gave him and his family so much. Formal education, he decided, was not for him. So, in the summer of 1986—the same year a boy who would change Robert's life was born in Laredo, another Texas border town 140 miles southeast—Robert, much to the dismay of his non-English-speaking parents, passed up the scholarship and enlisted in the U.S. Army.

Since he'd enrolled in ROTC during high school, he arrived at basic training as a seventeen-year-old platoon leader, instructing men who were older. To compensate for the age difference, and his small size, he acted extra tough and earned the nickname Little Hitler. After basic training, he began to work as a watercraft engineer at Fort Eustis, Virginia, where he picked up a mentor, a sergeant major, who led him to work on military bases in Spain and England. On the bases, he played baseball and lifted weights. Little Hitler sported ropy arms. His neck, once nerd-thin, disappeared into his shoulders.

In the Azores islands, on a small U.S. Navy installation off the coast of Portugal, Robert met Veronica, a blond *gringa* from Arizona. The daughter of a navy man, Ronnie was the only female mechanic at the base. She was tough. While fixing the hydraulic system on a tugboat one day, Robert snuck up and slapped her neck with grease-shaft oil. She wheeled around, called him an asshole. "Fuck off!" she said. One week later they conceived a son.

Ronnie was twenty, already married to a soldier, and had a two-year-old son. Her parents never liked her husband. As far as they were concerned, he was a freeloader who drank excessively at the bar they owned in Arizona. They didn't like seeing their daughter be the breadwinner *and* the parent. And now here was Robert: didn't drink, didn't smoke, would do anything for her.

But adultery in the military was a serious crime; at the discretion of a military court, it carried felony time and a dishonorable discharge. The chiefs read Ronnie and Robert their rights. They owned up to the affair. Ronnie's husband flew to Portugal; furious, he stomped around the base, drank, got in fights, and broke windows at Ronnie's house. No one liked her husband. So the chiefs held a meeting to arbitrate the love triangle, and let Robert and Ronnie walk away with reprimands. When the husband called Ronnie's mother and said, "Your daughter's a whore!" Ronnie's father grabbed the phone and said: "You weren't even born from a woman! Two freight trains bumped together and you fell out of a hobo's ass!" From there, the separation went smoothly.

In 1991, Robert's four-year military contract neared its end as the First Gulf War started. Robert saw other soldiers reenlisting and collecting $10,000 bonuses. He was willing to reenlist, until the U.S. government offered him citizenship instead of the bonus. Robert didn't care much about citizenship. Like his father, he'd always think of himself as Mexican; and, besides, his resident-alien status entitled him to a U.S. passport. But he still took the denial of the bonus—and the offer of citizenship as a substitute for the money that other soldiers received—as an insult. How could he serve his country for four years and not get citizenship automatically? So he declined reenlistment, walked away with neither the bonus nor citizenship, and returned to Texas with Ronnie and the boys, where he got a job as a diesel mechanic in Laredo—a border town neither of them knew.

IF IT WAS YOUR FIRST time, you drove south on Interstate 35, passed San Antonio, and expected to hit the border, but the highway kept plunging south. Texas hill country flattened out into a plain so fathomlessly vast, it gave you a feeling of driving down into the end of the earth. One hundred twenty miles later, and still in America, you reached the spindly neon signs of hotels and fast-food joints, gazed back north, and felt as if what you'd just traveled through was a buffer, neither here nor there. To the west, several blocks off I-35, rows of warehouses colonized the area around the railroad track. To the east, upper-middle-class suburbs gave way to sprawling developments, ghettos, and sub-ghettos called colonias. Go two more miles south, and I-35 dumped out at the border crossing, 1,600 miles south of the interstate's northern terminus in Duluth, Minnesota.

Robert and Ronnie were small-town people. Sprawling Laredo, with its 125,000 residents, was a big city compared to a place like Eagle Pass, which had a population of fewer than 20,000.

"Oh well," Ronnie sighed. "We'll try it for a year or two."

A few months later, while recovering from a work-related hand injury, Robert saw an ad for the Laredo Police Department. He enjoyed public service more than working for a company. But he had to be a U.S. citizen to be a cop. He didn't see any benefit to citizenship, aside from this policing career, and wasn't feeling especially patriotic after his snub by the military. He wondered: What would his father do? His father would shut up and do right by his family. Land the career, move forward. So Robert studied, took the test, and took the oath of U.S. citizenship.

When he joined the force, the Laredo Police Department employed about two hundred officers. Cops purchased their own guns. Uniforms consisted of jeans and denim shirts, to which wives sewed PD patches. Each patrol covered an enormous area. Squad cars called for backup, and good luck with that. But aside from domestic spats and some armed robbery, the city saw little violence. Across the river, Nuevo Laredo, with its larger population of 200,000 people, wasn't much worse. Drug and immigrant smuggling were rampant. But a smuggler's power came less from controlling territory with violence and intimidation than from the scope of his contacts in law enforcement and politics, and his ability to operate across Mexico with government protection. In exchange for bribes, politicians and cops refereed trafficking and settled disputes.

Mexico's narcotics industry was well organized. The business consisted of two classes: producers and smugglers. On the western side of Mexico, in the fertile highlands of the Sierra Madre Occidental, *gomeros*—drug farmers—contracted with smuggling groups to move shipments north to border towns. In the states of Sinaloa, Durango, and Chihuahua, an ideal combination of altitude, rainfall, and soil acidity yielded bumper crops of *Papaver somniferum*. Those poppy fields—some with origins in plantings made by Chinese immigrants a century earlier—produced millions of metric tons of bulk opium per year. Marijuana, known by its slang, *mota,* was Mexico's other homegrown narcotic. When the marijuana craze hit the United States in the 1960s, *mota* came chiefly from the mountaintops of the Pacific states of Sinaloa and Sonora, then expanded to Nayarit, Jalisco, Guerrero, Veracruz, Oaxaca, Quintana Roo, and Campeche. The irrigated harvest for *mota* ran from February to March; the natural harvest from July to August. All *merca,* merchandise, had to reach the border by fall, November at the latest. Americans didn't work during the holidays.

The large, curving horn of Mexico was anchored on two great

mountain chains, or cordilleras, both rising from north to south, one on the east facing the green Gulf of Mexico, the other sloping westward to the blue Pacific Ocean. Between these mountain ranges, a high central plateau tapered down with the horn to the Yucatán Peninsula. Eons ago, volcanoes cut the plateau into countless jumbled valleys with forests of pine, oak, fir, and alder. The coastal lands were tropically humid, but the plateau had a climate of eternal spring. It should've been eminently fit for man.

Instead, Mexico's future would be full of conquests, dictatorship, revolt, corruption, and crime.

When Robert and Ronnie arrived in Laredo in 1991, the major crossings along the two-thousand-mile border between Mexico and America—from east to west: Matamoros, Nuevo Laredo, Juárez, and Tijuana—were controlled by "smuggling families" that straddled the border and charged a tax, known as a *cuota* or *piso,* which was in turn used to pay the bribes that secured the routes for trafficking in drugs and immigrants. Fights broke out between the families, and there was some spillover violence, but there were no cartels, not yet.

Patrol officers in Laredo PD seized large quantities of narcotics and saw some dead guys left in the front yard. But nothing too graphic. The young cops, making their nine dollars per hour plus overtime, were cocky. They had no awareness of the larger world; everything revolved around them. Places like Florida, Colombia, Mexico City, Guadalajara, and Washington, D.C., were a world away, and changing. Drug-war politics were in flux. In Laredo, Robert and his partners knew little beyond their squad cars.

As cops came up in PD, some set their sights on SWAT; others tried out state agencies like Child Protective Services and found that they didn't mind dealing with domestic nightmares. Robert liked drug work because of the local impact. A drug arrest wasn't mere pretext. You weren't just taking a guy with dope off the street. That guy also committed assaults and robberies to get drugs. If the guy was a big dealer, maybe he used kids as drug couriers and to operate "stash houses," the places where dealers kept their drugs and money. Robert would stop a guy with a gram of coke or a pound of weed, or bust a house that sold heroin to local Laredo addicts. He'd get his picture in the *Laredo Morning Times* perp-walking a guy to the local jail. He felt like he was "sweeping the streets of crime." He'd turn on the TV, see some Nancy Reagan–type person telling everyone, "Say no to drugs!" and feel like Superman.

THE LUMP-SUM PAYOUT RONNIE GOT when she left the military took some weight off her and Robert's life together. They paid cash for a mobile home in South Laredo. Robert's salary covered bills.

Still, they were a young couple with two kids, trying to make it in a new city. There was plenty to fight about. One of about one thousand white people in a city where bloodlines and patronage determined jobs and social circles, Ronnie was more of an outsider than Robert. As a stay-at-home mom she felt isolated. Life in Laredo wasn't fulfilling. That was their biggest fight: She wanted to get out. When she did go looking for work, she felt lucky to get hired at a doctor's office, where she was told, "You know, I like it that you're not from here."

Later, Robert would learn to divide the cop persona from the father-husband. But in his twenties, the machismo kicked in at home. *I'm the man and you'll obey. I'm going out tonight. There's nothing you can do about it.* Ronnie was dominant herself, until she grew sick of fighting and relented. "Okay," she told him one night, "have a good time." Taken aback by her capitulation, Robert worried about what she was going to do when he got home. He rushed back an hour later. *Is that all it takes?* Ronnie thought.

If Robert's bravado failed to impress his wife, his little brother

Jesse saw him as a hero. Jesse, feeling as though he could please their parents only by matching Robert's accomplishments, dropped out of high school in eleventh grade and came to live with Robert and Ronnie in Laredo, where he got a job as a high school security guard. Jesse wanted to become a cop, too, but he was young. Robert advised him to get an associate's degree in criminal justice at Laredo Community College. But Robert hadn't gone to college, and Jesse was eager to start a career. There were openings at the police academy in Uvalde, near Eagle Pass. In the summer of 1997, Robert gave Jesse some money, and his old service weapon, a .357 Magnum. Jesse completed the academy but failed the written test, then failed it again. If he failed a third time, he'd be barred forever from a job in Texas law enforcement.

Meanwhile, after hundreds of drug arrests, fourteen cars wrecked in hot-pursuit chases, and a dozen minor fractures, Robert was awarded Officer of the Year.

A week later, Jesse bused up to Wisconsin, where his parents were doing factory work that fall. He spent the weekend with them, showing no particular signs of depression, then returned to the family house in Eagle Pass and shot himself in the heart with Robert's service weapon.

Rumors emerged in the aftermath of Jesse's death. A girlfriend might've been pregnant. He might've been messing around with drugs, might've owed people money. Robert put his fist through a wall, then stalked around Eagle Pass looking for people to speak with about Jesse, until his father said, "Déjale." *Leave it. Don't investigate.* So Robert took Jesse's prized possession, a Marlboro jacket he'd sent away for, and bundled up his grief.

The Officer of the Year Award came with an opportunity. The Drug Enforcement Administration offered Robert a role as a task force officer. He wouldn't make the pay of a federal DEA agent. He'd remain a cop, collecting salary from Laredo PD. DEA agents, who had college degrees, made twice as much in base salary as task force officers. Agents also earned monetary awards for major investigations, sometimes as much as $5,000 per case. The only incentive for task force officers was overtime pay—an extra $10,000 or $12,000 a year for the crazy hours. Win an award, lose a brother. Get a promotion, make the same pay. But now Robert would have the power to investigate drug traffic and make arrests anywhere in the country. He talked to Ronnie. "I'll travel and won't see you or the boys much. But it's temporary. I can bust my ass for awhile." Eric, the older son, was in third grade; Trey, the younger, was in first. Ronnie knew this arrangement made her a single parent. "Okay," she said. "Take four years."

For a young cop who believed in the drug war, joining the DEA was a big step in his career. It would be nothing like he expected.

2

Flickering Candle

Freeze there: See Gabriel Cardona march backward, away from the stun grenade and the Laredo safe houses, away from the Texas jails and the Company lawyer, back to that zone of impunity. See *la policía* clear out a restaurant so an enemy ate alone, idle prey, practice for a new soldier. See a pickup truck: Hear the screams of the bound men inside who killed Gabriel's boss's brother fade to the *whoosh-whoosh* of towering flames. See Gabriel, months earlier, arrive at the training camp, primed for the work but not yet a *frío*, his aptitude raising eyes among *la gente nueva*, the new people.

And keep rewinding, back a decade, to Laredo, Texas, in the mid-1990s. It was as hopeful a season as there had been in the oldest ghetto of the poorest city in America. A city of new immigrants and Mexican-Americans whose mother country, next door, was finally set to democratize after seventy years of one-party rule. A city on its way to becoming one of the busiest trading posts of the world's greatest economy.

September mornings arrived at a cool ninety-eight degrees—"the late-summer cold spell," locals joked. Mrs. Gabriela Cardona—known among her children as "La Gaby"—rolled out of bed quietly. Best to let the drunk sleep it off. On her way to the bathroom, with its ceiling that caved in a little more each year but never broke, she slapped the feet of her four sons, who slept together on a queen-size mattress. "Es-school! Es-school! Es-school!" she yelled in her accented English, and flicked water on the boys—ages eleven, ten, six, and four.

Despite La Gaby's troublemaking brother and her good-for-nothing husband, neighbors considered the Cardonas a capable family. La Gaby inherited an old family house across the river in Nuevo Laredo, and she occasionally collected rent on it. She worked hard, and always had a job. CPS never visited their address.

If she was going to have problems with any son, she doubted it would be with the second. Gabriel had started reading earlier than other children, consuming every volume of the *Sesame Street* series and *Selfish, Selfish Rex,* a parable about the virtues of sharing. He ran about in Batman shoes, scored perfect attendance at both regular school and Sunday school, and read the Bible. Teachers remarked on his generosity, and how he looked out for smaller kids.

"Oralé, al agua pato!" La Gaby yelled. *Listen up, hit that water duck!*

During elementary school mornings Gabriel showered with his older brother, Luis, while La Gaby shouted soaping instructions from the kitchen: "Cabeza, cuello, arcas, wiwi, cola, pies." *Head, neck, armpits, penis, butt, feet.* Combing the boys' hair into Ricky Martin pompadours, she repeated the instructions until they learned to do it themselves: "El partido por la orilla, lo demás pa'ca y levantas al frente." *The part should be on the side, the rest toward here, and raise it up in the front.* Then Gabriel helped his younger brothers get dressed, ate a breakfast taco of egg and chorizo, grabbed his note-book, and ran outside, where a tree dropped sour oranges and threw shade on the multiplying kittens that shat in the dirt by the rusty gate in front of 207 Lincoln.

Situated on a bluff overlooking the Rio Grande, El Azteca—their six-square-block neighborhood known simply as "Lazteca"—was 250 years old. The streets were narrow, the sidewalks high: a closed feel. Early morning was Gabriel's favorite time of day. Dawn came quiet in the hood, as cops and Border Patrol switched shifts. He preferred it to the chaos of Lazteca by night, when the streets came alive with the spotlights of beating helicopters and the squeal of tires as drug runners and coyotes—immigrant smugglers—tried to outrun the authorities.

Interstate 35, the biggest smuggling corridor in America, began a hundred yards from the Cardonas' door. On the way to school—north along Zacate Creek, west through the I-35 underpass that led to J. C. Martin Elementary—Gabriel and Luis passed men coming off night shifts packing narcotics for the drive north, illegal immigrants looking for a ride to a hotel, and the daily queue outside the bondsman's office. Such were the signs of Lazteca's economic health. And like any friendly neighborhood, generosity was community. Fathers and boyfriends and uncles and brothers came home after a successful trip to Dallas, giving here, giving there, buying pizzas. La Gaby would tell the boys, "Vacúnalo!"—*Get a lick out of him!*

Uncle Raul, the smuggler who blasted speedballs, injecting heroin and cocaine at the same time, was always in and out of prison, but Raul taught Gabriel and his friends to play football. Gabriel was the quarterback. One of his homies from Lazteca, Rosalio Reta—younger by three years and shorter than a kitchen table—was always trying to prove himself to the older kids. He took big hits and sprang back up, smiling, his huge cheeks swelling like avocados around the upper-lip birthmark. They played violent video games like Mortal Kombat, and listened to the rap music of Tupac Shakur.

On the way home from school, Gabriel and Luis played along Zacate Creek's slimy bank. If they came home stinking like fish, they received a beating from La Gaby, who always stood at the ready with an extension cord in hand, nose active. But she had a soft core. Gabriel and Luis's best friends, the Blake brothers, were allowed to sleep over whenever they brought La Gaby a bottle of Big Red soda or a Coke. She cried when CPS moved the Blakes to foster care in Brownsville after their mother was picked up again for heroin.

Mr. Cardona was good for certain things. An out-of-work security guard, he took Gabriel and his brothers to the park for barbecues and out riding bikes. He played guitar and sang. On weekends they walked across the border to visit extended family in Nuevo Laredo, passing from the fresh air of America to Mexico's wilder aromas: carne asada, horses, old leather. With air-pump guns, the cousins played "shooting." Gabriel would catch pellets in the face but never relent. They called him *loco,* crazy.

GABRIEL'S AMERICANNESS GAVE HIM A special status south of the border. The North American Free Trade Agreement, which took effect in 1994, eliminated tariffs on goods traded between Mexico, the United States, and Canada. Not only could Wal-Mart now ship raw materials to Mexico, manufacture goods with Mexican labor, and reimport the finished product to American consumers without penalty, but it could also establish retail outlets in Mexico and drive mom-and-pop stores out of business. Wall Street smiled. Investment flowed. American goods lined the shelves of supermarkets and U.S.-style department stores all over Mexico: Adidas and Kodak; Coke and Cheetos. Willie Nelson poured through speakers. All-day dry cleaners set a new pace. As cheap corn and wheat imports from the United States hurt Mexican farmers, rural Mexicans flocked to northern cities for work in *maquiladoras,* foreign-owned factories, where they became inundated with American consumer culture. McDonald's, Pizza Hut, and even Taco Bell lit up skylines from Monterrey to Mexico City. The tendency was to idealize everything American and discount everything Mexican.

After family visits, when the Cardonas returned to Laredo, Gabriel's father became insecure, then violent, having seen himself through the eyes of his Mexican family: an American who did no better than they did. Gabriel and Luis watched their drunk father beat their mother, punching her like a man would hit another man. When Gabriel went to school with a palm imprinted on his face, his teacher asked if he was okay. He nodded. He knew the rule: *No te identificas.* Don't say anything.

One night, La Gaby stabbed their father with a kitchen knife, then kicked him out for good. Gabriel was proud of La Gaby for being strong. He resented his father for drinking while his mother worked, and didn't consider his leaving any great loss. Though a sense of deep loss came a few days later, on Gabriel's tenth birthday, when Tupac Shakur died from gunshot wounds. Pac was his *perro,* his dog. Even years later he would feel *coraje,* rage, at whoever pulled that trigger.

IN JUNIOR HIGH, GABRIEL WON certificates of excellence for outstanding performance in math and English. Several of his adoring female classmates remembered him as the person to beat in seventh-grade algebra. He had a head for numbers, and a talent for memorization. His English teacher asked everyone to memorize a song and perform it. Gabriel appeared in class with a fake diamond nose ring, and a blue handkerchief around his head. The class rolled in laughter as he sang Tupac's "How Do U Want It?"

He quarterbacked the football team through two undefeated seasons, and dreamed of becoming a lawyer. In the summer between eighth and ninth grade he enrolled at Workforce Center, through the Texas Migrant Council, and made a hundred dollars a week. He gave money to La Gaby, and purchased Polo shirts and Tommy Hilfiger boots for himself. He bought a bus ticket to Brownsville to visit a girlfriend whose family had moved away. They went to South Padre Island and ate pizza. Gabriel Cardona appeared to be one of those rare Lazteca kids whose energy might take him somewhere other than prison. Looking at the industrious fourteen-year-old, no one could have imagined that the $896.10 he made during the summer of 2000 would be his first and last legal income.

NAFTA, meanwhile, meant huge changes in cross-border trade, with tens of thousands of trucks coming through Laredo every week. Laredo's population doubled during the 1990s, making it the second-fastest-growing city in America after Las Vegas, and the largest inland port in the Western Hemisphere. More than 75 percent of Fortune 1000 companies invested in Laredo's transport facilities that warehoused Mexican goods before they headed north.

But aside from some extra minimum-wage jobs in the warehouses, none of the new revenue seemed to make it into the pockets of the working class. With a median income 30 percent below the national average, and 38 percent of its residents living below the poverty line, life for most of Laredo, still a front-runner for poorest city in America, had changed little after NAFTA's passing. Despite the new orgy of commerce, it remained a giant, unimproved truck stop.

If the city of a quarter-million people didn't *look* as poor as it was on paper, it was because the black market buoyed the legitimate one. Many of Laredo's small businesses—perfume and toy stores; used-car lots and restaurants—were money-laundering fronts. The Mexican Mafia, a California gang with a strong Texas presence, owned slot machine halls known as *maquinitas,* and a bustling chain of beer drive-thrus, Mami Chula's, staffed by bikini-clad teens who accepted tips like strippers. Other big gangs, such as the Texas Syndicate and Hermanos de Pistoleros Latinos, known as HPL, also owned businesses. The tallest building in town belonged to the DEA.

Gabriel stopped looking forward to their Mexico visits. His family didn't have much, but he still felt bad going across in his Sunday best to see cousins who had nothing. Some of them picked pockets, washed cars, or performed sidewalk spectacles for tourist change. He did like sneaking out of church with his cousin, putting chewed gum on a stick, and fishing cash from the donation box. But Mexico, he felt, was dirty. Flies buzzed around garbage. He smelled urine, saw gang graffiti on brick walls, and watched plastic bags blow against fences, trapped like wounded birds. He didn't like having to be careful where he sat or roamed. His opinion would change, later, when he got some money. But for now he appreciated America for its relative glimmer.

When high school started, he hoped to become quarterback of the junior varsity football team. No Laredo team had ever made it past the third round of state playoffs; in most years, Laredo carried the dubious distinction of being the largest city in America not to have a football player win an athletic scholarship at any level. Still, a Laredo kid was a Laredo kid: five foot seven, not very fast, but played hard. Gabriel had read *Friday Night Lights,* the famous book about Texas high school football, and he dreamed of entering that world, of experiencing the American rite, as H.G. Bissinger wrote, of playing under the "full moon that filled the black satin sky with a light as soft and delicate as the flickering of a candle." He dreamed of something glorious to fill the blah of life.

The boy grew up handsome, talented, and popular. His ego knew little of rejection. So when the coach benched him in favor of a sophomore, he quit. It was a decision in which loads of portent would later be vested. Had he been a starter, he would've stayed in football, remained after school for practice, and kept getting the grades required for participation. Instead, after leaving practice that day, he hooked up with two brothers connected to Laredo's street gang scene, smoked pot for the first time, and drove around vandalizing houses.

A few days later some terrorists knocked down some buildings in New York.

3

My Dad Does Drugs

Shortly after September 11, Robert Garcia was in the doctor's office getting another round of steroid injections. His full head of black hair survived military service, the threat of a dishonorable discharge, early fatherhood, the struggles of marriage, and the stresses of a street cop. Now, at thirty-three, the thick hair was coming out in quarter-size patches.

It was pretty clear that drugs were to blame.

When Robert joined DEA as a task force officer, he started traveling up I-35 to "the checkpoint"—a kind of second border crossing twenty-nine miles north of Laredo where Border Patrol agents applied random levels of scrutiny to vehicles, more so to cars and trucks driven by Hispanics. Connecting with the entire system of U.S. interstates, I-35 ran up through San Antonio, Austin, Dallas, Oklahoma City, Des Moines, and Minneapolis. But it all started at the checkpoint, where the largest busts were made. Sometimes *tons* of narcotics were seized. As a street cop Robert made small drug busts within the city. His first months at DEA gave him a wider lens. Where, he wondered, is all this stuff coming from?

By 2000, six years after NAFTA was implemented, trade between Mexico and the United States had tripled, to $247 billion, and the four bridges that connected Nuevo Laredo to Laredo saw 60,000 trucks go north per week. Because every truck stopped for a search was a drag on global commerce, NAFTA eased friction for smugglers, too. Blizzards of white powder now came packaged in bounties of fresh citrus; boxes of plastic bananas, five-dollar sunglasses, and spice jars; as well as countless other goods. Some traffickers hired trade consultants to determine what merchandise moved across the border most swiftly under the new regime. Did a perishable get through quicker than a load of steel?

In the basic drug-interdiction formula, the DEA busted a smuggler coming across and offered to reduce his charges in exchange for his help busting the northern buyer—in places such as Detroit, Brooklyn, and Boston. To account for the time lost during interdiction and to ensure that the deal seemed genuine to the northern buyer, the truck was then flown north on a DEA jet. Or, if there was enough time, an undercover agent, like Robert, would drive the drugs to the point of sale. The DEA called these busts "controlled deliveries."

Young, and often mistaken as Middle Eastern due to his dark coloring, Robert had a flexible appearance that made him a top choice for undercover jobs. With DEA, he worked and traveled constantly. He went undercover with smugglers from Mexico and Jamaica. He grew his hair long and wore Jesse's Marlboro jacket. A typical two-year DEA employee in Laredo—"a target-rich environment"—saw as much action as an eight-year agent in New York.

Some DEA task force officers like Robert—those who'd been "loaned out" from a local agency and weren't full federal agents—complained about the difference in pay. But the pay differential never bothered Robert. He was a cop from Mexico who was now working with U.S. federal agents, going undercover in New York City, and getting training that he would bring back to Laredo PD. If you were only in it for the money, he thought, then, yeah, you'd always be pissed off about the job. But what did he have to complain about?

Between jobs Robert squeezed in tourist activities, and sent photos to his mother. The Statue of Liberty. The Empire State Building. The Hard Rock Cafe. He made many big busts, and posed with agents for trophy shots.

Two million in cash!

A ton of cocaine!

At first the busts were exciting. But time passed, and Robert became jaded by the lack of impact his busts, or any busts, had on overall drug traffic. Even if he did one controlled delivery per week, the effect on the drug supply would be meaningless. Even drug war optimists conceded that, at most, interdiction halted 10 percent of drug traffic. Robert guessed the interdiction rate was closer to 5 percent or 2 percent. Either way, there was no such thing as a good year. Only in isolation, divorced from any context, could a bust shown on the nightly news appear important. Where there was demand, he discovered, supply found its way. Prohibition? It was a legal fiction.

He couldn't square the government's outlay with his new knowledge about the results of interdiction—until he realized where the money to fight the war on drugs came from. After 9/11, the Laredo DEA office transitioned from a "resident-agent office" that drew on local hires to a "district office" that recruited agents from all over the country. Eight agents became forty. DEA wasn't the only drug squad in town, just the main one. Laredo PD, the Texas Department of Public Safety, the sheriff's office, the Justice Department's Bureau of Alcohol, Tobacco, Firearms and Explosives (ATF), U.S. Immigration and Customs Enforcement (ICE), FBI, and Department of

Homeland Security: They all pursued the same targets, and all ran on drug money. Seizures of cash and equipment could finance half an agency's budget, sometimes more. The yin and the yang.

Drug traffic spiked, in spite of enhanced enforcement, but it was hard to argue with the war's economic agenda. A trafficker could serve time in a forfeiture-financed prison after being arrested by agents who drove a forfeiture-financed car and earned forfeiture-financed overtime in a forfeiture-funded sting. Who in Washington would get too worked up by a self-financing war? There was little downside to supporting the war. No wonder that, among politicians, out-toughing one another on drugs was a bipartisan practice.

When agencies weren't fighting with each other over cases and money, they were fighting over credit for busts and prosecutions. Mostly, agencies cared about being first to report a bust to Washington. Even within DEA, agents and task force officers backstabbed one another, poached informants, and refused to share information that would enhance the overall effectiveness of interdiction. The office had an open floor plan, yet rarely did an agent know what the agent sitting next to him was working on. To an efficiency-minded engineer, the futility of the larger war on drugs was impossible to ignore, and everything Robert had spent the past decade doing struck him as futile.

Robert's time in DEA was supposed to be four years. It dragged on, and the work drained him. He and Ronnie moved the boys to a three-bedroom house in a new subdivision of Laredo called Los Presidentes, and Robert's hair began to come out in patches. Where he'd once taken pride in soldiering for a cause, he now understood that border policing was not so much about achieving policy—*No drugs! No immigrants!*—as it was a symbol of state authority. The border was a theater, a stage on which many stories could be told. Busts—visible though misleading indicators of progress—won votes for incumbent politicians, fed a hungry press, and neutralized political challengers who tried to portray the border as out of control. September 11 opened the federal wallet, adding a new and lucrative plotline to the border narrative: smuggled terrorists.

"Middle East terrorists could arrive at any moment!" the sheriff of Webb County, home of Laredo, yelled to anyone who'd listen. Robert watched, fuming, as the sheriff, a guy who never put cuffs on anyone, held press conferences at the river as if he were the last line of defense against Armageddon. The sheriff waved a piece of fabric, which he said was an "Iraqi military patch" found in the brush by a local rancher.

Four years into his DEA stint, Robert was at the doctor, getting steroid injections for his hair, when he said it aloud for the first time: "The war on drugs is a big fucking lie."

THE WAR HAD BEEN A lie for two hundred years. America's earliest attempts to regulate vice regulated price only: economics by other means. In 1802, Little Turtle, the chief of the Miami Indians, made a speech to Thomas Jefferson about the effect that alcohol had in Native American communities: "Father, the introduction of this poison has been prohibited in our camps, but not in our towns, where many of our hunters, for this poison, dispose not only of their furs, but frequently of their guns and blankets, and return to their families destitute."

Legislators passed laws to stem the flow of alcohol into Indian lands. But the Indian demand for whiskey remained; and the pelts that Indians offered in exchange for whiskey could be sold dearly back east. Laws that prohibited the sale of whiskey to Indians merely inflated alcohol prices in Indian territory, such that a 25-cent gallon of whiskey in St. Louis could be sold by a fur trader a few hundred miles away, in what is now Iowa, for $64. The fur traders—such as America's richest man, John Jacob Astor, whose American Fur

Company controlled 75 percent of the fur trade—benefited the most from early prohibition.

Astor's company lobbied for exceptions to Indian prohibition, insisting that the company's boatmen, the ones who traveled up the Missouri River to purchase pelts, required whiskey for personal use on their long journeys. So exceptions to the law were legislated, and boatman permits were issued—in effect, permits to smuggle. In 1831, only one in every hundred gallons of whiskey brought into Indian country was covered by a permit.

A decade later, the Indian Office reported that more than a hundred Indians died in drunken brawls in Sioux country during one year; and that entire Indian villages would starve if the whiskey trade continued. The Indian Office appointed a roving agent to interdict illicit liquor on the Missouri. Even though the agent didn't find much liquor during his year in the field, his presence slowed the flow of alcohol up the Missouri, prompting Indians, finally, to raise their prices on pelts, and fur traders to complain to the government.

The lesson of early prohibition was clear: Where there was demand, supply found its way. In future attempts to regulate vice, the only question would be which community bore the black-market burden—as consumers of the vice, suppliers of the market, or both. Who would the Indians be?

ROBERT'S STRESS-RELATED BALD PATCHES DISAPPEARED after a round of steroid injections, then returned. He got more steroid injections and his hair grew back. He latched on to a drug load that took him from New Jersey to Chicago to San Diego, a big case he worked obsessively. The whiteboard above his desk at DEA—a mess of pictures and strings and note cards—grew like a graduate-level math proof that could be worked forever but never solved. He assembled binders on not just the "dopers" he tracked but their relatives, and memorized every address.

As Robert's DEA career stretched to six years, he became leery of who the boys brought home from school. All families of the boys' friends had to be vetted to see if Robert had arrested a father or an uncle. He also ran every neighbor through the system, knew the criminal history of every family that lived within a mile. It turned out that the next-door neighbors, whose twin boys Eric and Trey played with, did business with drug suppliers across the border.

While Robert was away, as often as two weeks per month, Ronnie raised the boys. In most Mexican households, men did the outdoor work and women kept the home. Ronnie took what she liked from her husband's culture but left that tradition behind. The boys learned to cook, clean, and do laundry. Everyone contributed.

She, Eric, and Trey talked and laughed. But the moment Robert returned home, the dynamic changed. His mood was shitty. If anyone made a noise, he reprimanded them. Trey, the blood son, obeyed. Eric, the stepson, had less reverence. Eric snuck around behind Robert and mocked him.

Be quiet!

Drop and give me twenty!

Robert and Ronnie programmed Eric and Trey not to tell people what dad did for a living. Since Robert often unwound by doing projects around the house, the Garcias told neighbors that Robert was in construction. But one day, while giving a class presentation on his family, Eric slipped and said, "My dad does drugs." The teacher called Ronnie: "Ma'am, I'm a little concerned."

4

The Noble Fight

Rohypnol, roofies, the date-rape drug: It used to be called Spanish fly. In Laredo, kids called the party pills "roches" because they were made by Hoffmann–La Roche, the Swiss pharmaceutical company. A powerful tranquilizer, roches were illegal in the United States but easily obtainable across the border, where one could buy a prescription for $5, and 100 pills for $50.

Gabriel had been hanging outside Martin High one afternoon when a slightly older girl named Ashley drove by with her friends and offered him a ride. The girls stopped at a gas station to buy cans of Sprite, and spread a bunch of pills on the hood of the car.

There were two kinds of girls in Laredo: hoodrats and *fresas*. A *fresa*—literally, strawberry—was a preppy, often light-skinned Latina from Laredo's wealthier north side. The *fresa* wore lip gloss, while the hoodrat wore bright red lipstick. Where the *fresa* preferred sweaters and fur-lined boots, the hoodrat stomped around in Nikes and cutoff T-shirts. Where the *fresa* feigned reluctance, said *no soy puta* before pulling down her thong, the rat gave up the *pepa* without a hassle. Ashley was a hoodrat, *del pueblo, pal pueblo:* from the hood, for the hood—at her core, a sweet girl from one of Lazteca's most shattered, CPS-worthy homes.

When one of her friends offered Gabriel a pill, Ashley said: "No! He's not taking any." But telling Gabriel not to do something only ensured that he did it. As they had, he crushed a pill, poured the powder into a soda, drank it down, and BOOM!

Thus began a routine: Cranking the stereo, Ashley and Gabriel drove around and talked for hours. One roche became two, then three: an instant good feeling, a cruising mood. Chatty. No worries. No shame. Ashley became Gabriel's *ruca,* his girl. A steady date but something less than a girlfriend, she dedicated the song "Dilemma," by Nelly and Kelly Rowland, to him.

The pills, which were used largely for recreation, not rape, worked differently on different people. Some became emotional and cried. Others went nuts, hallucinated, jumped off bridges. For Gabriel, the roches relaxed and desensitized him. On Sunday nights, everyone went to San Bernardo Avenue, a cruising street next to Martin High, one block west of I-35, where the owners of customized Chevy S10s and Dodge Rams showed off their butterfly doors and Forgiato rims that cost more than the cars themselves. Gabriel would note who owned which ride, making a mental catalog of Laredo's biggest smugglers. His courage amplified by the roches, he walked down the middle of San Bernardo, against traffic. Swerving between the low riders as they roared by, the world seemed harmless.

Later during freshman year, Gabriel was walking in the hall when a member of a gang called Movida bumped into him on purpose. Many in Movida had played football with Gabriel in middle school. But Gabriel's older brother, Luis, was in the rival gang, the Sieteros. When Movida saw Gabriel hanging out with the Sieteros, they begrudged him for it. Every few weeks he cut his hair at Nydia's Salon—Movida turf. One day they saw him there and asked what he represented. "I'm not into little kids' shit," he said, mimicking what he'd once heard his uncle Raul say. "I represent my hood, Lazteca." The boys of Movida said they had no problem with Gabriel. But now their opinion had apparently changed.

That same afternoon, Gabriel asked Luis for the keys to their mom's Escort so he could leave school and escape a potential confrontation with Movida gang members. As he walked through the parking lot he heard people behind him cussing him out. When he turned around, he saw two dozen Movida members walking toward him, and prepared for a beating. As they approached, Luis—short, with a hulking physique—came outside and stepped in between Gabriel and the mob. The leader of Movida threw a punch at Luis, who ducked and came back with an uppercut that knocked the boy down. He stood up, pretended to walk away, then turned around and slashed Luis's eyebrow with a sucker punch.

After the fight broke up, Gabriel felt humiliated. He knew you never let someone else fight your fights, and vowed to make sure it never happened again.

Gabriel started hanging out with the Sieteros, going to their parties, and looking for opportunities to be useful. The gang needed guns, such as .380s and 9-millimeters. A Laredo cop sold guns out of the trunk of his car. He had law enforcement catalogs for the kids to peruse, and would call them with news of special inventory. The cop—who lived on Lincoln Street, a block down from the Cardonas—even had grenade launchers and the flash grenades to test them.

FOR MORE THAN A CENTURY, Laredo ran on the old *patrón* system of political favoritism. J. C. Martin, the namesake of Martin High, was Laredo's mayor from 1954 to 1978. The original *patrón,* Martin maintained power by stewarding immigrant-friendly policies for the mostly Hispanic city. No ID cards. Abundant public housing. Loose limits on welfare. Martin could make millions of dollars disappear into a city-street department that paved only the road surrounding his mansion. He was corrupt as hell, but he brought out the vote.

The poorest areas of Laredo—the west side, home to Martin High; south-central, home to Lazteca; and the south side, home to the absolute worst ghetto, Santo Niño—were all bound by geography: the river and the border. After the city's population doubled during the 1990s, to nearly 250,000, real estate, still controlled by the oldest and wealthiest Laredo families—the Martins, Brunis, Killams, Walkers, and Longorias—remained some of the highest priced in Texas, which helped keep the middle class lean and locked the poor out of land ownership.

In addition to the official ghettos in central and south Laredo—Lazteca, Siete Viejo, Cantaranas, the Heights, Santo Niño—Laredo was ringed by communities, or camps, called "colonias." After World War II, developers began using agriculturally valueless land to create these unincorporated subdivisions without infrastructure or utilities, then sold the properties to immigrants who made low payments but didn't receive title until they made the final payment.

There were no members-at-large on the city council, no one representing politically significant voting blocks. Each neighborhood, rather, was a ward with its own councilman. The councilman would build a community center, or maybe improve a playground, then get reelected again and again on a hundred votes. Not even the mayor could propose a city-wide ordinance.

"Almost everyone here's Hispanic, and even the handful of gringos are assimilated," said Ray Keck, the president of Texas A&M

International University. The gringo son of European immigrants, Keck grew up just north of Laredo, went to Princeton University, married a Hispanic woman from Laredo, and then taught at the Hotchkiss boarding school in Connecticut. "Since there's little ethnic tension, there's an easier, more natural system of subjugation, and the social classes tend to stagnate."

Every school in Laredo has a colonia affiliated with it, and the colonia kids are bused in. Whenever crime becomes a political issue, local media blame the colonias, depicting them as havens of depravity and filth. Never mind that Laredo's biggest criminal families often came from the upper classes on the fancy north side. La Gaby knew it, same as Robert and Ronnie Garcia knew it. When a kid from United North or Alexander High got in trouble, you never heard about it, because his parents were related to attorneys and judges. The wealthy walked away with a lecture while the average José sat in the county jail.

In the Laredo Independent School District—which contained Martin, Nixon, and Cigarroa high schools—97 percent of students were considered "economically disadvantaged," and the other 3 percent just didn't fill out the paperwork. At Martin, the principal acknowledged that he fostered two groups: those who would go into the drug business, and those who would chase them. Cops, agents, lawyers, judges, court workers, probation officers; not to mention diesel mechanics, truck yard owners, and warehouses that stored seized contraband for the government—the list of jobs created by drug prohibition was long.

But everyone, it seemed, was mixed up in *something*. Laredo's council members lived on kickbacks. Judges favored dealers who supported their campaigns. The bail business was the biggest hustle of all. Bondsmen often split their money with prosecutors who helped recover seized vehicles and get their clients deals. For a fee, a corrections officer at the Webb County jail helped arrestees get their bail lowered. The corrections officer's son was Laredo's district attorney, though the DA was never implicated in the scheme.

On its high knoll—surrounded by coconut-less palm trees; adjacent to a huge port and a prized smuggling corridor—Lazteca, also known as the Devil's Corner, was magnificently positioned for a jack of black-market trades. Immigrants. Narcotics. Cars. Weapons. Cash. Here, in Underworld University, a brave and resourceful boy was a useful thing.

ONE NIGHT, DURING THE SUMMER between Gabriel's freshman and sophomore year, the Sieteros were throwing a party when the girlfriend of the gang's leader screamed from a seated position on the ground. When people came to help her up, she said she'd been hit in the face by "a short kid" who was drunk.

Twelve years old and still under five feet, Rosalio Reta worried that his given name sounded girlish. A fan of *The Simpsons*, he'd recently changed it to Bartolomeo. Friends and family now called him Bart.

Bart's large family was typical of Laredo's poor. His father, a construction worker, and his mother, a beautician, both born in Mexico, earned a combined $400 a week and received $1,200 a month in food stamps. The second of eight children—four boys, four girls—Bart was born in Houston. He lived across the street from the Cardonas and attended J. C. Martin Elementary until second grade, when his family's house burned down. The Reta family moved one neighborhood north, to Siete Viejo, where their dilapidated wood-frame mobile home lacked windows and doors. In the bedroom that Bart shared with his siblings, his favorite item was a Navy SEAL poster he stole from a local recruitment center. At night, when the family fell asleep together while watching TV, Bart would leave and walk to a nearby housing project where Sietero gang members gathered to smoke weed, drink beer, and play basketball beneath the twenty-four-hour safety lights.

Bart ventured out on these nights because he wanted to live his own life. He was tired of not having what he needed, of forgoing dinner on some nights so that his little sisters and brothers could have more food. To have something, he learned, you had to work for it. He was willing to work. He joined the Sieteros, and became a favorite of the gang's leader.

But now, at the party, Bart chugged Presidente brandy in the backyard when that same leader approached him, pulled out a gun, and put the barrel to Bart's head. Disrespecting a gang leader's girlfriend was grounds for a beating; hitting her in the face could warrant something worse. Some of the Sieteros discussed taking Bart to a nearby field and shooting him. One gang member said killing Bart wouldn't be smart because the girls at the party would tell on them.

Gabriel stood nearby, waiting for an opportunity to intervene on behalf of his childhood friend, the tough kid who always played football with the bigger boys and just wanted to fit in. Several gang members began to beat Bart, who tried to fight back but couldn't. Gabriel eventually broke it up, and dragged Bart away.

After that evening, Gabriel and Bart began to distance themselves from the Sieteros and spend more time with each other. While they walked near Gabriel's house in Lazteca one evening, Movida did a drive-by.

Gabriel had been shot at twice before; he would hear the bullets whistle past and imagine *The Matrix,* imagine that if he only raised his hand here, extended it there, he might just catch one. He would feel a chill, a tremble, and then battle mode entered. But this time he was hit on the back and head with shotgun fragments. Getting *shot,* he now discovered, was different than getting shot *at*. He didn't feel the tiny fragments when they entered. Just burning and cold drips.

Then humiliation, a tingle of rage on his lips, the unbearable feeling that someone had the upper hand.

TWO TEENS SHOT IN DRIVE-BY, wrote the *Laredo Morning Times*.

The cops recovered casings from the scene and said the investigation was ongoing. Investigation my ass, Gabriel thought after getting out of the hospital. When he retaliated, shooting one of his rivals in the leg, it was a big turning point for the fifteen-year-old. He became known as a *vato de huevos,* someone who had the balls to pull the trigger, a *gatillero.* Most important, he now fought his own fights. People felt safe in his presence. His friends wanted to be around him. When absent from a gathering, people asked after his whereabouts. The respect was intoxicating. He started to carry a gun.

His body changed. His bronzed, hairless chest was still concave, but his shoulders now popped. His lips grew plush; his nose straight and strong; his hands hard. He traded the Ricky Martin pompadour for the newer hairstyle, the Eminem fade.

Like any teenage boy developing a posture and attitude toward the world—a man's personality—cultural models imparted to him life's bitter realities and the noble ways of coping. In the shack next to his mother's house at 207 Lincoln, Gabriel and Luis watched *Blood In, Blood Out,* a movie about teen relatives from East Los Angeles, repeatedly. After the movie's characters get in a lethal fight with a rival gang, their paths diverge. Paco goes to the military and becomes a cop. Miklo goes to prison and becomes a gang leader. Gabriel understood the message of Paco: You can come from the hood and still make something of your life. But he identified most with Miklo. The heroic way the character stays true to his code and becomes the leader of his gang—"the baddest man in prison"—was an appealing fantasy.

On the wall of the shack, Gabriel scribbled lyrics and poetry by Tupac Shakur. He took off his shirt, smoked weed, and listened to "Hit 'Em Up," "Still Ballin'," and "Hail Mary"—songs about street life and getting revenge. Tupac wrote his best songs in prison, lived the life he rhapsodized, battled dirty cops, and survived assailants. Gabriel danced and shadowboxed with the music.

Five shots couldn't drop me—I took it and smiled . . .

"Turn that *Two-pack* shit off!" La Gaby would yell from across the dirt driveway, but Gabriel ignored her. As he moved around spinning, punching the air—his jeans sagging below the waistband of his plaid Tommy Hilfiger boxers—ideas sprang into his mind; principles crystallized into code. It was about being *en la punta del cañón,* at the front of the barrel.

Be the guy who goes first!

Die for the homies!

Gabriel's close friends frequented the shack. The boys—Gabriel, Bart, and another close friend named Wences Tovar, known as Tucan for his mighty nose—plus a cast of associated homies from Lazteca and Siete Viejo traded issues of *Vibe* magazine, and followed every twist of hip-hop's East Coast–West Coast beef. Reading about the homicidal music mogul Suge Knight and the corruption of the Los Angeles Police Department, they saw their own habitat reflected in that celebrated ether. The music wasn't just *called* gangsta rap. It was real.

Even more so when Carlos Coy—aka South Park Mexican, a Houston local—hit it big with songs like "Thug Girl" and "Illegal Amigos." South Park Mexican, wrote the *Houston Press,* "was a hero to the shaven-headed brown kids in baggy print shirts and jeans, those sons of yard men, road builders, roofers and dishwashers, the youths caught between two cultures but not particularly valued by either." SPM became a conduit for their rage and despair, but also for their dreams. He rapped for *all the crazy muthafuckas.* He let them know he'd been lost and needed help just like them. That's why those who followed him were *the sickest, most ill people in this world,* because that's who SPM wanted to help and change. He dropped outta high school cause he was tired of *selling crack to your homeboy's mom, and feeling like a worthless wetback*. As a soon-to-be eighteen-year-old high school freshman, SPM also worried about going to jail for statutory rape.

Gabriel and Luis used the shack to entertain female friends. On the outside of the shack, facing Lincoln Street, they hung a poster of a curvy Chicana lusting over a bottle of Bud Light.

When sophomore year started, a truant officer found rolling papers and a bullet in Gabriel's pocket. It would be the last day he set foot in Martin High.

5

Overachieving Bitch

Ronnie Garcia continued to struggle in Laredo. The city was rotten with domestic violence, and she didn't need to be a cop to see it. After working as a receptionist at the medical office for several years, she took a new job as an administrator and recruiter at Texas A&M International University—known as TAMIU, *Tammy U*. Ronnie's close friend there was the mother of Trey's best friend. The woman wanted to switch careers, and had just passed her nursing test when she told her husband she was going out to celebrate. He said no. She went out anyway. He met her in the front yard that night and slit her throat, killing her.

The father got life in prison. The eight-year-old son, Trey's friend, moved between his grandmother's house and the Garcias' new house in Los Presidentes. On the first Christmas after his mother's murder, they were opening presents when the boy broke down. Ronnie held him for hours at a stretch. But it was hard to know what to do. She called her own parents in Arizona. "Robert's never home!" she complained. "This boy is inconsolable!" "Oh quit it, you little overachieving bitch," her father would say, using their private rough language but not meaning it unkindly. "Slow down, honey. You can't be everything to everyone."

Through tumult, an unwavering ethic yoked Robert and Ronnie to one another in a way that could alienate them from the crowd, particularly Robert's crowd. From speeding tickets to arrests, Laredo cops bent the rules and traded favors with the powerful. Robert didn't play such games. Ronnie appreciated his rectitude, even if it limited their social life to a tiny circle of cops and federal agents.

At DEA, all the narcotics and cash and cars in the evidence room could finance a second agency. Temptation lurked, as it did at many of Laredo's law-enforcement agencies, and Robert never knew which of his colleagues would fall. An agent might stay clean, but when his kids grew up and he needed extra money, he skimmed cash off a bust. When the money was counted, the arrested doper would say, "No, there was more there than that." But the doper was a criminal, so the agent got away with it. And that was the first step toward ruin, because if the agent got away with skimming money once, then he did it again. He might wriggle out the second time, too. It was always that third time when he found himself talking to a prosecutor and bidding his colleagues farewell. It could be an agent from a legacy law enforcement family, or a father-son scheme. It could be an old partner, someone you thought you knew like the back of your hand. But then if you looked at the back of your hand every five years, it changed.

The Garcias' thinking: The system isn't fair but opportunity exists. Don't be a freeloader. Serve the community and it'll serve you. Get a job, suck it up. Get another job. Educate yourself. Keep moving. There was nothing political or ideological about it. Their guiding principle, rather, was a self-made couple's intolerance for laziness.

The Garcias weren't religious. Nor did they worship money. Respect and power, Robert had learned, were arbitrary and elusive. If the work didn't drive you, there was no point. He didn't hate guns but he didn't like them, either. Ever since Jesse's suicide he had no interest in them. He would rather cook than hunt, rather weld a new smoker for Sunday barbecues than customize a car. In his garage-turned-man-cave/office, he stood behind the bar and entertained friends with football on the big screen and music on the old jukebox.

On weekends, Robert spent as much time as possible with the boys. He and Trey wrestled in the morning. Eric, the stepson, resented their closeness. At thirteen, Eric had walked into Robert and Ronnie's bedroom and asked if he could change his last name to Garcia. Before Ronnie could answer, Robert said no. When Eric turned eighteen, Robert said, he could do whatever he wanted.

"You're being a fuckin' asshole," Ronnie told him.

Maybe so. But a name, in Robert's mind, didn't matter. It was how you brought them up that mattered. As the oldest son among his own siblings, Robert never called his father—Robert Sr.—"Dad." He called him Beto, short for Roberto. This formalness had nothing to do with a lack of affection. It was about respect. If you wanted to raise a baby, treat him like a child. If you wanted the kid to work with you, to help look out for the family, treat him like a man. Sentimentality, in Robert's mind, wasn't a prerequisite for good parenting.

For this reason, Robert intimidated Eric and Trey. He didn't tell them much, or show emotion. But he had his ways of caring. While they worked on projects together, Robert asked the boys questions about school and life. The three of them tiled the bathroom, and built a wall around the house. In the front yard they planted trees and flowers, and installed a sprinkler system. In back they built a deck, an outdoor bar, and a new shed. Trey was the athlete. But Eric, the gringo, learned Spanish better than his Mexican brother, and became a better craftsman. "You don't need to know how to do everything," Robert would tell them. "Just know what's involved in doing it, so you know how much to pay someone else. Otherwise you pay too much."

To those neighbors crowding around them in the subdivision, Robert and his boys were a marvel of discipline. When neighbors alluded to hopes of doing similar projects on their houses, Robert would say: "You buy the materials. We'll come over and do it."

Since he sent Laredo youth to jail on a daily basis, he brought a special vigilance to fathering. In this regard, Ronnie adapted her husband's style. Together they micromanaged where other parents trusted. They had to know who the boys would be with, where they were going. Cell phone numbers for friends and parents. Pickup and drop-off times. Trey complied. The younger boy was like his father, couldn't tell a lie if he wanted to. Eric, now in high school, was different.

"Where you going, Eric?"

"Out."

"With?"

"Friends."

"When you comin' back?"

"At some point."

As a white kid attending one of Laredo's tougher schools, United South, Eric struggled more than his parents realized. His English classes were taught in Spanish. Boys dressed in baggy jeans and Scarface T-shirts, flashed gang signs, and didn't give a shit. Eric, not a naturally aggressive kid, was bullied, and this made him angry. Robert taught the boys to remain calm in the face of aggression, to fight only when forced, but it wasn't so simple.

Eric's best friend became a father at thirteen. Seventh graders drove their parents' trucks to school. Eric certainly didn't wish to imitate all the debauchery he saw around him, but he envied the liberties enjoyed by his ungoverned classmates. To Eric, it was as if no one in Laredo were watching, except for his own dad, Little Hitler.

Eric, now sixteen, was smoking a little pot and doing a little drinking. His classmates did more. That year, United South expelled fourteen students for drugs and violence and stationed drug-sniffing dogs at all entrances, earning it the distinction of a "persistently dangerous school" under President George W. Bush's No Child Left Behind Act.

From the *Laredo Morning Times:*

United South hugs the Mexican border on the city's south side, and sits in a solidly middle-class neighborhood. But some of its students commute from colonias—unincorporated border settlements where impoverished residents live without public utilities.

Without running water, some students come to school unbathed for days, said Dago Carmona, a drug counselor at United South. Some work for or are related to members of the heavily armed drug cartels in Nuevo Laredo, Mexico. . . .

"It makes it hard on teachers, because some of them are afraid," Carmona said.

It's true that colonias contained illegal immigrants, but the media overplayed it. The biggest criminal families often came from those "solidly middle-class neighborhoods" where immigrant parents spoiled their children to give the next generation more than they had. As a TAMIU recruiter, Ronnie visited the high schools and saw this phenomenon firsthand. She generally found kids from colonias better behaved than their richer classmates; in the best cases, she attributed this difference to the example set by having two working parents. In many families from the Garcias' neighborhood, and in richer families from the north side, the mother stayed home, but it rarely meant greater oversight.

ONE FALL AFTERNOON, IN 2003, someone offered Eric a roche and told him to cut it in half. Instead, he took the whole pill and then fell out of his chair in math class. When security arrived a few minutes later, Eric was still lying in the aisle.

Robert met them in the hallway. In the parking lot, Eric and Robert got into it, pushing and yelling. At home, Robert made him take three drug tests—*three*!

Ronnie returned from work and watched from the kitchen. Here we go again, she thought. The prior spring, when Robert was away on an undercover job, Eric had come home from school all pissy and flung open the refrigerator door with such force that he put a hole in the wall. "Why can't you control your emotions?" Ronnie had asked while Trey looked on. When Eric said, "Shut up, bitch," Ronnie, not a small woman, reared back and clocked him across the face with a closed fist. She kept the incident between her and the boys, lest Robert's reaction alienate Eric for good.

"Don't worry!" Eric now shouted to his imaginary audience as he peed into cup after cup. "Robert is on the job! He'll get to the bottom of this case if it's the last thing he does!"

As his stepson ranted, Robert thought, You never know what you have at home. The carpenter can be great but his own furniture falls apart. The best mechanic in town breaks down on the highway. Watching Eric spin out of control, Robert wondered if he'd been too reluctant to let the boys make their own mistakes. You needed to monitor them and be strict. But they needed to go out there and fuck up on their own. The yin and yang. When Eric, still ranting, threw a wild punch, Robert tackled him, cuffed him, and ordered a squad car to take him to juvenile detention for an overnight stay. Had it been any other cop calling, dispatch would've thought it was a joke.

6

Underworld University

I begin my day at five a.m. as a dispatcher for a medical transportation service," Gabriela Cardona explained to Judge Danny Valdez when summoned to juvenile court to answer for her second son's truancy at reform school. "Judge, I don't know what he does or who he sees. He goes to Nuevo Laredo and doesn't return until four in the morning."

Back in 1987, as a young judge, Danny Valdez created the first gang summit in the Martin High cafeteria. The gang leaders would come in, shake hands, share a pizza lunch, and then return to hostilities a week later. But the initial hopeful stir the gang summit always created meant terrific PR, and the summits became regular features of springtime at places like Martin High and United South. Judge Valdez knew other ways of reforming bad kids; a week in juvenile detention, for instance, could help straighten a kid out. But since Laredo's juvenile detention center had only twenty-four beds, most offenders were released to their parents. Word on the street: *All you need is a parent to show up and they let you go!*

By the early 2000s, as street gangs with cross-border ties proliferated, Judge Valdez now dealt with one of the country's highest rates of youth arrests for violent crimes. Gangs used to fight with their fists; now they fought with weapons. A youngster was arrested for a violent crime in the city, on average, every other day.

But what Judge Valdez saw in his court, largely, were single-parent families going to hell. Parental involvement, he knew, went a long way. He tried ordering parents to sit with their delinquent kids in school, say, for a morning or two per week. The strategy could be effective, unless it was unrealistic for a parent to follow her child to school, which in most cases it was—as it was for Gabriela Cardona.

For her son's truancy, Judge Valdez fined La Gaby two hundred dollars and told her to accompany Gabriel to his reform school on Tuesdays and Wednesdays. He also ordered Gabriel to attend the Military Disciplinary Program, a weekend "boot camp" that enforced the consequences of delinquency and disrespect.

"Disrespect for what?" Gabriel asked his homies back in the shack on Lincoln Street.

"America, *güey*!"*

The boys laughed. Laredo devoted every February to a month-long celebration of George Washington's birthday, but these kids from Lazteca had no reverence for it. The driving principles of America, they believed, were waging economic wars and plundering other societies. Veterans Day supposedly commemorated lives lost in the war for freedom. But what freedom? they asked. Oil had nothing to with freedom!

On Televisa, a Mexican TV network, they watched captured

---

* Literally an ox or a beast, *güey*—pronounced "way"—is border slang for "dude," or "idiot," depending on how it's used.

smugglers on both sides of the border paraded in front of the camera amid bales of marijuana and bricks of cocaine; money; and guns. Far from cautionary examples, they considered the handcuffed men to be *pesados,* heavyweights.

EIGHTEEN MONTHS PRIOR TO GABRIEL and La Gaby appearing before Judge Valdez, the rolling papers and the bullet had landed him in Lara Academy, the first layer of Laredo's overburdened reform system. At Lara, a World War II veteran spoke about the horrors of war and the importance of an education. He described pulling limbs out of the South Pacific and confronting Japan's kamikaze pilots, who believed that to die for the emperor was to live forever. It was a weird way of thinking, the veteran said, but the suicide bombings on 9/11 were similar to the kamikaze missions. He concluded by saying that environmental influences were no excuse for delinquency.

When Gabriel showed up to Lara Academy buzzed one Monday morning, after a weekend of drinking, he was transferred to the next layer of the reform system—the Juvenile Justice Alternative Education Program. At JJAEP, known as "the Alternative," mobile homes converted to classrooms formed a square around a basketball court. Students worked on learning modules at their own pace. For this stage in the system, somewhere between high school and prison, Judge Danny Valdez and the other juvenile judges who oversaw JJAEP struggled with just how prisonlike the Alternative should be. For instance, video cameras trained on the students were a source of controversy. Were the cameras advisable safety precautions, or too Big Brother? Did they negate the sense of confidence and self-worth that the staff tried to instill in students? It was hard to say. Mostly, the cameras captured sex during recess, and footage of the girl who gave out blowjobs after school.

But the teachers and supervisors made it clear: If you didn't learn to behave, you *would* be sent to Texas Youth Commission, TYC, juvie—the junior prison that prepared you for the big house.

When Gabriel tried to reenroll at Martin High, as a sophomore, the principal advised him that it was better to catch up on credits in the Alternative, then return to Martin and graduate with his class. If Gabriel felt frustrated by the principal's dismissal, he was also too busy with underworld pursuits to dwell on his school failures for long. Accompanied by Bart, or some other associate, Gabriel stole cars in Laredo and sold them across the border to a man named Mario Flores Soto, known as Meme Flores, whom he met through a Lazteca family.

Meme—pronounced "MEH-may"—headed one of Nuevo Laredo's criminal organizations. Until then, Gabriel had only seen the money to be made from drugs going north. Meme showed him the other side: Mexico's demand for smuggled cars and weapons. From the 9 mm he graduated to bigger guns like the Mini-14, an assault rifle.

Uninhibited, thanks to the roches, which he now took with increasing frequency, ingesting as many as five per day, Gabriel stole cars and trucks with a methodical efficiency that sometimes dissolved into quick frustration if he felt a partner wasn't sharing an equal load of the risk. Having established a reputation as someone who was "always down to ride," ready to tackle any criminal opportunity, Gabriel felt that others in his circle, like his older brother Luis, wanted the benefits without the risks. When Gabriel forced Luis to steal a truck from a gas station, his brother tried to pull himself together. Luis walked into the gas station, but then just kept walking, past the vehicle and into the night.

Bart was the only homie whose fearlessness and work ethic matched Gabriel's. The day Gabriel "jacked," or stole, a customized Ford F-150 pickup truck from Lazteca, Bart was in flip-flops but he

still sprinted behind the truck and threw himself into the b
people from the neighborhood looked and laughed.

NOW, SENTENCED TO THE MILITARY boot camp for skipping the
Alternative, Gabriel, sleepless and still drunk from the night before,
was determined to "win" the boot camp when La Gaby dropped
him at the first weekend session. He forgot to bring his own water
bottle—a boot camp rule—and almost passed out from dehydration
during the marching, running, push-ups, and sit-ups. During the
break a congressman addressed them: "Half of you are not going to
finish high school. I've seen a lot of good people end up in bad places,
and we don't want that to happen to you."

Gabriel partied again that Saturday evening and refused to return to boot camp the next morning, so his mother called the cops.
A boot camp sergeant, seeing the police escort, went hard on Gabriel
that day.

Get back, get back, you're too slow!

I can't hear you!

Faster, faster!

Fall in!

The motivational yelling was thought to be effective because
these kids lacked an authority figure. But the sergeant didn't want
Gabriel there if he wasn't going to obey orders. He made it clear to
Gabriel that if Gabriel wanted, he could quit, then go through the
same boot camp in TYC. "Okay," Gabriel said, and walked outside,
as if to wait for a ride to juvie. When the sergeant went back inside,
Gabriel ran to Lazteca, and juvie waited. After getting caught for a
drive-by with Bart, a month later, at the end of 2003, Gabriel finally
landed in TYC. "We meet again," said the sergeant. After a few
weeks of juvie—where Gabriel saw Ashley, the one who introduced
him to roches, now pushing a broom across the cafeteria floor—the

probation officer cut the seventeen-year-old a break and sent him to rehab, the "youth recovery home." But all Gabriel saw in rehab were drug fiends. He didn't feel he belonged, so he escaped.

All the while, he never felt like a gangster in training. Nor like he was making a conscious decision to go one way or the other. It was never "This or that." It was always just "Okay, let's do this." You get thrown out of high school and placed in reform school. You get thrown out of reform school and placed in the Alternative. You get thrown out of the Alternative and sent to juvie. By then you are long gone, and the system appears to be funneling you from one stage of dereliction to the next. Nothing, it seemed, could halt his slide.

In Gabriel's mind, this perpetual state of delinquency, bouncing between reform schools and underworld pursuits, led somewhere. His trouble with school was no proxy for failure. A militant work ethic burned through the fog of the roches, and shaped into ambition the energy released by their powerful effects. He ran guns and made money. He stole cars and made money. During slow times, he and a friend broke into an abandoned theater in Lazteca and stole boxes of clothes and other goods stored there by local merchants. When you found a calling, Gabriel believed, you devoted yourself to it. And though he'd never felt beholden to any group, he now felt as though he were drifting toward some entity that merited his respect.

This activity with Meme, Gabriel thought, "wasn't kid shit no more." *No slinging nicks and dimes. No stupid beefs.* Meme and his associates in Nuevo Laredo were serious men who stuck to codes and took care of their own. Meme's partner resided in a Nuevo Laredo prison where his cell had leather furniture, a kitchen, and a flat-screen TV. Friends visited. Women entertained while guards brought beer. How terrible was that?

So when Gabriel broke free of rehab and sprinted through the onion fields of Webb County, kicking up clouds of dust on the way back to Lazteca, he didn't ditch the system aimlessly. He ran *back* to these enterprises, which benefited his mother, aunts, uncles, and brothers in the form of cash. His criminal lifestyle also meant he met new people constantly, and affiliated with desirable underworld elements. Whatever dreams he'd had, at six or eight or ten, of becoming a lawyer, of wowing audiences with his charisma . . . well, he was taking his talents elsewhere.

It was now 2004, and, according to underworld rumor, a new group with a "suicidal philosophy" was taking over Nuevo Laredo. Some referred to them as *la gente nueva*—the new people.

TO GABRIEL, ONE LAZTECA "HOODIE"—A homeboy from the neighborhood—stood apart from the others. Richard Jasso was the closest thing Lazteca had to smuggling royalty. A couple years older than Gabriel, Richard lived across the street with his wife's family. Richard didn't work for a gang, didn't have to. When he was six, he started smuggling immigrants with his grandmother. At eight, his father took him on coke runs to Houston.

At sixteen, Richard registered a "ghost company" called R.J.'s Trucking Inc. It specialized in shipping bulk loads of Mexican pottery and plastic scrap, which he could buy cheaply at the border and use as a "cover" for his marijuana loads. He shipped tons of marijuana to places like Georgia and North Carolina. He searched online for companies in those states that dealt in pottery or plastic scrap, and listed them as buyers on the shipping manifest, the "bill of lading," which contained a phone number for a female friend who answered in a sexy secretary's voice: "R.J.'s Trucking."

Richard purchased used Freightliner trucks, then stole permits and license plates from other trucks that looked like them. Instead of paying $8,000 apiece to buy cargo boxes, he rented them from a guy who waited two weeks before reporting the box stolen. By then Richard had taken a load or two north, and left the cargo box in some area where the cops could easily find it and return it to the owner. By seventeen, Richard had introduced roughly fifty tons of marijuana into the States.

But marijuana was just a start. Now, at nineteen, thanks to a connection brokered by his sister's husband, Richard was adding a more lucrative product to his business: cocaine. Richard bought a new line of trucks, as well as insurance and permits, hired a full-time mechanic at a thousand bucks a week, and rented a warehouse in San Antonio, where he and his brother-in-law now spent most of their time. Richard transitioned from the hood-chic style of Guess jeans and Polo boots to the business-casual uniform of DKNY pants and Steve Madden shoes—"the preppy college guy look," as he referred to it. He offered to take Gabriel, who was still working for Meme, on as a bodyguard, errand boy, and courier.

Richard represented much of what Gabriel wanted. He was married to a woman who came from a family of hustlers herself. Richard had partied in Miami Beach with one of his cocaine clients, a Cuban gentleman who supplied South Florida. In Lazteca, Richard told exotic stories, set in places like "Ocean Boulevard," about being at the Mansion nightclub and drinking Cristal champagne straight from the bottle while the most beautiful women you ever saw, dressed in the classiest clothes, made the air taste sweet. It wasn't bullshit, either. Gabriel and Luis, who also worked for Richard, saw Richard's setup in San Antonio. They saw how the VIP sections at the most popular clubs, like Planeta Bar-Rio and Ritmo Latino, were always reserved for Richard and his brother-in-law and whoever tagged along. How Buchanan's scotch and Patrón tequila were always on the table, and how Richard handed envelopes of several hundred dollars each to the person in charge of security, the waitress, and the club manager, who made his office available for activities that required discretion. One time, when Richard brought his mother to a Los Tigres del Norte concert at Planeta Bar-Rio, a couple occupied the table he wanted near the stage. Richard offered them two thousand dollars to move. A Volvo, an Avalanche, a GMC Denali, and a Jeep Grand Cherokee. Joe Brand, Versace, Hugo Boss, Lacoste, Prada, GBX, Fendi, Rolex, and custom jewelry. Family dinners at the best Mexican restaurants with the mariachis playing requests all night. Richard lived a dream.

He had lots of "weekend girls" who loved his warehouse of cocaine. The manager at Embassy Suites also loved him. The carousing led to fights at home. But his wife and kids lacked nothing. His mother-in-law, a friend of La Gaby, drove a new SUV. Every time Richard dropped another five thousand dollars at Toys "R" Us, the cashiers asked if he didn't want to adopt their kids. Gabriel noted the lust in the hoodrats' eyes when Richard drove his Hummer through Lazteca, Assassyn chrome wheels glimmering in the sun like knife blades spinning. Even Richard's wife's friends flirted with him openly. Handsome in a way that was less thuggish than Gabriel, but somehow also less delicate, Richard was a gregarious guy with the magnetic quality of someone who made you feel better about yourself, whose beaming, big-toothed smile seemed to say, "I'll show you a *very* good time."

In Lazteca, if someone owned a flashy car, such as a Tahoe or Escalade, customized with nice rims, a stereo, and tinted windows, people considered the guy to be *se mueve,* pushing, and he was respected. But if he had multiple such vehicles he was considered to be *se mueve pesado,* moving heavy, and that label came with a different level of respect. In the eyes of the community, Richard was a model young man, a young *pesado* who was "about his business." In Lazteca, to be about one's business was about the best thing you could be. Gabriel envied him.

In Richard's employ, Gabriel's awareness of success expanded from trappings—Versace, Mercedes—to behavior. How did power act? How was it established and how was it maintained? Richard had a business frame of mind. He was social, always on the lookout for upstate buyers, *piojos* who could bulk up his bottom line. Richard made his aptitude for violence known, but left it to others whenever possible. Gabriel saw how carefully Richard formed trust, and how quickly it could be broken. Richard even accused his own wife of "ripping loads," stealing drugs from him. Loyalty was fleeting in a world with such large amounts of money at stake.

Richard, now managing operations at the San Antonio warehouse, made $15,000 a week, sometimes twice that. And yet he seemed to think that paying Gabriel $300 a week and covering the clubs was adequate. What about the loads Gabriel ran to Austin? Did Richard think Gabriel was too dumb to know he deserved commission? Well, maybe the next shipment would have to go missing, and maybe the shipment after that as well.

In a traditional, arm's-length smuggling deal between professionals—in which the Laredo drug supplier hires a transporter to carry a drug load to a northern buyer—it's quite hard for one party to rip the other off. Both supplier and transporter protect themselves with something called a "letter." The supplier wants to protect himself against the transporter selling the drugs to another buyer, pocketing the entire sale price, then claiming that the vehicle crashed or that the load was seized by law enforcement. The transporter wants to protect himself against the supplier—who might be an informant—"dropping a dime" on him, reporting the details of the transporter's vehicle to the cops. In the "letter," the transporter writes the details of the vehicle he's going to use to transport the load, seals the letter in an envelope, and gives it to the supplier. The supplier can open the letter, later, *only* if something goes wrong with the deal. If the transporter returns with a story about a vehicle crash or a seized load, the supplier can confirm the story by opening the letter and comparing the vehicle details to, say, police paperwork or a report in the news. But if the deal goes as planned, the supplier must return the letter to the transporter unopened.

Normally, Richard used a letter with his transporters, but not with Gabriel because Gabriel was an old friend and he only moved small loads.

And so, with his childhood friend Wences "Tucan" Tovar, Gabriel jacked fifty pounds of weed from Richard and pushed it north, all the way to a connection in Springfield, Illinois. He jacked another load—two hundred pounds—and drove it to San Antonio. This time, however, the dope was concealed in a steel box inside the gas tank. They bought an electric saw, and parked in a nice neighborhood. Sparks flew as they tried to cut the tank in half. People gathered in their yards to watch. When the sparks ignited the fuel, the truck caught fire. Gabriel scrambled for a pail and a hose while spectators ushered their children inside, but the flames engulfed the truck too quickly so Gabriel and Wences ran away. Gabriel told Wences not to come around the hood for a couple of weeks. He told Richard that Wences had been arrested.

Tucan in the pen? It was plausible.

Born in Texas and raised in Lazteca until the age of ten, Wences moved across the border to Mexico when his dad "caught" a smuggling charge and had to flee. Wences moved back to Laredo at fifteen. Following his own early stints in Lara Academy and JJAEP, Wences applied to return to Martin High. The principal gave him one last chance not to fuck up. But when a sophomore challenged him to a fight over a girl, Wences cut open the guy's cheek with a punch. The guy said Wences hit him with brass knuckles, which wasn't true, but Wences landed in county jail for a few months, then pleaded guilty to aggravated assault and got probation. Word spread: Wences took a "felony two" charge—a second-degree felony—and walked away with only probation!

"Get a job!" his mother screamed. Wences labored at Expediters

Inc., a warehouse on the west side, but didn't like working for minimum wage. He cared about having enough money to own a decent ride, smoke pot, entertain preppy girls from the north side, and buy some flashy jewelry, the thick chains, *esclavas,* that were prized in the hood.

Having lived on both sides of the border, Wences, like Gabriel, had a wide network, and they would need it, because their association with Richard would not last much longer.

MOST OF GABRIEL'S SOCIAL LIFE now took place across the border. In the Nuevo Laredo nightclubs, where teenagers from Mexico and the States hung out, the hoodrats beckoned, their sweat-soaked tanks clinging to their breasts as they thumb-hooked booty shorts and hula-hooped their hips to Daddy Yankee's "Gasolina." They guzzled Budweiser and grinded against whichever baller's pocket showed the "gangster bulge" of a good week. The long-braided *fresas* congregated in the corner and sipped Boone's Farm, the bottom-shelf wine, while the rat waited for DJ Kuri to announce the next lap dance. Purple strobes flashed electric on rolling asses; eyes pulsed, teeth glowed.

There was a cap culture among border youngsters. On occasion Gabriel wore an L.A. Dodgers hat for "La Amalia," the Nuevo Laredo neighborhood controlled by Meme. Americans with a little money, especially those connected to prominent gangsters like Meme, had power in the Nuevo Laredo club scene. Most Americans went to Señor Frog's, which was stricter on security, more of a hookup scene. Clubs like 57th Street had less security, so they attracted a more thuggish crowd.

But as long as Gabriel didn't piss off the wrong people, his work for Meme Flores, which had continued while he worked for Richard, made the clubs a veritable zone of impunity. One night, roched out and feeling untouchable, Gabriel approached an enemy at the 57th Street nightclub and said, "What's up, fucker?" This enemy was a former friend. But following a disagreement over a gun swap, the friend had become hostile, at one point sucker-punching Gabriel, then threatening his younger brother. Gabriel had trusted the fool. And now this. *Nah*.

The roches having severed any last thread of restraint, he called the enemy outside and pummeled the larger boy to the edge of consciousness. It was the worst beating Gabriel's crew had ever seen. The boy was driven back to Laredo and airlifted to San Antonio that evening. Gabriel now had the reputation of someone who nearly killed someone with his hands.

On the American side of the border, back in Lazteca, Gabriel's business relationships frayed. Richard Jasso, suspicious over the missing loads, stopped giving Gabriel work. Smuggling, Gabriel learned, was a tough game. The moving parts, the responsibilities.

His separation from Richard was a setback. But he still had Meme—the cars, the guns—and who knew where that might lead?

PART II

The Company

The ladder of promotion was marked out in a straightfor-
ward, arithmetical way: the taking of captives—in single
combat, and scored as to quality—for presentation for death
on the killing stone.

—*AZTECS*, INGA CLENDINNEN

7

Original Vice Lord

In the beginning, on a brutal morning in June, when the South Texas heat congealed in the sky and baked the floodplains, there were only the stirrings of a city, an inkling of identity. Were they American or Mexican? Should they settle on this side or that? Did it matter which Laredo they lived in?

It was 1853, after America won the Mexican-American War. In the mid-1840s, James Polk had turned his political career around, and won the White House, when he perceived public sentiment in favor of bringing Texas into the Union. He continued the westward expansion—"manifest destiny"—by attacking Mexico, and winning California and New Mexico in 1847. Now, six years later, after Laredo residents had been given the choice to stay north of the Rio Grande, on what was now American territory, or move across the river to Mexico, a reporter for a new newspaper, the *New York Times,* came to Laredo and observed an American surgeon shoot two men in a bar.

The surgeon fled across the border, where his captors put him in leg irons and shipped him back across. In Laredo, he was placed on a box and hanged. The *Times* reporter saw cattle raids and military encampments, violence and rough commerce. What was the effect of this demoralized frontier life on character? he asked. "People grow used to it—reckless of life, ragged, and saucy. The attention is called to getting whereof to clothe and to eat. The practice of carrying weapons, imposed by a few upon all, makes them suspicious and hasty."

Since the end of the Mexican-American War, both countries had been expanding their legions of customs inspectors and border patrols, which turned Laredo and Nuevo Laredo into corrupt tariff-collecting towns. The mouth of the Rio Grande—where the great river empties into the Gulf of Mexico, two hundred miles southeast of Laredo—was becoming one of the busiest ports in the world. But Laredo and Nuevo Laredo remained trading posts, which meant that every new regulation presented a new smuggling opportunity: coffee, sugar, bacon, and even cotton. When the Civil War began, European ships waited in the Gulf to exchange their cargo for the outgoing Confederate cotton that helped finance the war for the south. When Union warships attempted to blockade the cotton trade and cut off Confederate financing, cotton smugglers traveled through Laredo instead.

Smuggling went both ways. Mexico's prohibition of tobacco, following its independence from Spain in 1821, translated into enormous premiums for American tobacco merchants. During the hostilities that followed the end of the Mexican-American War, Mexican authorities seized 565 bales from Samuel Belden, a New Orleans tobacconist. Belden petitioned U.S. president Millard Fillmore, demanding that Washington intervene on his behalf. Others filed similar grievances. Although better than what today's Mexican drug lords could hope for when their dope is seized, Belden's outcome was less than satisfactory. Decades later, in 1885, the U.S. government awarded Belden $128,000 on a $500,000 loss.

During the second half of the nineteenth century, as Laredo

developed new industries—oil, ore, and onions—the industrial revolution turned the city into a place of some significance. Bridges connected the countries. Railroads brought immigrants. French and Lebanese merchants. Swiss saddle makers. Polish grocers. Czech tanners. Italian hoteliers. In 1880, Anheuser-Busch established one of its first distributorships in Laredo. But the city remained a trading post. War and policy would always be hatched elsewhere; Laredo was the border frontier's petri dish of implication. No trade would affect the city as narcotics would.

IN THE 1870S AND 1880S, Civil War veterans hankered for the morphine they got on the battlefield, and doctors discovered cocaine's value as an anesthetic. The pharmaceutical business, led by companies such as Parke-Davis, built consumer interest in dope and coke, and the drugs became health problems.

During the first decade of the twentieth century, states experimented with regulation while support grew for federal prohibition. In 1912, the United States and a dozen other nations, including Germany, France, Italy, China, Japan, Russia, Persia, and Siam, signed the International Opium Convention at The Hague. The first international drug treaty, the convention committed its participants to suppress opiates and rid society of "hop heads." Two years later, the United States restricted access with the Harrison Narcotics Tax Act.

The first U.S. narcotics agents had low-paying, low-status jobs deep in the "miscellaneous division" of the Treasury Department, which was charged with other distinguished duties like ensuring the quality of margarine. When early Supreme Court decisions held that the Harrison Act prohibited doctors from prescribing even "maintenance doses" of opium or coke, narcotics agents arrested thousands of physicians and closed clinics—driving addicts to shady suppliers, and creating a lucrative black market.

U.S. drug policy was rooted in morality and panic about public health. But Mexico's antidrug law, adopted in 1916, grew partly from security concerns—or at least xenophobia. For decades, Chinese immigrants had been arriving in Mexico's Pacific Coast cities. Some paid fifty dollars to be smuggled into California. Others remained in Mexico, and some headed into the interior, settling in Sinaloa and Sonora. There, in the Sierra Madre mountains, they found a climate to ply the trade they knew well from home: poppy cultivation.

Post-1916, the growers and traffickers of the opium that was in such demand in the States lacked a black-market regulator to supervise the illegal market for narcotics. Colonel Esteban Cantú filled that void. A cavalry officer who campaigned against the Yaqui Indians during the Mexican Revolution, Colonel Cantú took control of the Mexicali Valley. Part of the northern Baja Peninsula, Mexicali was a popular destination for American tourists. Cantú trained a private army of 1,800 men, and projected a sense of order to Americans who had reservations about their safety while visiting Mexicali's red-light district.

Cantú's primary revenue came from taxing vice—sex, drugs, and gaming. The Tecolote Gambling Hall paid him $15,000 a month. A syndicate of Chinese opium dealers paid $45,000 to get started, and another $10,000 a month. These "taxes," Cantú argued, "moralized" vice by keeping the forbidden trades safe; financing public works and education; and liberating vice tourism from reliance on a corrupt and feckless central government in Mexico City.

A utilitarian outlaw, Colonel Cantú didn't plunder or pillage; didn't steal or menace. As Mexico's first vice lord, he innovated a centuries-old role in Mexico.

PRIOR TO THE SPANISH CONQUEST of Mexico, in 1519, merchants paid "tribute" to the dominant warrior elites, such as the Olmecs,

Toltecs, and Aztecs. The Aztecs, a wandering tribe that claimed to come from Aztlán, a mythical region in the northwest of Mexico, began as mercenary warriors for whichever tribe ruled the prosperous lake region around what is now Mexico City. Eventually, the Aztecs established their own city-state. Through the fourteenth and fifteenth centuries, the Aztec empire stretched across much of Mexico. Under Aztec rule, sophisticated cities hosted vibrant merchant economies. Governors regulated the trading markets, and adjudicated business disputes.

In 1519, when Hernán Cortés docked at Veracruz, in the Gulf of Mexico, the Spanish removed the Aztec warrior elites and leveled the empire. The natives who survived the Spanish conquest, and the disease that came with it, awoke to a new world. The *encomienda* system assigned zones of natives to serve individual Spanish colonists, "local nobles" known as *encomenderos,* who reported to the Spanish Crown.

Under Spanish rule, the natives upped their intake of pulque, a high-octane drink fermented from cactus. Imbibers blacked out, lost control, and became violent. Pulque, it was said, cast "the spell of Four Hundred Rabbits." The Spanish Crown, worried that lazy natives produced only enough crops to pay the royal tribute, granted *encomenderos* the power of *reparto de efectos:* a monopoly to sell imported luxury items, such as horses and chocolate, to natives at inflated prices. The *reparto de efectos* coerced natives into accelerating production of valuable exports, such as wheat. In the seventeenth and eighteen centuries, the industrial potential of a zone was regulated by what became known as *caciquismo,* local-boss rule. A warlord with strongmen, the *cacique* morphed, during the nineteenth century, into a military man like Colonel Esteban Cantú.

As Cantú organized Mexicali into Mexico's first zone of vice, the United States made serious changes to its trade policies—changes that would mold men with Cantú's inclinations into very different criminals.

During the early twentieth century, trade protectionists and liberal-trade advocates in America debated between a closed economy and an open one. Ever since the Civil War, tariffs, the hallmark of a closed economy, provided half of U.S. government revenue. But in 1913, the "opens" won: Congress approved the Sixteenth Amendment, instituting a national income tax. This tax reversed the way America financed itself. By 1920, falling tariffs composed a mere 5 percent of national revenue, while income tax supplied more than half the country's budget. This policy transformation prompted changes at the border.

On the enforcement side, this change in economic policy meant that the U.S. Customs Service acted less like a department of economic security, collecting tariffs, and more like a security force with a mandate to stop smuggling. Between 1925 and 1930, Customs personnel grew by a multiple of six. On the criminal side, smuggling shifted from evading tariffs to evading prohibition. Increased enforcement pushed up prices for prohibited goods. Mexican border towns expanded to facilitate illegal trade. In 1930, Congress created the Federal Bureau of Narcotics, or FBN, as an agency of the Department of the Treasury. The FBN fought opium and heroin, and successfully pushed for cannabis criminalization with the Marihuana Tax Act of 1937. By then Colonel Cantú had retired to California. The golden era of vice traffic was just beginning.

WHEN AMERICAN PROHIBITION PUSHED ALCOHOL underground, a youngster from the Gulf Coast began smuggling whiskey and *sotol* (cactus moonshine) up to Texas. In the 1940s, Juan Nepomuceno Guerra graduated to gambling, prostitution, and opium. World War II renewed the U.S. demand for morphine. Nepomuceno Guerra joined a coterie of *contrabandistas* such as the heroin king, Jaime Herrera Nevarez; Pedro Avilés Pérez, one of the first Mexican smugglers to expand into cocaine; and Domingo Aranda, who moved mule trains of tires, sugar, coffee, and anything else rationed in America during the war years.

Heroin still surpassed cocaine in demand. In New York and Chicago, the Jewish-Italian outlaw crew of Lucky Luciano, Bugsy Siegel, Frank Costello, and Meyer Lansky sent Siegel's girlfriend, Virginia Hill, to Mexico. She cozied up to officials, bought a nightclub in Nuevo Laredo, and shipped heroin north. In 1948, the FBN declared Mexico the source of half the illicit drugs in America. Nepomuceno Guerra organized a network of smugglers that would become known as the Gulf Cartel.

During the 1950s and '60s, narcotics traffickers slid into an alliance with Mexico's one-party government, the Partido Revolucionario Institucional—the Institutional Revolutionary Party—known as the PRI, or "Pree." At that time, the United States had little to say about drugs and corruption in Mexico. It was the Kennedy era, the height of the Cold War. Cuba, Russia, Vietnam. Similar to post-9/11 America, national security got all the attention. The CIA station in Mexico City—a hub of Soviet espionage, and a base for Cuban agents—was the CIA's most important base in Latin America. Mexico's federal secret police, Dirección Federal de Seguridad, the Directorate of Federal Security, was a criminal incubator that organized protection for traffickers on a national scale. But the DFS also shared intelligence with the FBI and the CIA. Ignoring corruption and trafficking was a condition for this assistance.

It was only after President Kennedy announced the Alliance for Progress, a multibillion-dollar aid program intended to strengthen ties with Latin America and fight leftist groups, that the Mexican government invited the FBN to open offices in Mexico. It was a token gesture, however. Mexico's attorney general said: no "buy cases" allowed; no FBN agents testifying in Mexican courts; and traffickers could only be arrested *prior* to delivering the drugs—a rule that nullified drug interdiction.

Here was a lesson that would play out several times over the next fifty years. Was it realistic to expect a dictatorship to repay a little financial largesse from abroad by suppressing the only source of income for millions of peasants? It was not. U.S. aid, or investment, or whatever it would be called, instead bought only the *appearance* of cooperation, temporarily, until Mexico's one-party government returned to regulating its drug industry in the safest way possible: selling smuggling routes to traffickers in return for bribes. And still, the Americans set up law enforcement offices in Mexico with the stated intent of attacking supply, while largely ignoring the demand at home.

In 1969, Richard Nixon picked up the antidrug ball and played with it. His Project Intercept inspected more vehicles at the border, slowing commerce. The idea was to prod Mexican businessmen interested in normal commercial relations between the countries to pressure the Mexican government to get serious about drug prohibition. But the program carried an unacceptably high price. Screwing up the economy to catch a few more drug loads: Was Nixon crazy?

In the 1970s, the second wave of Mexico's narco-bosses began to take over. On the eastern side of Mexico, Juan Nepomuceno Guerra continued to expand his dominion over the Gulf Coast and the Texas border crossings, in partnership with his nephew, Juan García Ábrego. On the western Pacific side, in the states surrounding the Sierra Madre Occidental, the domain belonged to several traffickers of the Guadalajara Cartel—men such as Ernesto Fonseca Carrillo and Rafael Caro Quintero. Chief among the Guadalajara crew was the godfather of Mexican traffickers, Miguel Ángel Félix Gallardo. Born in 1946, Félix Gallardo—known as El Padrino, the

Godfather—had been a cop and a governor's bodyguard in the state of Sinaloa. El Padrino's close working relationship with authorities made it seem as if he *was* the government, as if the drug trade, like oil and other industries of that era, was nationalized.

Mexico's authoritarian PRI was created in the 1920s, in the aftermath of the Mexican Revolution. For all its other faults, the PRI was well equipped to manage a country with a large criminal element. All government positions relied on PRI patronage. Within law enforcement, careers were assigned through party connections. Politicians or cops who did business with a criminal that lacked the PRI's blessing would be told to stop; if they persisted, they were killed. The PRI's system of regulating the narcotics industry assured traffickers that a few large bribes protected their business at all levels, from Mexico City up to the border. Men such as El Padrino and Nepomuceno Guerra paid the Directorate of Federal Security, the Federal Judicial Police, the attorney general, and the local police commander.

As part of the deal, known as the Pax Mafiosa, the PRI required that criminals adhere to certain principles. Since violence negatively affected the PRI's popularity with the electorate, with gringo tourists, and with Washington, traffickers had to operate more or less peacefully. This arrangement meant no dead people left in the streets; no media scandals; periodic imprisonment of low-level traffickers; and investment of drug revenue into poor communities.

By managing the black market, the PRI minimized violence, but this relative peace would be short-lived.

IN 1973, NIXON CONSOLIDATED SEVERAL drug-control agencies into one superagency, the Drug Enforcement Administration. At the same time he prevailed on Turkey, then the world's premier opium producer, to prohibit that drug, which in turn inflated the value of Mexican opium. In 1977, when Mexico saw that there might be money and political benefits in the antidrug agenda, they agreed to let the Americans spray crops. Operation Condor appeared to be a success: In addition to putting 39 helicopters, 22 airplanes, and one executive jet in the coffers of Mexico's attorney general, the crop eradication seemed to work. Strong herbicides like paraquat, which kills green plant matter on contact, reduced Mexico's share of the U.S. marijuana market from 75 percent down to 4 percent, and its share of the U.S. heroin market from 67 percent to 25 percent. To Americans, Mexican drug growers being marched off their land made powerful media images. By pasting "dark, gun-toting foreigner" on the face of what had hitherto been an unclear enemy, those images began to cement the terms of the war.

Mexico also got nice publicity for its cooperation, but it reduced the American presence after Operation Condor was over, and said that DEA pilots would no longer be able to fly unescorted through Mexican airspace. The Directorate of Federal Security—which the Americans still relied on for intelligence—coalesced, once again, around El Padrino's centralized control of the drug industry.

In Washington, the drug war remained a mostly secondary interest. Jimmy Carter, never a fan of prohibition, was concerned with reducing U.S. dependence on Middle East oil and striking a deal for Mexican oil. But Washington's priorities always shifted back to drugs whenever national security was implicated. In the early 1980s, the overseas smuggling route for cocaine, from Central America to Florida, turned Miami into a war zone. In 1982, Vice President George H. W. Bush announced the South Florida Task Force, a multiagency effort that emphasized interdiction and prosecution of smugglers. American politicians from the East and Southwest complained that the task force wasn't solving the problem but displacing it: Drug traffic now moved through California, Arizona, and Texas. So the task force concept expanded to five other regional centers: Los Angeles, El Paso, New Orleans, Chicago, and New York.

As cocaine traffic shifted to Mexico, El Padrino's control of the Mexican drug market began to fall part. In 1985, El Padrino was blamed for the torture and murder of DEA agent Enrique "Kiki" Camarena, whose face appeared on the cover of *Time*. Operation Leyenda, a huge DEA investigation, sought to bring everyone responsible for Camarena's death to justice. Several capos, including Ernesto Fonseca Carrillo and Rafael Caro Quintero—El Padrino's associates in the Guadalajara Cartel—were arrested. The DFS was disbanded, leaving Mexican traffickers to fend for themselves, and set up new protection arrangements with whomever had the power to make such deals.

To Americans, the Camarena tragedy seemed, ironically, like progress. But the dramatic overreaction to Camarena's murder set another drug war pattern: Like a cartel boss's capture, or his subsequent escape from prison, the murder of a single DEA agent was the kind of micro-event that would blur America's ability to see what was happening in Mexico.

The same year of Camarena's death, a major earthquake in Mexico City sent the value of the peso plummeting, and left Mexican cops, among others, desperate for dollars. In the past, when a dollar bought twenty-four pesos, corrupt police didn't do much dirty work for the drug traffickers who paid them bribes. But as the value of the peso fell, senior police officials started providing substantive labor to traffickers, such as security and smuggling.

In 1987, El Padrino—sensing the breakdown of Mexico's system-wide impunity for traffickers—convened the nation's top traffickers in Acapulco and divided the trade routes among them.

The Tijuana route went to the Arellano brothers.

Juárez went to Amado Carrillo Fuentes, known as Lord of the Skies for his innovations in aerial smuggling.

The Pacific Coast went to one of El Padrino's protégés, Joaquín

"Chapo" Guzmán. Chapo grew up in the Sierra Madre mountains during the 1960s. As a boy, he sat at his mother's table and drew stacks of fifty-peso bills on rectangles of coloring paper. "Keep them safe for me," he told her when he ran outside to play in the hills. It was there, among cannabis and opium ranchers, that Chapo— Shorty—left school in the third grade to work.

The Gulf territory, along with northeast Mexico, remained with the Gulf Cartel and Juan García Ábrego.

El Padrino's "privatization" of the drug industry created a new landscape of independent, competitive subsidiaries. Without a central authority to reinforce the benefits of compromise, the men who ran these regions gradually traded dispute resolution at the talking table for a more aggressive style. In the late 1980s and early 1990s, territorial skirmishes broke out between Chapo Guzmán and the Arellano brothers of Tijuana. There were kidnappings and car bombings. In 1993, Arellano assassins converged on the airport in Guadalajara to assassinate Chapo as he was catching a flight. Chapo escaped when the hit men gunned down a Roman Catholic cardinal instead, creating the sort of catastrophic publicity that the PRI deplored.

But the PRI was on its way out.

Opposition parties were winning state elections in Mexico. Each year, beginning in 1989 and accelerating through the 1990s, more and more power dispersed among local politicians such as state governors, who could now form new patronage networks with traffickers. For a while, the PRI managed to retain some control over the drug industry by micromanaging corruption agreements. Raul Salinas—the brother of PRI then-president Carlos Salinas— personally conducted auctions to sell off protection areas during the early 1990s, essentially subcontracting out to local officials the right to extort traffickers. But the PRI would gradually lose its monopoly on the authority to anoint traffickers and guarantee protection.

Traffickers, meanwhile, no longer knew whom to pay. Did bribing one law enforcement group guarantee cooperation from another? In this new environment, many traffickers preferred to hire private armies rather than outsource ineffective protection to the state. What state? By 1995, current and former law enforcement members would comprise half of Mexico's nine hundred armed criminal bands.

From warrior elites to *caciques* to Esteban Cantú and the contemporary capo—the narco-state, when it arrived, was five centuries in the making. Poverty and wealth, supply and demand, national security, free trade, and the exigent morality of world power— whatever war came would be as irreconcilable as the agendas that defined it, and restraint would not be a tenet of the new cartel ethos.

Many would link the modern-day Mexican Drug War to 2006, when a new president launched his assault against the cartels. Some would say it started here, a decade earlier, when the decentralization of Mexico's political system set in motion the most violent criminal organization in modern history.

Others would say it began with dinner.

8

Bank of America

In the eyes of world power, Mexico's one-party government was an ugly beast, outdated. So, on a February evening in 1993, when the seventy-year-old PRI faced its first viable political rival, limousines dropped the thirty richest oligarchs at the finance minister's mansion high above Mexico City, in the fancy Polanco neighborhood, where President Carlos Salinas presided.

The evening's agenda was how to fund the embattled beast, the PRI. Salinas wasn't running again; the constitution prohibited it. But the left was making a serious challenge to the PRI. The PRI couldn't afford to rely on government funding in the upcoming campaign, as it had in the past. If all went as planned, Mexico, via NAFTA, was about to expand its economy and could no longer afford to be seen as a state-party system. The oligarchs agreed that a leftist notion like campaign finance reform was a small price to pay for the money they stood to make when Mexico went public, turning their corporate holdings into attractive purchases for wealthy conglomerates abroad.

Since taking office in 1988, President Salinas had privatized 252 state companies. In exchange for sweet regulatory deals, the oligarchs paid high prices for those companies. Salinas returned their largesse, paving the way for more than a dozen monopolies. Among the guests that night were the new cement baron and the new soft drink baron. Carlos Slim, soon to be the world's richest man, was the telephone baron. After Slim bought Telmex, the Salinas government authorized a phone rate increase of 247 percent.

Yes, they all agreed, save the Beast. The oligarchs would finance the PRI themselves.

A campaign chest of $500 million was thrown out as a figure. Someone suggested $25 million per man. The TV tycoon said why not make it $50 million? A few guests balked. Not everyone had done as well as the TV tycoon, whose Televisa enjoyed 95 percent audience share.

Carlos Slim said he supported whatever figure was decided. But why all this fuss? Why couldn't the funds be collected in private, anonymously?

In a country where half the population lived in poverty, there would be questions, Slim knew, as to how these thirty magnates—all middle-class businessmen before the privatization—could come up with $25 million each for the PRI. People would wonder what favors they got, or would get. What idiot held a banquet? It would turn into a scandal when charges of corruption surfaced.

Slim understood something about Mexican history that his fellow oligarchs forgot. As Mexico's Nobel laureate Octavio Paz said, the Mexican Revolution, from 1910 to 1917, was a struggle between opposing principles: nationalism versus imperialism; labor versus capital; democracy versus dictatorship. It was a struggle between a state-managed economy and free markets. Mexico's northern intellectuals wanted a strong central power. Southern peasants fought for social justice.

The conservative armies of the north won. Post-1917, the new Mexican state aimed to keep order in a country riven by warring fiefdoms and local-boss rule, by a history of *caciquismo*. But how to achieve that stability? It would be done by writing some meaningless phrases into the constitution. To placate the left, the new rulers created six-year terms with no reelection. Under the logic of the new constitution, one ruling party would guarantee peaceful continuity. The only check on PRI power would be the kind of empty socialist rhetoric—enshrined in government-commissioned murals by artists like Diego Rivera—that made liberals feel better despite being ignored on most important issues. Ironically, observed Andrés Oppenheimer, a leading Latin American journalist, the new revolutionary state would maintain law and order, and extinguish Mexico's historical sweep of dictatorships and revolt, by creating yet another dictatorship.

And now, with foreign cash flooding Mexico in anticipation of the 1994 implementation of NAFTA, Wall Street and Washington sided with Salinas and the oligarchs—and vice versa. European investors had focused on opportunities in the new markets of the former Soviet bloc, and paid little attention to free-market reforms in Latin America. The future of Salinas and Slim's Mexico lay closer to home: with America. To hold up their end of the deal with Washington, however, the oligarchs needed to deliver stability. Well, that was thought to be no problem. Mexico's revolutionary potential was feather-light—until the banquet.

The oligarchs rolled out, having settled on $25 million each. Hours later, the publisher of a financial daily called *El Economista*—in his capacity as businessman rather than journalist—attended a breakfast organized by a business lobbying group, where the cement baron and the department store tycoon talked openly about the previous evening's fund-raising banquet. News of the event soon landed on the front pages of *El Economista,* the *New York Times,* the *Wall Street Journal,* and the *Miami Herald,* threatening to ruin NAFTA. Salinas, the banquet proved, was not propelling Mexico into a free-market democratic society, but further into an oligarchic system marked by a mafia-style secret society. The blowback was mighty: another devaluation of the peso, a crash of Mexico's stock market, and a peasant revolt in the southern state of Chiapas.

To President Bill Clinton, NAFTA was the deal of a century, a centerpiece of Clintonian prosperity. Over the objections of angry unions, domestic producers, and political foes like Ross Perot, Clinton kept NAFTA alive with a $50 billion bailout for Mexico. Even when it was alleged that Raul Salinas, the Mexican president's brother, colluded with the Gulf Cartel to have his own brother-in-law, the majority leader of Congress, killed, and police arrested Raul's wife in Switzerland as she tried to remove funds from a $120 million bank account, NAFTA backers in Washington saw little reason to dwell on Mexico's burgeoning criminal class.

Washington shunned comparisons between Mexico and Colombia. Mexican traffickers were nowhere near Pablo Escobar's level of power. Chapo Guzmán was in prison. So was El Padrino. Those guys weren't running for office, as Escobar had done in Colombia. Washington was still proud of the manhunt that led to Escobar's 1993 death. But Escobar's fame eclipsed his true legacy: The resources poured into his pursuit revealed the killing of a single drug lord as an end in itself, a symbol detached from the drug war. The only entity more invested in Escobar's outsize legend than Escobar himself was the American government, which needed to justify turning Colombia upside down to kill him. Mexico was about to become a country of Escobars—mass murderers and bad cops elevated to world-historical status by a media-besotted society bent on getting the criminals it deserved.

But it was not only Mexico's myriad police forces that were vulnerable to corruption; it was soldiers as well. Created in 1986 to provide security for the FIFA World Cup, Mexico's Grupo Aeromóvil de Fuerzas Especiales, or GAFE, the Special Airborne Forces Group, became Mexico's elite military squad. During the 1990s, GAFE soldiers attended school at Fort Benning, Georgia, and Fort Bragg, North Carolina, under a program overseen by American general Barry McCaffrey. Known as the School of the Americas, the program was intended to train Latin American militaries to counter perceived communist subversion. Trained by veterans of the counterinsurgencies in El Salvador and Guatemala, about 3,200 GAFE officers—the equivalent of Green Berets—learned rapid deployment, aerial assaults, marksmanship, ambushes, small-group tactics, intelligence collection, prisoner rescue, and communications. In late 1993, in the wake of the infamous oligarch banquet, the Mexican government enlisted GAFE troops to crush the Chiapas uprising in southern Mexico. Within hours of GAFE deployment, thirty Chiapas rebels were killed, their bodies displayed on a riverbank with ears and noses sliced off.

After Chiapas, GAFE officers formed an antinarcotics unit that coordinated with DEA and FBI. But members of the GAFE narc squad quickly formed their own drug-trafficking group, another police mafia.

BY THE MID-1990S, WITH THE overseas route to South Florida shut down, following the Reagan-era focus on Miami and Colombia, more than 90 percent of U.S.-bound cocaine came through Mexico. The Mexican profit margin on coke appreciated, then appreciated again, and again, as Mexico became more valuable as cocaine's byway to the bank of America. Mexicans leveraged their position until they became the "owners" of South American cocaine. Where they once made $2,000 per kilo working as mules for the Colombians or Peruvians or Bolivians, they could now buy a kilo from Colombia for $2,000 and sell it for five times that at the border, ten times in Dallas, or twenty times in New York. Clinton's focus on chasing away domestic methamphetamine—another low-weight, high-value product—shifted production of that drug south of the border as well. As the millennium approached, Mexico was becoming the Bordeaux region of the drug trade.

By 2000, cross-border trade between the United States and Mexico would quadruple, to more than $250 billion. But Nuevo Laredo would see a disproportionate share of the new commerce—more than twice the trucking activity of Tijuana or Juárez. The increasingly fractious cartels of Mexico coveted the new power that NAFTA gave the eastern Gulf Cartel.

When Gulf Cartel leader Juan García Ábrego, the first Mexican trafficker to make the FBI's Most Wanted list, was arrested by Mexican authorities in 1996 and extradited to the United States, leadership of the Gulf Cartel fell to two men: Osiel Cárdenas Guillén and Salvador "Chava" Gómez Herrera.

A onetime car mechanic who also worked as a *madrina,* or informant, for the Policía Judicial Federal—Mexico's federal police force—Osiel was skilled at using law enforcement against his smuggling rivals. Osiel was the Gulf Cartel's primary earner. Chava Gómez maintained control of the smuggling corridors. But Chava, Osiel believed, asked for money too often. He'd call and say: "Oye, Osiel, necesito que me mandes $50,000." *Hey, Osiel, I need fifty grand.* This arrangement made Osiel feel like Chava's employee. "Mi compadre ya me tiene hasta la madre," Osiel would say. "Me exige como si él no pudiera generar sus ingresos." *I've had it with my buddy. He demands money like he can't generate it on his own.*

The man Osiel hired to kill his Gulf Cartel coleader was a young GAFE soldier. Arturo Guzmán-Decena became the first employee—"Z-1"—of the Gulf Cartel's new enforcement arm, Los Zetas.

"What type of workers do you need?" Guzmán-Decena asked.

"The best armed men there are," Osiel replied.

"These are only in the army."

"I want them."

Word of employment spread. Recruitment methods were bold, and included intercepting military radio frequencies to inform soldiers about the benefits of "shifting bands." GAFE soldiers knew Osiel as "Fantasma," "Ingeniero," and "Matamigo"—the Ghost, the Engineer, and the Friend Killer. They heard their former colleagues were calling themselves Los Zetas and making *cañonazos de dolares,* cannonballs of dollars.

Typical among the recruits was "Z-7," known as Mamito ("the Gentleman"). In 1994, when he was sixteen, Mamito joined GAFE and later worked as part of the narc squad. In 1999, when the Mexican government prosecuted him for corruption, Mamito deserted the military, went to Tamaulipas—the northeastern Mexican state that contains Nuevo Laredo—and found work with Osiel, collecting debts, carrying out assassinations, and overseeing drug shipments for the Gulf Cartel.

In 2002, when Z-1 was killed by the Mexican army in a restaurant, another former GAFE soldier, Heriberto "Z-3" Lazcano, took over. Distinguished for his movie-star looks and tactical brilliance, Lazcano was known as "El Verdugo" ("The Executioner"). He ran Los Zetas with another former GAFE man, Efraín Teodoro Torres, "Z-14," known as "Catorce" ("Fourteen").

Los Zetas soon numbered about fifty former soldiers and a few nonsoldiers. There were rumors about the origin of the name "Zeta," which means "Z" in Spanish. Some said it was a radio call sign. Others believed Osiel called his enforcers the Zetas because *z* was the first letter in *zapatos,* shoes. "A man without shoes cannot walk," he was fond of saying, charmed, surely, that a once-shoeless child now commanded an army of boots. The Zetas wore black tactical uniforms and bulletproof vests. Shoulder patches featured a *Z* super-imposed on the state of Tamaulipas, encircled by the words: Special Forces of the Gulf Cartel. Osiel sent the Zetas to Nuevo Laredo with instructions to establish control.

In the old days, Mexican police used informants to track how much the local narco-boss made in the "plaza"—a town or area through which drugs passed in exchange for a tax paid to the con-trolling authority, the cops—and adjusted the monthly payola ac-cordingly. The term *comandante* did not refer to the drug lord but to the police commander, whose power included having the office of the attorney general, the army, and the PRI behind him. A drug lord lasted for as long as he could keep up with bribes and beat away competitors. But as the Zetas, on behalf of the Gulf Cartel, swept northeast Mexico—"cleaning" the states of Coahuila, Nuevo León, and Tamaulipas—they transformed the old system of corruption.

One day, a young federal prosecutor named Carlos Hinojosa was called to a meeting with other local law enforcement officials.

"Don't interfere with trafficking," Catorce, the Zeta leader, told them. "La Compañía will work freely." *La Compañía*—the Company—now referred to the larger corporate entity formed by the combination of the Gulf Cartel and its enforcers, the Zetas.

As a prosecutor, it had been Hinojosa's job to process complaints and make decisions about whom to charge with crimes. He also served as liaison between the prosecutor's office and the cartels. He knew all the traffickers, and collected the bribes. But those days were over, he was told now. The bribe would no longer be a matter of negotiation. Many cops, hearing this, switched sides, dropping the pretense of public servant and joining La Compañía outright. Ca-torce approached Hinojosa: "So, are you working for them or are you working for me?"

What did it take to join the Company? Hinojosa wondered.

As long as Hinojosa generated income for the Company he was

welcome, he was told. When he stopped generating income, he was no longer welcome. It was that simple. So the bespectacled Hinojosa became a Company accountant. He collected money from the smugglers who worked for the Company or did business with the Company. Hinojosa's new colleagues in the cartel called him *Jotillo,* Little Faggot. It was unclear whether this nickname demeaned his status as a back-office man, or referred to actual homosexuality.

In the early 2000s, the Zetas arrived in Nuevo Laredo to a black market already transformed. The old smuggling families had given way to larger smuggling groups. The groups originated with families but included recruits from their local communities. As drug traffic spiked, these groups carved up Nuevo Laredo and divided the spoils of taxation. Now the groups faced a choice: They could operate under Zeta rule, paying a smuggling tax to the Company, or they could get *borrado del mapa,* erased from the earth.

The leader of the first group, Los Chachos, refused to cede his territory. He was found facedown in a ditch, naked but for a leopard-print thong.

The second group, the Flores Soto gang, was led by Meme Flores, the man who bought cars and weapons from Gabriel Cardona. Meme became an ambassador to the Zetas in Nuevo Laredo, in charge of sourcing cars and weapons and doing whatever else the Zetas asked of him.

The third group, Los Tejas, included two rising stars in the border underworld: the Treviño brothers, Omar and Miguel. But their boss in the Tejas didn't want to cooperate with the Zetas. So the Zetas approached Miguel Treviño instead.

ONE OF THIRTEEN CHILDREN, MIGUEL Treviño grew up in a working-class neighborhood of Nuevo Laredo where he did odd jobs for the wealthy while his father managed ranches. They never starved. Every Treviño son was taught to hunt. As a teenager, Miguel learned the drug business from his oldest brother. He traveled back and forth to Dallas on I-35, mastering that four-hundred-mile stretch of highway that could make a kilo of coke, or an eighty-pound bundle of pot, 100 percent more valuable.

After a car chase in 1993, Dallas police arrested Miguel, then nineteen, in a pink Cadillac with a broken steering column. He paid a $672 fine for evading arrest. But when his oldest brother was convicted of marijuana trafficking in Texas and sentenced to twenty years in prison, Miguel was furious. America treated Mexicans like shit. Miguel tattooed *Hecho en Mexico*—Made in Mexico—on the back of his neck, and a cobra slithering down his forearm. He returned to Nuevo Laredo and worked as a cop, feeding info to the Tejas, then joined the Tejas with his brother Omar. Miguel controlled a neighborhood called Hidalgo, a crucial staging point for smugglers in the north-central section of Nuevo Laredo, just east of the railroad tracks that cross the river and shoot up the west side of Laredo, zipping past Martin High. In the late 1990s and early 2000s, neither Miguel nor Omar Treviño was known beyond their small corner of the Nuevo Laredo underworld—but that was about to change.

"The narcos frequently act with loyalty toward their bosses, but it's just camouflage," writes Ricardo Ravelo in his biography of Osiel Cárdenas. "Acting loyal or honest doesn't mean being one or the other. Even if the mafia has its rules, there are no values. In this agitated environment, the premise that keeps them going is *frialdad*"—cold-bloodedness. Though not a former GAFE soldier, Miguel must've felt that his value system, or lack thereof, meshed with the Zetas' cold-blooded, take-all approach to business. To cement a role for himself in the Zetas, Miguel murdered his Tejas leader, then eliminated the leader's family as well.

Miguel and Omar Treviño were two of many who joined the

Zetas when they came to Nuevo Laredo to take over. But the Treviño brothers did what successful gangsters do: acquire power through ruthlessness. Miguel, now in his early thirties, rose in the Zeta ranks by maintaining tight control over Nuevo Laredo, always erring on the side of caution when he encountered perceived enemies.

One night, in early 2004, he mistook two American teenagers for adversaries.

9

The New People

W hat are you doing here?" the man who looked like Rambo asked again, English and Spanish bleeding into one another. He took a grenade off his chest belt, tossed it from hand to hand like a tennis ball.

"Nothing," Gabriel said, his jaw sore; his eyes hard, glazed, drifting.

"Where are you from?"

"We go to college in Texas," Gabriel said. "We work in McDonald's."

"Oh yeah? What do you study?"

"Law."

"Bullshit!"

"Yes, sir. I mean no, sir."

He stepped closer to Gabriel. "Se mira tranquilo. Demasiado tranquilo. ¿Porque?" *You look calm. Too calm. Why?*

"Yo no sé." *I don't know.*

"Hijo de tu pinche madre. Te crees bien verga." *Son of a fucking bitch. You think you're all that.* "¿Con quien jala? ¿A quién le andabas vendiendo la troca?" *Who do you work with? Who were you selling that car to?*

Earlier that night, Gabriel and Wences Tovar had taken a Jeep Cherokee to Nuevo Laredo. Wences said he had a new connection, a Mexican cop who would pay a little more than the standard rate of one thousand dollars per SUV. Sure, Gabriel said, always game to expand his network. He and Wences drove to the Nuevo Laredo police barracks, and asked for the cop. They met blank stares. So they left. It was dark. As they headed back to Guerrero Street, which would return them to International Bridge One and Texas, a Mexican police truck pulled them over. Gabriel and Wences were handcuffed, led into the brush, and told to stand still. The cops made a call.

La gente nueva, Gabriel knew, were cleaning Nuevo Laredo, wiping away past dealers and putting a halt to all local drug selling. If you possessed drugs, and they didn't know you, it meant someone was selling them to you, or you were selling them without authority. You'd be tortured until you spilled your source. Gabriel hurried to step through his handcuffs, arranging them at his front, and reached inside his jeans. He was about to throw the baggie into the brush, but thought better of it and swallowed all five roches instead.

A caravan of black Suburbans arrived on the side of the road, police lights flickering. These people didn't look like cops. They wore all black. Gabriel and Wences were blindfolded and put in the back of a truck. Ten minutes later they arrived at another place, got out, and were escorted into some kind of structure. The blindfolds removed, their eyes adjusted to a narrow, windowless room. It looked like a *caballeriza,* a horse stall made of brick. Beyond the open door was a circular driveway and what appeared to be a large ranch, an *ejido* with a bunch of small houses on it. They were left alone. More Suburbans arrived.

Gabriel and Wences had been searched for guns, but Gabriel still had his cell phone. He dialed his older brother.

"¿Qué onda, güey?" his brother answered. *What's up, dude?*

"They picked us up across," Gabriel said. "Now we're at some *finca* and I don't know whether . . ." Gabriel tried to spit the words but couldn't accelerate his speech.

More men were getting out of the Suburbans. In the illumination of headlights, a cloud of dust rose and hung in the air, moved forward, then dissolved. "Qué?" Gabriel heard his brother say before snapping the phone shut. From the shadow plodded a phalanx of men led by an individual wearing a gun holstered on one thigh, a knife on the other: Miguel Treviño.

"Who were you just calling?" Miguel asked.

"Nobody, sir."

"Don't bullshit me." Miguel threw his head back, flexed his neck, and looked down his nose with penetrating eyes. "Are you fucked up?"

"No, sir," Gabriel said, then glanced at Wences for confirmation. Terrified, and without roches to steel his confidence, Wences's sober eyes looked to Gabriel as if they had a conscience of their own, and wanted to get out of the sockets and run away. Gabriel pursed his lips, but couldn't stop himself: He erupted in laughter.

Miguel, surprised, knocked Gabriel down with a powerful hook. Gabriel fell; was helped up. More questions were asked, and more bullshit answers provided.

The grenade came out. Miguel left the horse stall.

Gabriel now told Wences that he loved him, and that it was good to have been friends. Wences, his heart beating wildly, couldn't understand how Gabriel remained so calm. Wences didn't want to die! Gabriel continued: It was a shame to go like this, but there were worse ways. They both watched Miguel confer with the others outside, holding the grenade against his hip like a pitcher cups a baseball.

A thought popped into Gabriel's mind: *Meme*.

"I work for Cero Dos!" Gabriel shouted, using the code name for Meme Flores: 02.

Miguel turned around. "What?"

"I bring him cars and trucks. I also cross *juguetes*"—toys, guns.

Miguel laughed. "Why the fuck didn't you say something?"

"I didn't know who we were dealing with. I didn't want to be saying something to the wrong people. Nuevo Laredo is still mixed."

"It's not mixed anymore. We're the only dominant ones."

Gabriel nodded. Miguel explained that the cop they tried to sell the *troca* to was a contra, an enemy, and had been *borrado del mapa* the previous day.

Thirty minutes passed, then Meme arrived.

"Yeah, he's my guy," Meme said. "Get him off."

Gabriel and Wences were uncuffed.

Meme introduced Miguel to the boys as a *comandante* for Los Zetas. Meme had never met Wences. But Meme told Miguel that he could vouch for anyone whom Gabriel called a *pareja,* a partner. Gabriel, Meme explained, was a stellar worker, a *firme vato* who supplied Meme with vehicles and guns from Texas.

In his mind, Gabriel now made the connection: All those stolen trucks and smuggled guns went, ultimately, to *la gente nueva,* the Zetas. Neither Gabriel nor Wences had heard of Miguel Treviño until this evening, but they now understood him to be a high-ranking member of the new cartel.

"You can call me Cuarenta," Miguel told the boys, referring to his Zeta call sign, Z-40. He slapped Gabriel on the back. No hard feelings, eh?

That night, Miguel, Gabriel, Wences, and Meme drove around Nuevo Laredo in a caravan. Gabriel smelled burning rubber and branches; outside, he saw ragged groups of huddled Mexicans stretching their arms over *tambos*, fifty-five gallon drums, nudging each other aside for access to the flame. The driver called ahead to a restaurant, and by the time they arrived it was empty.

Over dinner, Miguel elicited a sense of Gabriel's work with Meme, and inquired about the boys' legal problems in Texas. Wences, sober and still recovering emotionally from their near-death experience, didn't speak much. But Gabriel sensed an opportunity. Perhaps his connection to Meme could be converted into something bigger. Gabriel spoke to Miguel confidently, as if they were equals. Despite the pills, his youthful mind remained a trap for details and dates. He unfurled a litany of transgressions, as if enumerating bullet points on a resume: drugs, weapons, assaults.

Miguel listened. Boys like these could be useful.

A YEAR EARLIER, IN 2003, the Gulf Cartel leader and Zeta founder, Osiel Cárdenas, had been apprehended in Mexico. The DEA-led manhunt for Osiel, which lasted several years, entailed tracking Osiel's girlfriends and working with producers of the TV show *America's Most Wanted* during what DEA reports referred to as the "media blitz" part of the operation. The Zetas tried to break Osiel out of prison with a squad of helicopters, but the attempt failed when the weather turned bad and a pilot backed out.

If Osiel thought it was going to be easy to escape, it might've been because his cross-country rival, Chapo Guzmán, leader of the Sinaloa Cartel, had escaped one of Mexico's most secure prisons in 2001. Now, with Osiel in prison and Chapo roaming free again, the Company—the Gulf Cartel and the Zetas—faced its first real threat: Chapo wanted to expand his organization's reach east, beyond Juárez, to the most lucrative border crossing of them all, Nuevo Laredo.

In early 2004, when Miguel Treviño met Gabriel Cardona and Wences Tovar, he would've been aware of Chapo's ambitions. He also would've been aware of an American smuggler from Laredo who'd recently spurned the Zetas and sided with the Sinaloa Cartel instead.

In the 1980s, Edgar Valdez Villareal grew up on Laredo's wealthy north side and played linebacker for United High. Known as "La Barbie" for his blond hair and blue eyes, a look Mexicans refer to as *güero,* he was in a dope-dealing gang of rich kids called the Mexican Connection. La Barbie passed up college and joined a group of smugglers, shipping marijuana, then cocaine to Georgia and beyond. Indicted for smuggling in 1997, La Barbie relocated to Nuevo Laredo. In 2002, when the Gulf Cartel and the Zetas came to Nuevo Laredo and killed La Barbie's boss—the leader of the Chachos, the one who turned up dead wearing nothing but a thong—La Barbie staged a revolt.

From a DEA report:

> Edgar Valdez Villareal was advanced ("adelantado" or "fronted") 100 kilos of cocaine by the Gulf Cartel for which Valdez Villareal later paid. Valdez Villareal was then advanced 300 kilos of cocaine by the Gulf Cartel and later paid for those in full. Valdez Villareal was then advanced 500 kilos by the Gulf Cartel and only paid for 250. Valdez Villareal then convinced the Gulf Cartel to advance 1000 kilos. Valdez Villareal failed to make any payment for this shipment. The resulting debt, considered a theft, led to the initiation of hostilities. . . .

After killing a Zeta operative sent to kill him, La Barbie fled to Acapulco and joined a family of Sinaloa-affiliated smugglers—the Beltrán-Leyva brothers, who imported forty tons of coke per month through the southern Mexican port at Zihuatanejo. A Beltrán-Leyva underboss owned a marble business in San Antonio, Texas, which the organization used to smuggle coke to buyers in Atlanta and New York. La Barbie, together with Chapo and the Beltrán-Leyva brothers, decided to fight for Nuevo Laredo.

La Barbie, Miguel knew, was organizing soldiers, with the backing of the Beltrán-Leyvas and the Sinaloa Cartel, and a battle was coming.

Now, in the restaurant, Miguel asked who Gabriel knew in Laredo, and by his tone it was clear that he meant high-profile people in the underworld.

Gabriel thought back to those Sunday night cruises on San Bernardo Avenue, when he used to ask the older boys which ride belonged to which smuggler. He nodded and spit some names. Moises Garcia. Chuy Resendez. Richard Jasso.

Impressed, Miguel mentioned a training camp in southern Mexico. Gabriel appeared interested; Wences remained largely silent. Miguel said Meme would be in touch about coming to the camp.

Gabriel and Wences returned to Laredo, having met the deadly crew, *la gente nueva,* the Zetas, the ones who wouldn't take no for an answer.

IN LATE 2003, ROBERT GARCIA had returned to Laredo PD after a stressful six years in DEA. He served his stint with the feds, and stuck with it longer than most. He was glad to be done, glad to be finished with the constant travel. He was thirty-five and looking forward to spending more time with Ronnie and the boys. Trey had just started high school and Eric was a senior.

But if Robert envisioned returning to the small-town pace of the city he patrolled in the 1990s, he was mistaken. Murders and drug crime were up. Laredo was becoming America's car theft capital. Its juvenile crime was out of control.

Laredo's new chief of police, Agustin Dovalina, called Robert into his well-appointed office. Flanked by his deputies, Chief Dovalina joked that they were going to put Robert in a more relaxing job.

"What?" Robert asked.

They said they needed another detective in the homicide division.

If they expected resistance, they didn't get it. After drugs, the prospect of turning to murder came as a relief. Robert knew what homicide detectives did. There was a body. You helped the family with their loss, and tried to figure out what happened. He didn't need the willful ignorance of a drug cop to believe in the job. Murder was apolitical. The pressure of homicide work also appealed to him, as did the win-lose nature of the job: You either caught the murderer and locked him up, or you didn't.

"The cartel stuff," as he would later call it, was not on his mind when he took the job. Laredo law enforcement knew about the Gulf Cartel, the Zetas, and the Sinaloa Cartel. There had been intelligence floating around about cartel conflicts in Mexico. But there was no reason to think those conflicts would affect Laredo. To the extent Miguel Treviño was known at all among Laredo law enforcement, he was known as another "flunkie" in the Nuevo Laredo underworld, one of many local criminals who worked for whichever organization dominated the area.

Upon returning to Laredo PD, in the final days of 2003, Robert had no idea that a clash between two cartels would spill into Texas, turning his new job into something more than garden-variety homicide work, a fight for the city itself.

GABRIEL CARDONA, THE LAREDO YOUNGSTER whom Robert would soon meet, was also ignorant about the future. Since the ninth grade, Gabriel lived day to day. He had no idea where his association with Meme Flores, or his initial meeting with Miguel Treviño, would take him. At seventeen, he had stolen some cars, smuggled some guns, moved some drugs, and been in some fights. He was an intelligent thug, but a roche-addled high school dropout nonetheless, oblivious to the political twistings taking place above him and in far-off lands.

Gabriel's cartel initiation would unfold over the coming year. His first meeting with Miguel had taught him only that his underworld mentor, Meme Flores, was "deeper in the game" than Gabriel realized.

Neither Gabriel nor Robert could've known that, through a series of escalating events, they'd both be plunged into the inaugural battle of one of the most brutal wars in modern history, a war that would bring a standard of violence back to the Americas not seen since pre-colonial times, or ever.

With Gabriel set to go global, as a cartel member, and Robert set to go local again, as a homicide detective, they appeared to be on separate tracks.

They were heading right for each other.

10

Raising Wolves

E very morning at eight thirty, print and TV reporters filed
in to La Parroquia, a two-hundred-year-old coffeehouse in
Veracruz, Mexico, that overlooked the Gulf Coast. La Parroquia's concrete façade faced the busy port walkway in Veracruz,
where carts and stalls sold ices, sodas, and tourist trinkets. Barges
from all over the world offloaded electronics, furniture, and multi-
ton shipments of South American cocaine.

From Veracruz, the coke traveled north by plane to towns such
as San Fernando, Reynosa, and Matamoros. Once a week, plaza
bosses received the planes, each carrying 400 kilos, half a ton. They
unpacked 25-kilo suitcases, repacked the merchandise as one-kilo
bricks, and loaded the bricks into smuggling vehicles. Drivers then
took the vehicles north to Texas border towns like Brownsville and
Laredo, then on to distribution hubs in Houston and Dallas.

Here, in Veracruz, one of Mexico's largest drug gateways—and
therefore one of its most corrupt cities—the criminal elite controlled

the media, and La Parroquia was where it happened. By 9 a.m., tables filled with politicians, businesspeople, and anyone else wishing to be heard by local journalists, many of whom accepted money from entities outside the news organizations that officially employed them. Shoeshine boys crouched on the terrazzo floor. Men wolfed down huevos rancheros while a nurse roamed the café and charged five pesos to check their blood pressure. White-jacketed waiters poured steamed milk into glasses of thick coffee for a buzzy drink called *lechero*. Over the next four hours the day's news was gathered, invented, negotiated, and paid for.

The Zeta coleader, Z-14—Catorce—managed the Veracruz plaza. A smaller plaza like San Fernando—halfway between Veracruz and the border—might be worth $50 million a year as a gateway to border cities. Matamoros, a border city, might be worth twice that. But in Veracruz, a leading site of cocaine import, a competent plaza boss like Catorce could make several hundred million dollars a year. So Miguel Treviño traveled there in 2004 and learned everything he could about plaza management.

This is what Miguel apparently learned, and what he would apply when he returned to Nuevo Laredo:

SECURITY: Under Company protocol, the first task for any new plaza boss was to train and arm a security force. The cost of running a typical plaza ran about $1 million per month in peacetime, two or three times that during war. Expenses included bribes, payroll, houses, and equipment: .50-caliber weapons, thousands of magazines, grenades, bazookas, and bulletproof SUVs that cost $160,000 after customization.

Catorce insisted that a GAFE soldier train all recruits. Each trainee learned how to use firearms, walk in the brush, fight with a rival cartel, rescue a dead or injured partner, look after a boss, jump from moving cars, and speak in

Company radio codes. Training lasted two or three months. Each trainee made $130 per week. With salary and equipment, it cost $8,000 to train one Zeta soldier. As graduates, each soldier made $250 per week plus commission.

EMPLOYEE PERKS: Catorce offered his men an employee-investment program called *la polla*. A group could pool their money and invest in a load at the Company's border cost of $10,000 a kilo. If the kilo made it to Brownsville or Laredo, it sold for $12,500; $14,500 in Houston; $18,000 in Dallas; $24,000 in Atlanta; and $30,000 or more in New York. Like a futures contract, each *polla* was labeled with a city. One *polla* was for "Atlanta prices," another for "Chicago prices." Company men could make their own risk-reward calculations, allowing them to feel as though they owned a stake in the business.

PAYOFFS: The two most important law enforcement people—the boss of the federal preventive police and the boss of the federal highway police—made between $6,000 and $10,000 per month in bribes, while lieutenants made $3,000. Many journalists "reported to" a politician, and about 5 percent also "reported to" a cartel. At La Parroquia, politicians, many of whom took money from the cartels, paid off reporters who printed fawning coverage of their agenda and ghostwrote their guest columns. TV and print reporters made $1,300 to $3,300 per month—as much as eight times their salary.

In Veracruz, Miguel saw how a well-compensated media paid for itself. As punishment for tax evasion, two outlets of a popular sandwich chain might burn down in the same afternoon. The largest newspaper in Veracruz would run the next day's editorial on winemaking. Several bars could be sprayed with machine-gun fire in broad daylight, and the following day's front page would feature a thoughtful meditation on the city's street dogs. There was no telling what a journalist might find newsworthy.

REVENUE: The main source of revenue was the *cuota* or *piso*, the smuggling tax. To come through the plaza, immigrants paid a tax of $250 if from Mexico; $500 if from Central America; and $1,500 if from Europe. Coyotes, their escorts, paid $100. Drug traffickers paid $50 per kilo of marijuana (about $50,000 per ton) and $500 per kilo of cocaine (about $500,000 per ton). Some paid their tax in kind, such as 5 kilos for every 100. After "stepping on" a kilo of coke, making two or three kilos out of the original by cutting it with things like baby laxative, the cartel could make $50,000 per kilo by selling small amounts—known as *grampillas,* staples—to Veracruz townies.

The plaza boss also extracted tax revenue from businesses. Grocers paid around $1,000 per month. Pharmacies paid $3,000 per month; bars, nightclubs, and brothels two or three times that. The *piso* purchased more than protection; it also bought a buffer from government oversight. Whereas failure to pay the cartel tax could bring violence or legal problems in the form of a city inspector concocting health violations, dutiful payment meant that the grocer could sell alcohol twenty-four hours a day, that the nightclub could serve the underage, and that the restaurant could cut corners on health protocol.

If a business had an electric bill of 20,000 pesos per month ($1,300), the person in charge of the federal electric commission saw that the business paid only one-third of the bill. In return, the business paid the utility manager 1,000 pesos for fixing the bill, and 3,000 pesos to Catorce for ensuring that the bill would be fixed. For some, the spoils of anarchy justified the *piso*.

SPIES: *Panteras*—female informants—were crucial to Catorce's business. Tax revenue was reinvested in dancers and barmaids who could monitor subversive chatter and provide information about, and photographs of, the condemned. Hotel workers and taxi drivers also made great sources.

BANKING: In 2004, Catorce gave $12 million to Pancho Colorado, a respected magnate who owned an oil-services company in Veracruz called ADT Petros Servicios. Colorado bid on government contracts for work, such as remediation, that Pemex, the national oil company, outsourced. A generous man who also owned resorts and employed the mentally disabled because everyone deserves a job, Colorado was always smiling in La Parroquia. With the Company's $12 million, he bought the Veracruz governorship, which influenced the granting of oil contracts. Once granted, ADT's contracts required capital to be serviced. Catorce supplied the overhead, which returned in the form of clean government money.

Miguel returned to Nuevo Laredo, ready to tackle new opportunity. He would recruit soldiers, establish a culture of discipline, and dominate the territory.

BACK IN THE TRAINING CAMPS of Tamaulipas, in the summer of 2004, it was time to put the recruits in simulated raids and rid them of their bad habits. Hundreds of contras—Sinaloan enemies rounded up in raids—had been collected for the purpose.

"Bienvenidos, cabrones," Meme Flores told the recruits upon arrival at the training camp. "Ésta es La Compañía, la mera paipa de Mexico." *Welcome, brothers. This is the Company, the true shit in Mexico.* The approximately seventy young men, ranging in age from fifteen to thirty but dressed identically in jeans and T-shirts, sat on wooden benches and stared into his eyes. They listened. For the Mexican recruits, getting accepted into the Company, making good on promises to family, traveling in Mexico with respected men, returning home to parents and wives as a *somebody:* Whatever they fantasized about, it all seemed possible on this day.

Known as the *adiestramiento,* or the *'diestra*, the training camp was staffed with Mexicans, Israelis, and Colombians. A week earlier, Gabriel—one of the only Americans at the camp—packed into a caravan of Suburbans heading south through Mexico to the training camp near Monterrey. A month had passed since the meeting with Miguel, when Meme asked Gabriel to come to the camp. Wences hadn't been invited. In the caravan, Gabriel wore jeans and white T-shirts, as instructed, and left everything else behind, including his cell phone and wallet.

The *reclutas,* recruits, slept on hard cots, twenty-five to a compound, and were given a loaf of bread and a banana every morning. They swam, and negotiated obstacles: mud, tunnels, ropes, and walls. Twice a week, in the middle of the night, camp leaders roused the recruits to pull weeds for new soccer fields. In the morning run, whoever came in last owed one hundred push-ups. In the afternoon they played soccer, and then everyone took turns boxing. There was no shame in not knowing how to fight. You were there to learn.

They learned about weapons: how to work the double grip of the MP5 submachine gun, made by Heckler & Koch; how to shoot the Glock, the thirty-eight, and the FN Herstal; and how to reload the magazine on an AR-15 assault rifle without losing ground to the enemy. The Colombian mercenaries taught combat skills. How to trap a car in an intersection. How to jump between moving cars. How to shoot through armored vehicles by unloading a clip beneath the door handle. How to walk and shoot accurately at the same time, minimizing your profile. How to shoot a running contra, like leading a wide receiver in a football game. On the basis of these early drills, more than half of the seventy recruits were separated and trained for noncombat jobs, as lookouts and patrols. About twenty recruits remained to be trained as *sicarios,* assassins.

Having excelled in the "dry drills," Gabriel was chosen to demonstrate the first live exercise: take an AR-15 assault rifle, run into a house, and kill the contra inside. The other recruits who'd been designated as killers were invited into the house to observe from an adjoining room. Meme told the contra that if he survived, he'd be set free.

Gabriel, outside, breathed deeply, tightened his fists around the rifle, and charged in. When he came through the door, Meme jumped out and slapped the rifle out of his hands, then kicked the weapon toward the contra. Gabriel wrestled the contra for the rifle. Meme separated them and addressed the recruits.

"If you fall down or lose your rifle in a raid, never fight for the weapon. Your main disadvantage in a raid is unfamiliar territory. You don't know the surroundings. You don't know the position of the contras in the house. In the moment of entry, all you know is that one guy knocked you out. He might be the only one you need to neutralize. Or there might be others. You don't know. But that's okay. Your brothers are charging in behind you." Meme shouted: "Listen up! Never wrestle for a loose gun. Instead, pull your *cuchillo* and put the contra out by hand."

A new contra was brought in, and told that if he could knock Meme off his feet and wrestle Meme successfully for the AR-15, he'd be set free. When the drill began, Meme lost the rifle on purpose and kicked it toward the contra. As the contra scrambled for the gun, Meme unstrapped his *cuchillo* from his leg and stabbed the contra's thighs, stomach, and chest until he was dead. Meme stood up and caught his breath while two recruits dragged the dead contra away. Of the twenty or so remaining recruits, several walked out of the house and joined the others for training in noncombat roles.

Of those recruits who proved they could kill, each was assigned a *cuas,* a partner. Walking, shooting, eating, shitting—you and your cuas, short for *cuate,* pal, watched over each other at all times. Gabriel's *cuas* was a boy named Israel, whom Gabriel remembered from going to church as a child in Nuevo Laredo, when the Cardonas used to come across on weekends to see extended family. The *sicarios* gathered near the edge of a forest, thirty feet behind a line chalked on the ground. Beyond, in the woods, two contras were tied to each other at the waist and told that if they made it through the first round, successfully outrunning the gunshots, they'd be let go. With his *cuas,* Gabriel ran up to the line, eyes focused on the scattering targets. They stopped, put their left foot in front, as taught, twisted slightly at the waist, put their left hand on the barrel grip, raised their left elbow to heart level, aimed the AR-15, and released thirty rounds: *prrrrt.* They held position, switched the right thumb of their trigger hand to the right side of the grip, pressed the button above the trigger that released the double-sided clip, and simultaneously extended the four other fingers of their right hand to catch the clip as it released. With clip in hand, they turned their palm outward, thumb down, inserted the other side of the clip into the rifle, and released thirty more rounds—*prrrrt*—as targets continued to fall, dumping a total of sixty bullets in ten seconds. They fanned out, and the next two partners came in behind them. That, they were told, was how you held down territory and kept the contra at bay. If a recruit dropped a clip, someone yelled *"a mamar!"*—"suck it!"—and he and his *cuas* owed the Company one hundred push-ups while their brothers kept at it, contras dying by the dozen.

Meme's lessons aside, when it came to the torture and murder taught in the training camp, the Company's instructors led by example more often than they taught. Instructors threw around a phrase: "You see and do." And this approach fostered competition. As one recruit remembered: "Everybody wants to outdo the next man. They all want to do the best kind."

Psychology played a role in Company training, just as it had for the GAFE men schooled in Fort Benning and Fort Bragg. In the 'diestra', isolated for a month and trained to kill by cold method, the instructors reminded recruits of their longing for "riches and bitches." They had no job, no education, no future. By depriving pissed-off recruits of the world outside—of family and friends and girlfriends, of bedding and clothes—the *comandantes* encased them in psychic solitude; motivation by humiliation. They were forgotten, far from home. But now they were soldiers. And when they arrived at the plaza, they would arrive with a purpose, and release all their rage.

Finally, toward the end of camp, it came time to kill without any of the weapons they'd been trained in: no *corta* (handgun), *larga* (rifle), or *cuchillo* (knife). This was when the Company gauged your strength of mind, saw whether you could "lose your fear," and separated the *fríos*—the coldhearted ones—from those who would be put to other uses. Could you do it and still sleep?

The recruit chose among implements: a shovel, a hoe, a sledgehammer, a machete. By way of example, a *comandante* selected a machete and beheaded a detainee. Did that man ever kick! If done properly, a hoe took one or two hits; a shovel, several. You tried to hit the contra square in the head so he suffered little.

The tools were then put aside and you killed with your bare hands. To feel the body give out for the first time was, in the words of one recruit, "something else for real."

11

I'm the True One

W ith its vertically integrated systems and its young career men who charged up the ranks, the Company—unlike those dead-end, minimum-wage jobs in Laredo, and the even more dismal futures that awaited those from the Mexican side of the border—granted members the conceit that commitment would be recognized in compensation, job security, flexibility, and prestige.

Ranking Company men—the bosses and underbosses known as *comandantes*—referred to the young hit men, the *sicarios,* somewhat disparagingly, as *soldados,* soldiers: brutal errand boys who did what they were told. Officially, the *soldados* were known as "eles." *Ele*—"L" in Spanish—stood for *lobo:* wolf. Like their young mafiosi brethren in New York, or Naples, the cartel's Wolf Boys were willing to die not for any religious purpose but for money and power.*

---

* "Wolf Boys" is the author's phrase.

Most Wolf Boys were, in the vernacular of Laredo's Mexican-American youth, "straight Mexican." But as the Gulf Cartel and its Zeta enforcers rose as a single corporate unit in eastern Mexico, preparing to battle incursions from the western Sinaloa Cartel, a few American kids joined the ranks of Zeta *soldados* and became Company Wolf Boys themselves. Gabriel was among those early American recruits. Wences Tovar hadn't attended the training camp yet. But Wences became a low-ranking Company man in his own right, smuggling guns from Texas to Mexico for Meme Flores.

In the circles that Gabriel and Wences ran in, Company membership was monumental. The musician Beto Quintanilla, king of hard-core norteño music, a kind of Mexican hip-hop set to polka beats, sang hits about the Company's enforcers, and those songs blasted in the car of every teenager from Reynosa to Piedras Negras.

The money, of course, was a big part of the allure. For *sicarios,* the weekly salary—or *aguinaldo;* literally, "bonus"—was $500. Commission missions—solo jobs assigned outside the *operativo,* the normal patrol—were usually compensated at $10,000 each, possibly more depending on the importance of the target. A high-ranking cop, politician, or cartel rival, for instance, merited a higher bounty—to compensate for the increased difficulty of the job, but also for the risk: The greater the importance of the person killed, the greater the chance of that person's family or associates taking revenge.

While Gabriel's American citizenship meant a slightly higher status than his "straight-Mexican" counterparts, the basic qualifications for an effective Wolf Boy were universal. Like Gabriel, the ideal Wolf Boy had no children or serious amorous ties; like Gabriel, he could be in the streets at all times and go anywhere. Unburdened by conscience—whether because of youth, environment, nature, narcotics, or a combination—he was ruthless and free, a heat-seeking missile of black-market capitalism to be deployed against anyone who ran afoul of the Company, threatened its business, degraded its name, or challenged its leaders. Over the next two years, as the Sinaloa Cartel came east and battled the Company for the rights to the Nuevo Laredo–Laredo crossing, Wolf Boys would become plentiful, and life would grow cheap.

Assigned to the Nuevo Laredo plaza in the fall of 2004, Gabriel settled into Company life. He learned the roles and responsibilities, and what it took to rise. He learned the difference between a *comandante regional* (a state commander), a regular *comandante* (a plaza boss), a *comandante de mando* (a midlevel manager), and an *encargado de seguridad* (chief of security). As a mere *sicario,* or *ele,* Gabriel reported to Meme Flores, who was now the *encargado de seguridad* in Nuevo Laredo. Meme, in turn, reported to Miguel Treviño, the plaza boss. Below Gabriel in the hierarchy were the *halcones* (hawks, or lookouts) and *guardias* (patrols), younger boys and females who monitored activity in the plaza, tracked the movements of smugglers, and reported on the comings and goings of police.

The Company also employed a large finance team; each plaza had several accountants. One was in charge of payroll. One oversaw the local *tienditas,* small "drugstores" that sold narcotics to local Mexican users. Another accountant collected taxes from local businesses such as bars and pharmacies. Within each plaza, one accountant was allocated to each of the Company's two primary products: marijuana and cocaine. These accountants corresponded with "runners"—transporters—on both sides of the border, and reported to the plaza's lead accountant.

The *comandante regional,* state commander, audited the books of every plaza within his state regularly. The lead plaza accountant—responsible to the state commander—checked in periodically. *Come over to such-and-such place. Bring the book.* If there was a problem with the accounts, all the accountants would get together to see if it could be solved; if it couldn't, the plaza accountant would be killed by the plaza boss, and the plaza boss might in turn be killed by the *comandante regional*. It was rumored that once, in Monclava, the books were so dirty that no one showed up when called to a meeting. The entire plaza staff had to be replaced.

IN EARLY JOBS, WHEN ASKED to accompany Meme, or others, on hits or raids in Mexico, Gabriel was nervous. His jaw tightened; an AR-15 rifle felt no heavier than a paperback book. To take his mind off a mission he focused on the function and assembly of the weapon. He rubbed his sweaty hands against his pants until it was time to rush in. For commission missions—those solo jobs assigned outside the *operativo,* the normal patrol—the local Mexican cops often assisted Gabriel by setting up targets and clearing out locations. In one job, the cops patrolled the territory around a restaurant while Gabriel walked in and shot a contra in the head.

While the act of taking a life became routine, some work put a heavier strain on his mind. A Nuevo Laredo dealer who sold coke in one of the Company-owned *tienditas* had been underreporting profits. Gabriel and Meme tracked him down in his car. Meme pulled him out, pistol-whipped him, put him in the backseat of Meme's Jeep Cherokee, and asked Gabriel to restrain the guy while they drove to a house. Inside the house, Meme pulled the guy's shirt off and taped his eyes, arms, and feet, then threw him on the bed. The dealer kept saying he'd pay but needed time. He just needed some more *merca*—product—to make up the loss, he said. Meme said Gabriel could leave. The next day, when Gabriel asked Meme what happened, Meme said, "Se lo fumaron, pal guiso." *They killed him in the stew.*

Gabriel felt bad for the guy. It was one thing to kill a rival in a war, someone who worked for the other side. The people that they killed in the training camp were all rivals from the Sinaloa Cartel, or at least that's what the recruits were told. With this dealer, how much dope money could have gone missing if the *tiendita* he ran was just one of a dozen or more drugstores the Company had in Nuevo Laredo alone? But this stringency, Gabriel figured, showed the seriousness of the organization. *Por y sobre la verga* was the Company's motto. Older Company men repeated this phrase constantly; literally, it meant: For and about the "cock" or "dick." But the intended meaning was closer to: For and about the idea, or principle. The rules were the rules.

An enemy, or contra, typically meant a rival connected to the Sinaloa Cartel, or a cop who took money from the Sinaloans. But the definition of "contra," Gabriel learned, was flexible; it could also be a Company dealer or smuggler who stole money or drugs, or who underreported profits. A contra could even be someone who dared to date the ex-girlfriend of a ranking Company man. Under Zeta rule, the smallest slight was grounds for death.

THE COMPANY WASN'T *ONLY* ABOUT work. Partying was a big part of cartel life. When the Nuevo Laredo plaza "heated up"— was raided by the federal police—everyone except the *guardias* and *halcones,* who stuck around the plaza to see who divulged information to the government, dispersed for *franco,* vacation. On *franco,* many Company men retired to *La Zona,* or Boystown, a walled city of brothels that employed prostitutes from all over Latin America, some coming from as far as Brazil and Peru. There was a Boystown in Nuevo Laredo, and another in Reynosa, another border town 120 miles southeast of Nuevo Laredo. Both Boystowns were run (or extorted) by the Company, but they were also open to the public, patronized not just by Mexicans but also by busloads of gringos from Houston and Dallas. In the Boystown bars, a prostitute kept each patron company, and offered a *palo*—a "fuck"; literally, a stick—for between thirty and eighty bucks. There were many beautiful women in Boystown, and Gabriel couldn't understand why they worked there.

Many of the Mexican Wolf Boys patronized Boystown, but Gabriel could never see paying for sex. He preferred to spend his money in the Nuevo Laredo nightclubs, a few of which were known specifically as "ele clubs," clubs that catered to Wolf Boys—like Luxor and Eclipse.

At Eclipse, DJ Kuri periodically announced "El Pescadito": "This is the fish song!" DJ Kuri yelled over the microphone. "Go ahead and fish!"

One night, Gabriel cast his imaginary fishing pole across the dance floor and "reeled in" a fifteen-year-old from Laredo named Christina. She was a freshman at United High, the alma mater of La Barbie, the smuggler who challenged the Company, fled Nuevo Laredo, and aligned with the Sinaloa Cartel. Christina had a lantern jaw and dirty-blond hair. Her nose flared gamely at the nostril. She and Gabriel started seeing each other.

Christina turned out to be a friend of Wences's girlfriend. Although Christina went to United and lived in the north-side suburbs, the nicer part of Laredo, her family struggled while her father did eight years on a smuggling-related charge. Her uncles and cousins were also in the drug business, as smugglers and money launderers. What Gabriel saw, though, was a beautiful *fresa,* a preppy who carried her willowy frame in sheer blouses and tight wrap tanks, someone who looked as though she came from the better part of town, and being with her boosted his ego.

Christina's friends had high expectations for boys; they acted very *mamona,* stuck up. But Christina just wanted a steady boyfriend, and she made that clear to Gabriel. If Gabriel made her feel secure, she also inspired positive feelings in him. The soldier in him softened in her presence. He said, "People say I'm cold. But with you I'm different."

SEVERAL MONTHS OF WORK PASSED in Mexico.

Gabriel learned how to pay off Nuevo Laredo cops, get information he could use against Sinaloa enemies, and interact with the Company's command-and-intelligence center. "You don't enjoy what you're doing," he'd tell his older brother Luis when they spoke about killing people. But as a young man prone to feeling that his life lacked purpose when he wasn't hustling and making money, Gabriel did love the continuous action. As he tracked targets and kept in close touch with Meme, he liked the sense of having others rely on him. More than anything, he enjoyed giving money to La Gaby and his brothers, and wasting money on entertainment for his friends, the growing circle of hoodies—old partners in small-time crime from Lazteca and Siete Viejo.

For a friend who was now connected to the most respected men from the border underworld, the hoodies were at Gabriel's beck and call, available to run errands and provide rides whenever he asked for a favor. When Gabriel would take his friends to La Siberia, their favorite lunch spot in Nuevo Laredo, they left their car in the middle of the street. "I'm Meme's people," Gabriel would tell the guy at the door. Traffic came to a halt while they ate lunch, but no one honked or complained. A cop simply told drivers to reverse their cars and go around a different way.

In Nuevo Laredo, during Gabriel's first months of membership in the Company, he didn't perceive much of a war. The Company appeared to control the area. But now, in the spring of 2005, as the Company and the Sinaloans expanded their ranks, more intense conflict visited the border, and the Company's grip on Nuevo Laredo was no longer assured. Gabriel discovered that the impunity he once enjoyed diminished a little. On April 1, after being picked up for driving a stolen car and possessing cocaine, he landed in a Nuevo Laredo jail for ten days.

Power and authority can shift quickly in the cartel world. The phrase "I'm Meme's people" no longer bought Gabriel as much *palanca,* leverage, as it once had. During his ten days in jail, his status as a member of *la gente* kept him safe and conferred certain privileges. He got a bunk of his own, albeit roach infested, and money to purchase laundered blankets. He ate fried tacos and beef stew, rather than take scoops from the communal bucket of *rancho,* a thin soup of rice, potatoes, and beans. He saw how control of the prisons was critical to a cartel's control of the plaza. In the prisons, criminal networks mingled and joined forces, shared information, found new recruits, and killed enemies who landed inside—which meant the death could be written off as a "prison fight" rather than a murder.

On a Sunday afternoon in May 2005, a month after his release, via bribe, from jail, Gabriel woke up at Meme's house in Nuevo Laredo, a gaudy mansion known as El Castillo, the Castle, where Gabriel had been spending many nights. On waking, he thought immediately of Christina. She was getting angry. He was either busy working or in jail. A week would pass without communication. When he did finally call, she would threaten: *Come see me immediately or forget about our relationship!*

"Call Wences," Meme told Gabriel. "Tell him to come across."

"I don't want to come," Wences told Gabriel over the phone.

"Why not? You don't have a choice."

A load of weapons Wences was supposed to cross to Mexico had gone missing, Wences explained, and he feared the consequences. After the incident with Meme and the coke dealer, Gabriel didn't *disbelieve* that lost weapons could merit punishment. But he felt confident that Meme would not ask him to set up his own friend.

"Don't worry," Gabriel said. "I'll be there."

Driving toward the outskirts of Nuevo Laredo, Meme told Gabriel and Wences that they were going to meet "the men of Nuevo Laredo." Be serious, he said. There was a mission to do, money to make. "Take advantage of this. Ask for everything you want: ARs, vests, cash, cars. They'll give it to you."

Ten minutes later, Wences and Gabriel stood on a patio behind a nice house. A black Suburban backed into the driveway and parked, nose out. Two men got out; one faced the road, the other circled the car. Two others emerged from the truck and walked to the patio. They wore military fatigues, and camouflage hats tied beneath the chin. Gabriel was impressed: the all-black look had become a trend around the hood, but these guys were soldiers. He thought of Bart's SEAL poster, of the video games they used to play.

As the men approached, Gabriel recognized Comandante Cuarenta—Forty—Miguel Treviño. Gabriel had known that he worked for Miguel, even if orders came from Meme. But he'd hardly seen the man since that night, nearly a year earlier, when he and Wences tried to sell the truck to the wrong cop.

"Saludos, señor," the boys said.

"Mis Gabachos!" Miguel said, using his slang for Americans. He threw his head back and sighted the boys down his nose. *"No me llames 'señor.' Señor* is for the one in heaven. Call me *comandante."* He asked which of them would be his "man."

When Wences was silent, Gabriel jumped in and said, "Yo mero." *I'm the true one.*

Miguel touched Gabriel's chest and smiled. "Eres como yo, güey. Tú si eres frío." *You're just as cold as me, dude.* Then he touched Wences's heart; it beat fast. *"¿Tienes miedo?" You scared?*

"Me acabo de echar un pase," Wences stuttered, explaining that he'd snorted a line of coke that Meme offered on the drive over. Wences confessed that he thought he was going to get smoked for a load of lost weapons.

"Cómo crees, güey," Miguel said and laughed. "Eso pasa siempre." *Don't worry, dude. Shit happens all the time.* Miguel turned to Gabriel. "So, you think you're a badass?"

"Yes, Comandante."

"How many people have you killed?"

"I don't know."

Miguel laughed. "So many that you don't know? Do you know how many I've killed?"

"No, Comandante."

"I've killed more than eight hundred people."

Gabriel and Wences followed Miguel and Meme into the house for a meeting of Zeta *comandantes*.

After some talk, the men agreed that the war with their Sinaloa rivals needed to be fought in the States as well as Mexico. Sinaloan contras were jacking Company loads in Mexico, sneaking across the border, and establishing themselves in Texas, where they assumed that the law-and-order culture of America would protect them, or at least make retribution less attractive. Also, by flooding South Texas with money, the Sinaloans—through an allied smuggler in Laredo named Chuy Resendez—were getting Company smugglers to flip sides. All contras and defectors in Texas had to be eliminated, Zeta leadership decided. It could only be done with a strong presence on the U.S. side.

The *comandantes* looked at Gabriel and Wences, and asked them to find eight *Gabachos de huevos,* Americans with balls, who could attend a training camp and then join them in the plaza.

Which plaza? Gabriel wondered.

Until now, the only plaza he knew was Nuevo Laredo, where the cops not only looked the other way while he carried out assassinations but often helped him murder people. He and Wences just nodded: Yes, they would do it.

As the boys walked out, the *comandantes'* meaning became clear.

Miguel gave them $10,000, told them to buy a couple of used cars, and assigned them two commission jobs, for $10,000 a piece—in Laredo.

Laredo? As in *Texas*?

Doing missions in a place where the authorities took homicide seriously was not the most appealing prospect. But it was Forty asking, *Miguel Treviño,* and Gabriel understood the implication. To climb the ladder, he had to work in the States.

One of the men Miguel asked them to kill—a Nuevo Laredo cop named Bruno Orozco, who had defected from the Company and now worked with Chuy Resendez in Laredo—had killed Wences's cousin earlier in the year. Once timid, Wences now appeared bold and willing.

They would do the jobs, Gabriel told Miguel, and they would recruit more *firme vatos*.

Who's my man?

I'm the true one.

He was part of something now, and a Wolf Boy never said no.

PART III

Spillover

The first captive so offered made one a "leading youth," a "captor," marked by appropriate face paint, the right to wear a breechclout with handsomely long ends instead of the brief boyish affairs of novices, and a cape bearing a design in place of a plain mantle: no small reward in self-conscious and narcissistic youth.

—*AZTECS,* INGA CLENDINNEN

12

In the Dirty Room

Midnight closed in, the full moon set the river on fire, and the Treviño brothers were coming to collect.

Bzzz. Bzzz. Bzzz.

Mario Alvarado's cell phone skittered across the table again. On the third call he answered.

"You messed up," said Miguel. "You shouldn't have left. Why'd you leave?"

"You didn't tell me to stay or nothing," Mario mustered.

"You've got to pay this *cuenta*," Miguel said, referring to Mario's debt. "You owe a lot of money to the *gente*. Meet Omar on this side. Bring your Hummer, *pa entregarlo*"—for exchange.

Mario Alvarado, the young American, hung up. Two roads appeared before him. He could kiss the drug-smuggling business goodbye, and disappear. The *cuenta* was a million dollars. Would the Treviño brothers hurt his family for that much money?

Was Mario really asking?

Option two: Return to the Treviño brothers in Mexico, confront Miguel and Omar, hope they valued their *cuenta* more than Mario's head, and then rely on Wayo, Mario's assistant, to hustle up the debt while Mario offered himself to the brothers as collateral.

Mario Alvarado . . .

Most runners who smuggled bricks and bundles north were mere Company subcontractors: commission men. But Mario Alvarado was American, and he worked for himself. He bought coke and marijuana directly from the Treviño brothers in Mexico, which was like buying directly from the Company. This relationship made Mario more like a partner of the Company than an employee. Granted, he was only one of many runners who moved a piece of the approximately ten tons of coke that the Company sent across each week—about $100 million of product at the 2004 border price of $11,500 per kilo. There were bigger movers working the Dallas hub: José Vasquez, for instance, moved 1,000 kilos to Dallas every month. But José was a Company man making 3 percent per load. On a $20 million deal, Jose's $800,000 commission equaled Mario's profit on much smaller and less risky loads. A freelancer with "a direct connect," Mario "owned" the drugs he moved: The full price spread between the border and Dallas—or between the border and New York—belonged to him. As did the risk in the event, say, that law enforcement stopped one of Mario's drivers. For three years, Mario's privilege kept him motivated, a little smug as he hustled across the country, buying and modifying vehicles and expanding his network of northern buyers. On most days he was proud of his position. Tonight, hiding from the brothers, it felt like a sentence.

It began in 2002, when Mario was eighteen and selling enough dime bags of coke in Dallas to finance a hunting trip to Nuevo Laredo. A guide there named Adolfo Treviño, whom everyone called Fito—pronounced "FEE-toh"—charged five hundred dollars for a weeklong deer hunt on his ranch. Mario met Fito's brothers, Omar and Miguel. Fito and Omar called Miguel "Michael," but no one else did.

Miguel was a sure shot and a fun guy, generous with instructions about marksmanship. He snacked often on Rolo candy, seemingly addicted to the caramel-filled chocolates. When they posed for pictures with their kill, Miguel threw his head back, smiled thinly, and extended the pinkie and pointer fingers of his right hand—"throwing the goat" as it were. Miguel had dark eyes and high-chiseled cheekbones. He was not tall, but thick in the chest, arms, and thighs. The Treviño brothers carried guns in restaurants. They drove twice the speed limit. Cops never bothered them.

On return hunting trips, Mario felt at home in Nuevo Laredo nightclubs, where his gringo dollars earned him consideration he was unaccustomed to in Dallas. One night he ran into Miguel and Omar, who were dressed in black fatigues and riding around town in a caravan of Suburbans. It was now clear to Mario that the Treviño brothers were into more than hunting. They recognized Mario as well. "¿Qué onda, güey?" Miguel said. *What's up, dude?*

Mario thought: I want to work.

He asked Omar Treviño about getting kilos, and Omar said Mario could buy as many kilos as he wanted.

The economics were simple. It was a matter of paying $11,500 per kilo in Nuevo Laredo versus paying $18,000 in Dallas. Mario would have to cross the coke over the border himself. But the risk was worth the profit. He returned to Nuevo Laredo with $57,500 in cash and bought five kilos—eleven pounds—from the brothers. Mario and his man, Wayo, rented a stash house in Nuevo Laredo. To prepare the product to be smuggled across the border and up to Dallas, they designated one room for the first wrapping—"the dirty room." After the first wrapping, they took off their clothes and passed the drugs to the second room, "the clean room," then showered and put on new clothes before the final wrapping. On Mario's first big coke deal he made $25,000 in profit, then set about expanding his new operation.

Mario purchased pickup trucks from which he removed panels and lights. The trick was packing the drugs in a part of the vehicle where the body wouldn't lose its hollow sound when slapped. It got to where Mario was buying ten kilos per week. Then twenty. Then thirty-five. When the brothers saw that Mario was a reliable and steady client, they began to front, or advance, the youngster his kilos.

It wasn't long until Mario discovered he could trade guns for drugs. The brothers would take all the guns Mario could smuggle south. The profit on a dozen AR-15s—purchased for a total of $18,000 at a gun show in Texas and sold to the brothers for $30,000 in Mexico—covered one kilo *and* the payment to the "straw purchasers" who bought the guns for Mario at the Texas gun shows. With every dozen assault rifles Mario smuggled south, the "brick" was therefore free and the entire $18,000 sale price in Dallas was profit. Mario began moving fifty kilos per week to Dallas. He used a Buick Riviera, a Lincoln Navigator, a Ford Expedition, a Dodge Ram. When Nuevo Laredo started becoming more violent, in 2004, he rented a new stash house across the river, a cute pink house on Topaz Trail, an upscale suburban street on Laredo's expensive north side.

A diligent hustler was a hot commodity in the Company, and the Company's social fabric absorbed Mario. They invited him to barbecues in Nuevo Laredo, where up-and-coming *comandantes,* always looking to expand their own networks, schmoozed Mario. Any ranking Company man knew that in order to rise, and remain a welcome member, he needed to generate income.

"Nah," Miguel said when his Company colleagues tried to tempt Mario with better deals. "He's my *gente.*"

Mario was getting in deep, and it wasn't long before he started to learn about the downside of doing business with the Company. For

one, if he wanted to move the "white" he'd have to move the less prof-
itable "green" as well. Mario woke up in Dallas one day and found
1,200 pounds of marijuana on his doorstep unbidden. Lacking storage,
he kept the eighty-pound bundles in his mom's garage, unaware that
his parole-violating cousin was staying there. It was a depressing day
when, after the cops came to the house to retrieve his cousin on the
parole violation and discovered the pot in the garage, Mario's mom,
who'd been arrested with the cousin for possessing 1,200 pounds of
pot, called Mario from jail and Mario had to remind her to keep her
mouth shut. A few times, Miguel sent kilos that were no good, and
Mario had to pay anyway. Being *gente,* it turned out, meant taking the
good with the bad. The bad could be pretty shitty.

But there was one outcome he dreaded the most. And it came in
late 2004, when he had to call Miguel and say, "My calves drowned."
Ninety bricks of the white had been seized from his transporter on
the way to New York. Mario, having been fronted nearly two hundred pounds of cocaine, owed the Company a million dollars. He
went to Nuevo Laredo to try to make good with Miguel, to ask for
another load to make up the loss. But Miguel wasn't receptive. He
kept Mario overnight. In the morning, a panicked Mario left without permission.

Now, in the fancy pink stash house on Topaz Trail—surrounded
by the paraphernalia of a smuggling operation: Food Saver machines
and plastic wrap for vacuum-packing drugs; hollowed-out TVs for
transporting kilos; and a lifetime supply of tire shiner and Windex
for concealing aromas—Mario and Wayo reached a decision. Mario
would hand himself over to the brothers, and trade in his Hummer
for credit. Wayo would stay in Laredo and wait for instructions.

"We have to handcuff you," Miguel said when Mario returned to
Nuevo Laredo. "You might try to run off on us again."

They went hunting, and then Mario rode along on stash-house
raids. Mario watched Miguel respond casually to chaos and gunfire.

He rarely looked over his shoulder or surveyed a room before walking in. Miguel's *escolta,* his squad of soldiers, protected him; but on missions, Miguel went first, always moving toward the engagement with the same strutting brutality: chin up, toes out.

They gave Mario kilos to send across to Wayo, who brought them to Dallas. Ten keys here, ten there. Mario got his *cuenta* down to $120,000. He cut that number in half by giving them $60,000 worth of jewelry.

After four weeks of detention, they were at a restaurant when Miguel announced, "I'm going to let Mario leave now."

Mario was elated; paying his debt hadn't guaranteed his freedom, or even his life. Some in the cartel world were loath to let any debtor live. Those who'd been threatened over money tended to hold grudges. Suppose Mario decided to become an informant for the government?

But this prospect, apparently, didn't bother Miguel. For a drug kingpin in Chicago or New York, insulating yourself against the snitching of arrested subordinates was a constant concern. But Miguel had the greatest insulation ever: a two-thousand-mile border that divided the Company from American law enforcement, and ensconced it in a world of its own rulemaking. Besides, Mario was an American, and it was hard to justify killing a good American runner.

No, it made sense for Miguel to let Mario live. But someone else would eventually pay for this smuggler's reprieve

13

Garcia's Orgasm

For Robert Garcia, being a good cop was all about what he called the Mental Fuck. As a young patrolman, he learned the value of a good one. When he got called to testify, he always showed up early to court to banter with the defense attorney. He'd bullshit about a past case, or recall that time they had dinner, if they knew one another. Then, later, after being cross-examined, he'd swing by the defendant's table again, during the break, and joke some more. "Geez," he'd say, "you almost had me on that one!" And the whole time he could see the crook thinking, Isn't this lawyer supposed to be working for *me*? There it was, the Mental Fuck.

Defense lawyers taught Robert a lot. The best ones were nice in the early going of a cross-examination. They pretended to believe everything he said. Robert called it doing "a Columbo" on someone—giving a false sense of security to set him up for later.

The Mental Fuck, at its core, came back to control. He'd spend days or weeks preparing to testify, memorizing hundreds of facts and dates from a case that might share facts with other cases. When testimony day came, he wanted to burst through the doors, rush to the stand, and pour it all out. He always reminded himself to go slow.

The prosecutor called his name. The doors swung open. Everyone looked back. He strolled in, buttoned his jacket, unbuttoned it when he reached the stand. Adjusted the chair. Adjusted the microphone. Asked for water. Answered questions slowly. Saw where the defense attorney was going. Responded slower than the attorney wanted.

Trial was a big show. But it could be a beautiful dance when properly controlled.

Robert learned control in the squad car, during the early years, when federal agents he'd soon work with were still off at college. Every day he stopped people, mixed it up with criminals, learned how to talk to them, how to be easy, how to pretend, convincingly, that they were the ones doing the Mental Fuck on *him*. Later, he saw the college guys come, the ones who went straight to DEA or FBI without law enforcement experience. They'd be all uptight in the streets, using fancy words to sound authoritative, as if talking in a cop show. The criminals, like dogs, smelled that fear.

In the police station, in the interrogation room with informants and suspects, control came down to reading a personality. The gangster wanted his ego stroked. The reformed addict wanted to be a cop. The beat-up weekend girl just wanted to be heard. If he didn't find their motivation, he had nothing to play to, and then he'd be the one getting played.

Ten percent of the time, murder suspects broke down and cried at the station. Robert comforted them. They told him everything. The other 90 percent of suspects came into the interrogation room with a plan, a set of lies to tell. If Robert expected them not to lie, and jumped all over every line of bullshit, he got nowhere fast. The criminal knew how far he could push. Robert learned to let himself be pushed even further. He *wanted* them to lie, to get that shit out of their system. Because in between the lies there were going to be bits of truth. The key was gathering those nuggets and putting them in storage for confirmation and cross-checking. The hours-long back-and-forth, give-and-take of a great interrogation, well, for Robert this exchange was a kind of intellectual sex, Mental Fuck culminating in Mental Orgasm. He came out of the interrogation room thinking, Ah, give me a cigarette!

Switching from DEA to the Laredo PD homicide division reinvigorated Robert. He'd put all he had into the objectives of DEA. It had taken a terrible toll on him, and he felt as if the drug busts amounted to nothing. The goal of drug interdiction was too uncertain. Without attacking demand in the United States, he couldn't see the point of putting so many resources into stemming only a fraction of traffic. But violence spilling over was another matter.

When Robert transferred to homicide, in the last days of 2003, there was no cartel-related violence in Laredo. But, just a few days into his new job, there was a double homicide; a month later, a guy was ambushed on his front lawn; and shortly after that a guy was killed in his white Cadillac. All of these victims were known Laredo gangsters. It was clear, from the PD investigations, that the victims were somehow connected to organizations across the border, but it was unclear how. The murders were professional, and no suspects were located. Once, in mid-2004, Laredo PD picked up a top Zeta, unknowingly, and then let the guy go. As 2004 turned to 2005, the murder rate spiked in Laredo. Even national news picked up on it. And yet Robert knew the real numbers were worse than reported. Through informants he heard of cartel hits that would never be solved or even known about. Bodies that dropped in Laredo were being disposed of in Mexico.

Now it was June 2005, and just a week earlier, some guy had

walked up to the front door of a local gangster's house, rang the doorbell, and shot the gangster's thirteen-year-old son by mistake. A security camera on a school across the street captured the shooting, but the video was grainy. Laredo PD knew that one of the two cartel groups in Nuevo Laredo—either the Gulf Cartel and the Zetas, on one hand, or the Sinaloa Cartel on the other—was behind all of these execution-style murders, but they didn't know which one. The name Miguel Treviño had been coming up in informant interviews; he was apparently now a leader for the Zetas in Nuevo Laredo. The names of other cartel leaders were also known. But Laredo PD had no leads on the cartel battle. As for the bodies turning up in Laredo, it was hard to investigate murders ordered by people in another country, particularly a country where few in law enforcement could be trusted to cooperate with U.S. authorities.

On June 8, 2005, however, there was a small breakthrough. Robert arrested an eighteen-year-old named Gabriel Cardona at the scene of a broad-daylight murder on Killam Industrial Boulevard, off I-35 near the northern city limit.

IT WASN'T THEIR FIRST MEETING. Eight months earlier, shortly after Gabriel's eighteenth birthday, Robert interviewed Gabriel when Laredo PD picked him up for aggravated assault. Gabriel and another boy from Lazteca had done an unsuccessful drive-by shooting over some personal dispute that appeared unrelated to any gang conflict. The incident didn't stand out much in Robert's mind; drive-by shootings were daily occurrences. Gabriel had spent a couple of days in jail for it, if Robert remembered correctly, and then bonded out for $10,000 or $20,000.

Now, here's what Gabriel told Robert, and what Robert knew from his investigation at the scene of the murder on Killam Industrial Boulevard:

With Gabriel at the wheel of one of three cars, the hit crew, pretending to be undercover police, pulled over a former Mexican cop named Bruno Orozco in the middle of a busy road. Realizing they were fake cops, Orozco yelled for help. That's when another young man, named Wences Tovar, shot him nine times with an AR-15 equipped with a silencer. Leading the hit group was a man whom Gabriel said he knew as the Marine, or Z-47. The Marine left in one car and escaped cleanly. Wences left in the second car, which he abandoned near the border, along with the AR-15, ran into the woods, and got away. Gabriel peeled out, drove toward the border, and was stopped near downtown Laredo, after a small chase.

It had been a violent week on both sides of the border. On the Mexican side, Nuevo Laredo's new police chief was sworn in. "I'm not beholden to anyone," said the police chief, a former print shop owner and Chamber of Commerce president. "I think those who should be afraid are those who have been compromised." Three hours later, the new police chief was murdered in his car. On the U.S. side, the Sinaloans gunned down a Zeta at a Laredo Mercedes dealership. Then the thirteen-year-old boy, mistaken for his father, was murdered on his front lawn when he answered the door.

Now, in the interrogation room, across from Gabriel, Robert prepared himself for the Mental Fuck.

But he had little idea what to make of the kid, an American teenager who claimed to be connected to the Zetas. It wasn't uncommon for drug-trafficking organizations in Mexico to hire an American in Laredo to carry out a hit. That happened from time to time. But usually the guys who took those jobs were seasoned gangsters in their thirties and forties, guys from big American gangs like Texas Syndicate, HPL, or the Mexican Mafia. Those Americans weren't actually members of the Mexican cartel, they just ran with one of the gangs that took the murder contracts via some connection across the border. So at first, Robert had trouble believing it: Was an eighteen-year-old

American kid really working as a killer for the Zetas? Or was Gabriel Cardona full of shit? Laredo thugs, especially youngsters, were always lying about their underworld accomplishments.

Gabriel explained more about the murder on Killam. He told Robert that the day before he'd run into a friend in Laredo. No, he didn't know the friend's name, only his code—47. Gabriel's claim of not knowing his own friend's name wasn't automatically bullshit; people in the underworld often knew each other by code only. This friend, Gabriel continued, had asked Gabriel if he had a car, and, if so, whether Gabriel could help him kidnap a person in Laredo and take the person across the border to Mexico. "Just pick him up and take him across," Gabriel emphasized to Robert. Of the person to be kidnapped, Gabriel knew only that he was a policeman in Mexico, or a former policeman, and that he was wanted for killing Zetas on behalf of a major Sinaloa-allied distributor in Texas named Chuy Resendez.

The Chuy Resendez connection: To Robert, this detail sounded too specific to be made up. Robert didn't disbelieve that the original goal was to kidnap the guy rather than kill him. But the idea of Gabriel running into a friend, then tagging along on a mission of this magnitude—whether intended as a kidnapping or a murder—sounded like fiction.

Well, Robert had a confessing suspect in Gabriel, even if he didn't have the shooter, so he shifted the focus to Gabriel's own background.

"How much time do you have being a Zeta?" Robert asked.

"Five months, more or less," Gabriel said.

Robert wondered if Gabriel would speak about crimes he committed in Mexico. "How many people have you killed across?"

Gabriel said he had killed three people in Mexico.

"Did you kill all three at the same time?"

"No, two together, one separately."

"Policemen?"

"Just guys."

"Who was the last one you killed across?"

"They called him La Rata," Gabriel said, invoking the term—*ratas,* rats—that the Company used for the Mexican military.

"With a *cuerno* or a nine?"

"A thirty-eight."

"Close range?"

"As I'm closing in, if he turns I'll fire. If he doesn't turn, I'll shoot him in the head. In other words—"

"So you kill the guys and then what the fuck do you do?"

"The cops pick them up and throw them away. I'll be told, 'These guys are going to the *guiso.*' And it's no problem."

"And the cops escort you?"

"The cops set up an area, clear it out, and sound the sirens if there's a problem. That's the way it is across." Gabriel spoke in a frank, shrugging way. *What is one to do? It's just how it is over there.* "The military are the only people not on the payroll."

"So if the law over there stops you, if you're cruising, what do you tell them?"

"They knock on the window. I lower the window, but only this much"—pinching thumb and forefinger—"and ask what they want. They say, 'Get down.' I say, 'Why am I going to get down?' They say, 'Well, what are you doing?' I say, 'I am working. I am with La Compañía.'"

"¿La Compañía?"

"Yes. And they won't report anything."

"Are you armed?"

"When I am, I just tell them, 'Don't you see the gun?' And the guy won't ask more questions because he knows that if I'm carrying then I'm with them. He just asks for money. I give him ten or fifteen bucks."

"Tell me. From messing around on this side and doing drive-bys to killing people as if they were cockroaches—how the fuck do you jump from one thing to the other?"

"They told me five hundred dollars a week, ten thousand dollars a job, and you'll have all the power."

"But there's a war between two groups. Aren't you afraid the other group is going to pick you up?"

"The other side doesn't know who I am."

"Yes. But they'll find out eventually."

"Yes, eventually, they will. But that's why one knows what he gets into. So no problem. If they pick me up, well, too late. I'm already in it."

"Well, you know what you're facing here, right?"

"Yes, I guess I'm burned on this one," Gabriel said, as if he'd been caught skipping school.

Robert felt his aggravation getting the better of him, so he left the room and observed Gabriel on the video feed.

"Are you listening to this?" Robert asked Chuckie Adan, his partner in the homicide division.

Chuckie, also from Eagle Pass, was a few years younger than Robert, and had many children with a beautiful babe from Border Patrol. A former baseball prospect, Chuckie now carried the heft of a guy who poured two beers into a glass at once rather than waste time pouring each beer separately. Hardworking and irreverent, he paired well with Robert.

"What do you think he is?" Chuckie asked. "HPL? Texas Syndicate?"

"Says he's a Zeta."

"He *says* that," Chuckie said doubtfully. "But he's probably Mexican Mafia or some shit like that."

"Nah. He used to run with the Sieteros, that little gang in Lazteca and Siete Viejo. But it sounds like now he's part of a Zeta group working over here, taking orders from someone in Mexico maybe."

On the video feed, Robert and Chuckie watched Gabriel play with a pencil, a piece of paper. During Robert's first eighteen months in homicide, he spoke to several killers. Most were older criminals who gave up what they thought they needed for favorable bail treatment. The cocky ones sometimes alluded to other criminal accomplishments, but never specifics, and nothing like this. Nothing about cops helping out on hits, or sending bodies to the *guiso*. Nothing about weekly salaries. *La Compañía.* This kid was definitely different than anything Robert had seen during his career.

Gabriel stretched over the back of his chair, ran his hands through his hair, talked to himself. Robert knew that Gabriel knew that he couldn't be touched for what he'd done on the other side, and was trying to get under Robert's skin with it. *You think you're all-powerful, copper? You got me on this one, but you can't touch me on the others!* The kid wanted to stand up to the cops and be the Man, just like he was in Mexico. But he wasn't in Mexico. He was in the United States, facing murder charges as an adult. Out of nowhere, Robert and Chuckie saw Gabriel nearly break out in tears: The potential weight of this murder charge hit him. Ah, Robert thought, a crier. A sensitive little hit man.

Robert returned to the interrogation room and asked if Gabriel knew a guy named Catorce, referring to Z-14, Efraín Teodoro Torres, the original Zeta member who controlled Veracruz. Catorce's name had been showing up in Laredo PD reports, along with Heriberto Lazcano and Miguel Treviño.

"I don't know who that guy is," Gabriel said, looking surprised that Robert knew this name but also proud of himself for knowing someone of such importance.

"How about Miguel Treviño?" Robert asked.

"No, I don't know him," Gabriel said with a straight face.

"But isn't he in charge over there?" Robert asked, referring to Nuevo Laredo. "You have to know him."

"Nope."

Gabriel, it was clear, would now play dumb about everything except that which Robert could prove, and this pissed Robert off. Having intrigued Robert, initially, with some details of cartel life, Gabriel was now pulling back.

Robert picked up Gabriel's cell phone, checked the screen. "Both Forty-Seven and Forty keep calling you," Robert said. This information would've helped Robert, had he known the Zeta codes, but that intelligence hadn't yet come to him. He didn't know that 40—Cuarenta—referred to Z-40, Miguel Treviño.

"Forty-Seven is the Marine?" Robert asked.

"Yes."

"So then who's Forty?"

"A friend of Forty-Seven's."

Robert continued to scroll through Gabriel's contacts. "Who's A-One?"

"That's Ashley, a girl. I met her yesterday."

"How about C-One?"

"That's Christina, my girl."

"How about Guisos?" Robert asked. "Is that where they disappear the guys?"

"Yes. But I don't know his name."

"Who's Oh-Two?" Robert asked, referring, unknowingly, to Cero Dos, the call sign for Meme Flores.

"Juan," Gabriel said.

"Juan what?"

"Juan Gomez."

Robert showed frustration. "Don't fuck with me."

"Yes," Gabriel said. "No."

"Who from Los Zetas gives you orders?"

"The Commander."

"Which one?"

"Eliseo," Gabriel said, thinking of Efraín Teodoro Torres: Catorce.

"Is that his name or what they call him?"

"That's how he calls himself."

Gabriel's cell buzzed again: 40. "Who is this Forty?"

"I don't know."

"He keeps calling you, bro."

14

Corporate Raiders

Everyone in Miguel's *escolta*—his raiding party; literally, his escort—wielded an AR-15 assault rifle with a grenade-launcher attachment, four fragmentation grenades, and nine double-sided magazines; plus a .45-caliber handgun with four clips and a level-four bulletproof vest with two metal plates. Whatever confidence their equipment failed to inspire, it was hard to question a *comandante* who went first in raids, who never asked you to do something he wouldn't. Miguel was *la mera paipa,* the true shit. They followed him anywhere.

At midday, when it rained, they found a place to rest. When the sun reemerged they resumed their chase and slaughter of the con-tras—Sinaloan soldiers and smugglers, in the state of Tamaulipas, who worked for men like La Barbie, the Beltrán-Leyva clan, and Chapo Guzmán himself. As the raiding party went from place to place, littering the earth with darkening bodies, Miguel took on the appearance of an automaton.

In the *guiso* that followed raids, the sucking flames of the oil drums swallowed humans whole. The manager of the *guiso* cut out the bottoms of oil drums and set the drums in foot-deep holes in the ground. Both ash and oil seeped into the ground during the two or three hours it took a corpse to burn properly. Sometimes the scorched corpses, their faces twisted in a charred rictus of woe, were removed early and set upon the earth. *Soldados* kicked the black busts idly, like nudging a pebble, and the remains collapsed in soft explosions of ash. The *guiso* manager then shoveled heaping piles of ash onto pickup beds—a convenient way to dispose of the bodies, dust to dust as the truck motored down the highway.

Wences Tovar, the triggerman on the Bruno Orozco murder, was now one of the newest additions to Miguel's *escolta*. After Wences escaped the scene on Killam Industrial Boulevard, where Gabriel was caught and taken into custody, he fled across the border and lay up in a Nuevo Laredo hotel that later got raided by La Barbie's men in retaliation for the Bruno Orozco hit. The murder of Orozco, a valuable Sinaloan employee, made Wences a target. But Wences fooled La Barbie's people, left out a back entrance, and met Miguel at a gas station.

"You killed Orozco?" Miguel asked as he unwrapped a tube of Rolo chocolates.

"Yes, I did it."

"Have you been to the camp yet?"

"No."

Miguel threw his head back and looked down his nose at Wences approvingly. "You know what?"

"What?"

"You're not a *panochón*"—a pussy.

Wences nodded, proud.

Miguel gave him ten thousand dollars. "What do you want?"

"What do you mean?"

"You can have anything."

"What? Like food?"

Miguel and his men laughed.

Wences thought about it. "I don't have a car," he said.

"What kind do you want?"

"An Avalanche."

Miguel handed Wences a phone number and told him to take a few days of *franco*. "Call this number at nine every morning and nine every night. Don't miss a call. You'll be told when to reincorporate." He gave Wences the name of a hotel where the Company had a block of rooms reserved.

Later that evening, a pearl-white Avalanche appeared out front.

A week later, Wences incorporated with Miguel's *escolta*. Each day was a new raid, often many raids, busting down houses and killing Sinaloans. Rolling up to the house Wences would register the smallest noises, and steel himself against waves of adrenaline. Then stomping boots blew by like an ancient war cry. They went in through the back or the front, or sometimes they laid down cover fire while a *soldado* snuck up to the house and tossed a *piña*—a grenade; literally, a pineapple—through a window.

They did as many as ten raids a day. They'd take whatever they could carry after the contras were killed or captured. The loot—some combination of drugs, cash, guns, and jewelry—was piled on a table and split among the *escolta*. After a house was secured, Miguel would approach the most restless contra first and ask questions. Who do you work for? What do you do? Do you know so-and-so? How about so-and-so? He wanted addresses and names. He scribbled every piece of intelligence in a small notebook. He was always looking for the next house to raid. As conversation dwindled, Miguel would put his right hand on his .38 Special, tilt his head back, arch his neck, and shake his left leg, front to back, as if keeping time. The shaking leg: That was how Wences knew someone was about to die. Then Miguel would go to the second-most-restless contra, ask questions, and *poom*. Miguel's eyes circling for the next and the next and . . . *poom*. If the contra gave him what he wanted, the contra died quickly. If the contra held out, ears and eyes and limbs flew.

Each day, Miguel and other Company men logged newly gathered information at the Company's central intelligence office in Nuevo Laredo, known as *La Central*, where Miguel's binder of names, faces, locations, and other intelligence was constantly updated. He also got locations from his *panteras*, the female spies and lookouts. These ladies slept with the enemy, snapped photos, and wrote down addresses. His *panteras* were so valuable that when the Mexican federal police attempted to extradite one to the States, he waged open battle in the plaza to prevent it.

He was a farmer's son and a man of routine. Except for classic films with Mario Moreno, the Mexican comic actor better known as "Catinflas," Miguel didn't care for movies. He said they made people unrealistic about life. In *Proceso*, the weekly newsmagazine, he followed politics and cartel news, but he spoke of neither. At night, when they weren't working, he wore white crewneck T-shirts; jeans or clam-digger-style shorts; and Nikes or Reeboks. Once a month he rented a hotel and told his men to invite their families for the weekend. He abstained from marijuana and coke, only sniffed a bundle or tasted a brick to confirm quality when loads moved through the plaza.

Where they worked, in the livestock-rich environs of northeast Mexico, Miguel treated his crew to *cabrito*, roast baby goat in tacos—sending out for two hundred tacos at a time—and *cabeza de vaca en barbacoa:* a whole smoked cow's head from which the rich cheek meat was torn, shredded, wrapped in tortilla, and garnished with cilantro and onion. When near Monterrey, he sent bodyguards there to fetch massive quantities of *cabrito* from a famous restaurant called El Rey. Unlike other capos, Miguel didn't try to intimidate underlings with wealth. If a soldier, or a soldier's wife or child, or even a weekend girl, needed something, Miguel met the number without question, or sent a Company doctor immediately.

On *franco* they absconded to Tampico and the Playa Miramar. On that cobalt-watered coast north of Veracruz, under the shade of thatched *palapas,* it was always platters of *mariscos*, seafood, and beer. Once, when Wences, oblivious to tradition, asked for a cheeseburger, Miguel cracked up and said, "Si no estás en Boorger Keeng, güey!" and redubbed the boy "Hamburguesa."

On some weekends Miguel hunted for deer on his brother Fito's ranch and played basketball with his men. He visited his two pre-teen daughters from his first marriage; his son, Miguel, from his second; and his current wife, Maribel, and their son (also Miguel) and daughter. On other weekends, his bodyguards accompanied him to La Molienda, the racetrack where horses sprinted a quarter mile in seventeen seconds.

The quarter horses . . .

Miguel studied top bloodlines: Mr. Jess Perry, First Down Dash, Walk-Thru Fire. He learned how to buy into syndicates—shares in a top horse's future offspring. These shares were marketable commodities, liquidity being one hallmark of a good investment. He learned about "equine embryo transfers," in which breeders transfer embryos from an aging mare into a younger womb, harvesting foals from the impeccable genetics of a dying mother. Miguel tracked auctions and horses on a BlackBerry, calculating each horse's value by comparing how much he paid at auction to how much each horse earned at races and in breeding fees. Before auctions, the ponies went on the Internet. He examined pictures. Did it have an imperfection in its gait? Did its knees work properly?

An agent who worked for Miguel found front men to buy horses on Miguel's behalf—in Mexico and the States. Bucking industry practice, Miguel changed the names of his horses, once he owned them, to the names of cars: Rolls-Royce, Corvette, Bugatti, Jaguar, Porsche Turbo, Mercedes Roadster. Often, he raced a horse, then sold it back to the front man. When a front man, once contracted, refused to continue as a cog in Miguel's scheme, he would be eaten raw—killed—and a new front man would take his place.

The horse-racing hobby was a decent way to launder money. For one thing, expenses were endless. Boarding and feed. Trainers. Entry fees and private racing facilities. Bribes to jockeys and gatekeepers. There were so many ways to disappear cash! On most money-laundering schemes, if you paid "twenty cents on the dollar"—that is, pay twenty cents to launder one dollar, receiving eighty cents back in clean money—you did well. But here was a scheme where you could actually *make* money. For big races, a typical winner's purse was $400,000, and Miguel could fix races in Mexico in half a dozen ways. For instance, he could put a jolting device in his jockey's hand. Or, if he had a weak pony racing, he could pay to have the track packed extra hard to favor slower horses. Or he could pay gatekeepers $10,000 each to hold their gate for a millisecond longer while his pony shot out first.

Miguel's collection of quarter horses grew to several hundred. He bought a new ranch in Coahuila and called it La Ilusión. The trainers and breeders he employed knew not to raise the dangers of an overcrowded pasture—disease, injuries, fighting. Those trainers and breeders did whatever Miguel asked; after all, they made names for themselves in the industry by working for people who owned the best horses. El Comandante knew his business, and condescension was the gravest disrespect.

On Sundays Miguel went to church with his mother in Valle Hermoso.

15

The Clean Soul of Gabriel Cardona

Religion was for the ignorant, Gabriel believed, despite his religious upbringing. In his poor corner of America, he saw people submit to Catholicism, which, in his opinion, was "all about the religion and nothing about the people submitting to it." They submitted out of weakness, he thought, and became weaker. Same thing with Islam. All those promises of eternal life in paradise? It was the brainwashing used to attract adherents, as far as he could tell.

Zeta *comandantes* laughed at Al Qaeda. Those fools fought for a fantasy, sacrificed everything in preparation for the next life. But what were they really angry about? Certainly not about women showing a little skin, which should've been a source of joy. And not about men fucking each other. Smoking someone with AIDS made business sense, but a clean fag brought good money in Boystown. Nor did the terrorists have any legit beef with Judaism, a righteous faith that revolved around money. Ah! Being poor is what pissed the terrorists off.

Well, Gabriel could understand *that*. If you took a despairing, idle person you could convince him anything was the source of his misfortune. Modernity. Greed. America. Disobedient pussy. The desperate were full of rage, devoid of purpose, and eager to belong. Zeta brass knew this phenomenon well.

Ever since emerging from the training camp, Gabriel believed that you lived and died, and maybe there was a point but who knew? Everyone was motivated by rage. He knew that much. And surely it was better to focus that rage on attaining something real, now, because there was no more spiritual meaning in death than there was pride in a fast-food job. What mattered was legacy, that one's family and associates remembered a man with reverence as *un vato de huevos, murió en la vaya,* a man of courage who died on the go, not as a coward who flipped burgers but as a soldier who perished as bullets whizzed by on the battlefield.

Gabriel had his own religion—"the Law of Attraction," he called it. In sum, you got what you set your mind to attain. He set out to earn money and he earned it. He set his mind to working with Meme Flores, and the relationship turned into something more than he could've imagined. He set his mind on Christina, and got her, too. He thought of this faith in self-determination as his American trait, his birthright as a citizen, the United States, in his mind, being the epitome of fuck-the-world-let's-live-and-see-what-happens.

He'd said fuck the world, set his mind to attaining Bruno Orozco, and now he was in jail. He wasn't sure what this experience said about his Law of Attraction. But he knew the Orozco mission was a success, insofar as Orozco was dead; and jail, it seemed, was simply a by-product of that success.

Gabriel knew the county jail scene. In the fall of 2004, after getting caught on that drive-by, he spent a few days "on lock" in the Webb County jail, in downtown Laredo. But there he'd been housed in general population, "a mix of gangster day care and crime school," where everyone watched telenovelas in the afternoon and fell in love with the Mexican actresses. There were several sixteen-bunk dorms with a communal toilet, a dayroom, tables, a TV, a telephone, and frequent visitors. The jail was civilized, not unpleasant. This Orozco arrest, however, was different. Instead of going to the local Webb County jail, the state shipped Gabriel a hundred miles north to the Frio County jail in Pearsall, Texas, and segregated him in a corner cell without phone or commissary privileges.

Across the floor, over in general population, known as "GP," he watched the Jehovah's Witnesses come to the jail each day to proselytize. Every day, a self-proclaimed devil worshipper in GP would antagonize the Witnesses and spit hate: "Fuck God!" he screamed. "God sucks my dick!" Then, one day, Gabriel watched a smiling Witness extend his hand through the prison bars and say, loud enough for the whole floor to hear: "All is forgiven, my friend." Stunned, the devil worshipper rushed over, gushing with gratitude, and clasped the Witness's hand with both of his hands. This spontaneous reversal, the triumph of belief over atheism, affected Gabriel.

Bibles floated around the jail. He asked for one, read it, and found that he remembered much from those old Sunday school sessions where he scored perfect attendance.

Several weeks passed. He became *flaco* and *barbón,* skinny and unshaven, and grew his hair long for the first time since he was a kid. Through the slam of iron bars and the clatter of steel shutters, doubt crept in. Who were his friends? How could he save himself? What was he to make of this roche-free sleep, dreaming of slit throats, exploding heads, and burning bodies?

AS A HOMICIDE DETECTIVE IN Laredo, Robert and his partner, Chuckie Adan, had plenty of work even without cartel-related violence.

It was afternoon on a weekday in late June 2005. Earlier in the day, Robert and Chuckie had reported to the scene of a lifeless body half-concealed in the brush near Lake Casa Blanca, just off the Bob Bullock Loop, Highway 20, the road that rings the northern and western areas of the city. The dead girl wore a white T-shirt, and black sweatpants with a pink stripe down each side. The detectives observed a cluster of shallow contusions on her left cheek, and deeper cuts below her chin, above her eye, and at the base of her ear. The body—legs crossed at the ankle—looked as though it had been placed neatly in the brush, rather than thrown or dumped. It was almost as if someone had made a lame attempt to bury the child.

The young mother, who called in the missing-child report shortly before the body was discovered by a citizen looking at land near the lake, exhibited few signs of urgency when Robert and Chuckie visited the apartment. She said that she and her boyfriend last saw her six-year-old daughter the night before, around 11 p.m., when they went to bed and the girl stayed up to watch TV on the futon where she slept.

The boyfriend explained to Robert: "La niña es bien chiflada y nunca hace caso. Yo la busqué y no la encontré." *The child is very spoiled and doesn't listen. I looked for her and didn't find her.*

The mother suggested somnambulism: speculating that her daughter sleepwalked out of the apartment.

Robert consulted his notes: The girl was discovered shoeless and sockless. In contrast to the dirt-smudged ankles and bruised arms, the bottoms of both feet were spotless.

Sleepwalked? Four miles? Robert and Chuckie betrayed confusion.

The mother attempted to make herself cry.

IN THE FRIO COUNTY JAIL, Gabriel read the Bible and obsessed over Matthew 12:43. When an evil spirit came out of a man, it went through arid places, seeking rest, and did not find it. If, when the evil spirit returned to the man, it found the house of his soul swept clean—but as yet unoccupied by something new and good—the evil spirit brought seven other evil spirits to live there. Without something righteous to replace evil, Gabriel understood Matthew 12:43 to mean, evil not only returned but multiplied.

He called Christina every day, insisting she be home at 5 p.m., stacking her mother's phone bill with collect charges. Christina sent him a letter with a picture of the two of them, and sprayed her Lacoste perfume on the envelope. She was *empelotada,* in love, and he began to fall in love, too. If she wasn't home at five to accept his calls, he left angry messages.

In the cell next to him, a new inmate, a twenty-year-old woman, cried nonstop and pleaded to see the chaplain. When the chaplain was slow in coming, the woman begged the guards to let her kill herself. She cried and cried and the sound became unbearable. Gabriel finally knocked on the wall and asked what upset her so much. She didn't want to talk about it, she said. So he asked how much her bond was.

"Why does that matter?" she said.

"Just tell me."

Her bond was $500,000, and that's when Gabriel knew. Before she arrived, there was jail gossip about a Laredo woman named Yulianna Espinoza. She supposedly did nothing while her boyfriend beat her six-year-old daughter to death, then dumped the girl by a mesquite tree near Lake Casa Blanca. Begging death? Half-million-dollar bond? Who else could it be?

Normally, male and female prisoners didn't sit in side-by-side cells. But it was a small county jail. Laredo PD sent Gabriel there for his own safety, so he could be housed in a segregated unit, and the police sent Yulianna there for the same reason. Prisoners didn't like people who killed children.

"Look," Gabriel said, "you can't change anything. Mourn your loss but know life goes on." He asked if she had other children. She had two sons.

"So live for them," he said. He told her to turn her bible to Luke 2:19. It was about how the angel Gabriel taught Mary to have faith in what she couldn't grasp. Yulianna told Gabriel he was crazy. But her crying slowed. They became friends. Her cell didn't have a shower. So every other day the officers put Gabriel in her cell while she showered in his.

The boyfriend, also in the jail, sent Yulianna notes on sandwich paper. "I felt ugly when I would hit your kids," he wrote in one. In another: "Don't try to make it seem like I took away your girl. You know how she behaved and how she frustrated us both." He asked Yulianna to take the rap for her daughter's death.

"I still love him," Yulianna told Gabriel, and began flushing the notes down the toilet.

"Get off that *viaje*," Gabriel hissed: *Quit that way of thinking.* "The guy is full of shit!"

"But you don't understand."

"I do understand!" he said. "Your sons need you!"

They argued for several days until Yulianna relented. When she agreed to pass the remaining notes to her attorney, Gabriel gripped his Bible: *All the ways of man are pure in his own eyes, but the Lord weighs the spirits.*

16

The Kingdom of Judgment

As a federal prosecutor, Angel—pronounced "AHN-hell"— Moreno believed in the righteousness of American law more than Robert Garcia ever could. Robert, for instance, didn't care whether marijuana remained illegal or not; for all he cared, it could be punished with the equivalent of a traffic ticket rather than prison. But Angel Moreno wouldn't hear of it. Moreno dismissed arguments about drug legalization as liberal crap. Yet Moreno, whom Robert respected for his courtroom tenacity and willingness to chase hard cases, was one of the most important people in Robert's professional life. The two met for lunch, or after-work drinks, several times a year.

A career prosecutor with graying hair who looked like a Hispanic Donald Sutherland, Moreno emigrated with his family from Nuevo Laredo to Laredo when he was seven. He finished Marine Corps service in 1977—the same year Robert arrived in Eagle Pass, Texas, with his family. For Moreno, Martin High led to Laredo

Junior College, which led to Texas A&M International University and then law school at University of Texas in Austin, during the mid-1980s, around the time Gabriel Cardona was born.

As a young prosecutor, Moreno did capital murder cases and corruption cases. As an assistant U.S. attorney on the federal side—an AUSA—he spent a year in Washington, D.C., training incoming prosecutors. Back in South Texas, he handled drug cases along the border. In 2000, over the objection of his wife, he volunteered to participate in the U.S. State Department's plan to reform Colombia's justice system in the wake of Pablo Escobar's death. Moreno would, among other things, help Colombia establish programs for wiretapping, witness protection, and port security. His wife hadn't liked the idea of uprooting their five-year-old son to go live in a war zone for two years.

One night, Moreno and his wife saw the film *Proof of Life,* in which Russell Crowe's character goes to Latin America to rescue the kidnapped executive married to Meg Ryan's character. Moreno enjoyed the movie; in fact, it inspired him a little. At home that evening, after receiving a follow-up phone call from the Department of Justice to ask if he was interested in the Colombia assignment, Moreno told his wife that he'd like to do it.

In Colombia, Moreno quickly discovered that State Department bureaucracy stifled any possibility of achieving real reform. The State Department, Moreno saw, merely wanted him to spend his $88 million budget ASAP, and then leave the country. Moreno left Colombia a year early, when the Bush administration took office and summoned him back to Texas. But he did learn something while there.

What distinguished Colombia from other Latin America countries torn by drug trafficking and corruption, Moreno believed, was the dedication of Colombia's idealists. Moreno saw Colombian prosecutors and cops, the noncorrupt minority, get car-bombed and shot in their driveways regularly. And yet they continued to show up for work every day. Sure, drugs still flowed out of Colombia, but

Moreno came away from the experience believing that a small bunch of true believers could make real progress.

Bullshit, Robert thought. This drug war optimism was where Moreno, the prosecutor, and Robert Garcia, the cop, parted ways. Unlike Robert, the imperfections of the drug war didn't keep Moreno awake at night. In Moreno's view, just because prohibition wasn't a booming success didn't mean the alternative was superior. Moreno enjoyed a drink. But legalizing coke? Heroin? Why would you add more things to the mix of stuff that can screw up people's lives?

After coming back from Colombia, Moreno returned to his role as AUSA for the Southern District of Texas. One of four federal districts in Texas, the Southern District covered seven prosecutorial territories: Brownsville, Corpus Christi, Galveston, Houston, McAllen, Laredo, and Victoria. Moreno served as the district's "drug chief," running the office's Organized Crime Drug Enforcement Task Force, OCDETF, pronounced internally as "OHSA-def."

As the OCDETF supervisor, Moreno organized multiagency investigations of cartels on both sides of the border. He instructed agents and cops on how to gather enough evidence to make a federal case. He helped get warrants for searches and wiretaps. And, after busts were made, he negotiated with defendants and took cases to trial.

Moreno understood the reality of drug interdiction, that most drugs got through the border, but this didn't bother him as much as it bothered Robert. Nor did he see any great travesty in the fact that prosecutors like himself regularly cut deals with the worst capos, murderers, and smugglers, while low-level lackeys got much stiffer sentences. In Moreno's mind, if you accepted a drug-free society as a worthy goal, then you had to accept the realities of pursuing that goal. No system was perfect. Moreno preferred to focus on what went right. And OCDETF, when considered in isolation, was an efficient prosecutorial machine.

The OCDETF program grew out of the original idea for the

South Florida Task Force, established in the early 1980s. The goal was to dismantle drug syndicates by prosecuting their leaders. At bottom, OCDETF was a funding mechanism: It streamlined investigations of drug-trafficking organizations by forcing law enforcement agencies to powwow with each other, pooling intelligence before deciding where to funnel money. OCDETF avoided several agencies working independently against the same target, repeating one another's work and wasting resources.

About 40 percent of organized-crime cases in America were prosecuted in the southwest region of the United States, and much of that chunk was concentrated in South Texas. To agents and cops in Laredo, Angel Moreno was the gatekeeper at the federal level: the person who told you whether your leads could be parlayed into a Big Case—something to build an agent's promotional "package," to move up a pay grade—and, if so, what further evidence you needed for Moreno to open a case and get an indictment.

As "the face of the federal government in court," as Moreno put it, he was the judge before the judge. He held the keys to the Kingdom of Judgment. If an agent from DEA or FBI, or any other federal agency, needed a subpoena or a wiretap warrant to make a case, Moreno, Monk of the Fourth Amendment—that constitutional provision that prohibits searches and seizures without probable cause—was the guy who read the agent's affidavit and said yea or nay.

Now, at their lunch date, Robert and Moreno gossiped about cases. Robert mentioned the recent bust of Gabriel Cardona and explained what was known about the murder of Bruno Orozco. A Nuevo Laredo cop and former Zeta, Orozco betrayed the Zetas and channeled Zeta intelligence to a Sinaloan in Laredo named Chuy Resendez. Moreno knew about Chuy Resendez; everyone in Laredo law enforcement did. Chuy—pronounced "Chewy"—controlled the smuggling routes through Rio Bravo, a small border town just east of Laredo.

Robert said that, ironically, on the day before the Bruno Orozco hit, Cardona met a guy named the Marine, Z-47, at Jett Bowl in Laredo to plan the hit while the Laredo Police Department held a bowling tournament there. They laughed. Even more ironically, Robert said, Border Patrol raided the Laredo motel room where Cardona was staying that day. Illegal aliens were constantly being kept at the Hacienda Motel, so Border Patrol did periodic sweeps. Cardona, Robert explained, concealed the AR-15 in the trunk of his Jetta. All Border Patrol found in Cardona's motel room was an industrial-size roll of cellophane.

Robert described his interrogation of Cardona. The cop-assisted whackings. The *guiso*. *La Compañía*.

"¿La Compañía?" Moreno asked.

"It's what they call the Gulf Cartel and the Zetas now."

Robert said the kid claimed to be a Zeta, and that there were more like him, working both sides of the border.

"He told you this?"

"Bragged about it."

Moreno asked for more on cartel activity. Robert said he recently investigated a shoot-out at a Laredo soccer field. A team of Zetas tried to gun down a team of La Barbie's assassins, many of whom were also American teens from Laredo. Like Chuy Resendez, La Barbie was a Laredo local and everyone in law enforcement knew him.

"La Barbie has his own assassins now?" Moreno asked.

In the aftermath of the soccer field incident, Robert said, Laredo PD turned up assault rifles and grenades. During the interrogation that followed, one of La Barbie's guys, a twenty-year-old hit man from Laredo, flirted with the idea of becoming an informant, even gave Robert a copy of a video, not yet publicized, appearing to depict four Zeta operatives being questioned and then executed by La Barbie himself.

Later in the day, Robert stopped by Moreno's office and showed him the video. One Zeta talked about plans to kill the attorney general of Tamaulipas and the new police chief in Nuevo Laredo. Another Zeta talked about training camps. Subjects of discussion included the *guiso,* and the reasons behind the recent assassination of a Nuevo Laredo reporter.

After the video, Moreno pressed his lower back and laughed. "Well *that* was interesting." Where Robert treated atrocity intellectually, and expressed awe only if the social dynamic called for it, Moreno treated the violent criminals they dealt with as sort of amusing. He believed that you couldn't do this kind of work and not let it affect you. Humor was a way to internalize and process the violence without going crazy.

Robert and Moreno were accustomed to seeing cartels hire American gang members to carry out hits in Texas. But rarely did the cartels themselves handle violence in the States; they were wary of risking the political blowback, which often translated into heightened enforcement on both sides of the border. But even when they hired an unaffiliated killer, heavy artillery such as grenades and assault rifles were unheard-of. Recorded executions, American teen assassins—those things were definitely new.

"These fuckers are here among us," Robert and Moreno agreed.

The goal of OCDETF—the "kingpin strategy" of America's war on drugs—was to go after whoever in Mexico was ordering this violence: La Barbie, the Beltrán-Leyva brothers, or Chapo Guzmán; or a leader of La Compañía. Since the goal of OCDETF was to prosecute big cartel bosses, and because OCDETF investigations were expensive, a prosecutor, before requesting support and funding for an OCDETF case, wanted to make sure that arrests of low-level guys, such as Gabriel Cardona, would lead up the chain of command, and provide enough evidence, eventually, to bring charges, like RICO and conspiracy, against a top cartel boss.

But with no proven connection between Gabriel Cardona and

Company leadership, there was no OCDETF case to be made. Moreno and Robert needed more than one kid's tale of high-level connections. And without a clear connection to drug trafficking, Moreno wouldn't be able to convince DEA to agree to join a case.

For the time being Gabriel Cardona's murder charge for the Bruno Orozco hit would stay at the state level, and never touch Mexican organized crime.

THREE MONTHS AND ONE WEEK after the Orozco hit, a magistrate judge reduced Gabriel's bond from $600,000 to $75,000. Miguel sent someone to pay it. On September 14, 2005, one day after his nineteenth birthday, Gabriel walked out of jail and rode the jail bus back to Laredo, where he spent that first night of freedom with Christina.

"Leave it behind and start over," Christina whispered during their reunion. "We have us."

Maybe it was the summer of solitude in jail, or the positive role he had played in Yulianna's life. Or maybe it was something about reembracing the religion of his youth, or turning nineteen. Maybe it was just the detoxifying hiatus from the roches. But Gabriel thought of this cartel life, of how it risked everything, and he became emotional. He wasn't from a terrible family. They loved him. And he had a good girl who loved him. He'd seen enough movies to blame the absence of a superior male figure for part of his situation, which he recognized now as a kind of bondage.

He asked Christina: "Why do you prefer a *cagapalo* over a *calmado*?" A troublemaker to a civilized person.

Christina had never given that much thought. She guessed it was something to do with boredom. Or it was just the way she felt. She had no dad figure, and he had no dad figure. Gabriel was possessive, and she kind of liked that. She wanted to be protected. Unlike Gabriel's brother, and unlike Wences—indeed, unlike most of the assholes around Laredo—Gabriel never hit her and promised he never would. Why a *cagapalo* over a *calmado*? Where were the calm ones?

Gabriel, Christina knew, idealized the north side, where she was from. But he didn't understand it. Christina's family could afford to move to the north side only because her dad was in the drug business. Once they were there, he tried to get out; then they were going to lose the north-side house so he got back in and now he was in prison, too.

There was no fear in Christina's love for Gabriel. Still, she wondered: Was it okay to want a person like Gabriel, someone confident and handsome and tender, but also someone not like him? She didn't know the details of what he did to earn the money he gave her, but she knew it wasn't good. Her relation to Gabriel now put her in the center of gossip concerning underworld news. But on the Bruno Orozco thing, everyone knew that Wences pulled the trigger, not Gabriel. She didn't like what Gabriel did, but she loved him. Beneath that arrogance, she believed, he was just insecure. Every word from her mouth, every look, had an effect on him, and she enjoyed that little bit of power.

She didn't know how to articulate any of these thoughts. So, parroting her older girlfriends, she responded, "Los calmados son jotillos." *The calm ones are faggots.*

Then she lay back and offered him the *pepa*. The humid air doused them and they fucked till their nerves rang numb.

The next day, Yulianna called from jail to thank him and wish him well.

ROBERT GARCIA WOULD USE THE notes that Gabriel told Yulianna to save to force her confession:

Shanea, Yulianna's six-year-old daughter, was throwing a tantrum because she wanted to go to a cousin's house. Yulianna's boyfriend grabbed a belt and struck Shanea repeatedly. Yulianna watched, then turned her back. When Yulianna couldn't take it any longer, she went into the bedroom. Later, while helping Shanea bathe, she noticed the lacerations on her daughter's face and scalp. Shanea went to sleep, complaining of a stomachache, and never woke up. The boyfriend took the body from the house and came back without it.

Robert looked through the family's file. There had been signs. When visiting the apartment several times over the previous ten months, CPS had discovered a battered woman plus the usual hazards: floors covered with dirty diapers; exposed wires; tiny scarred bodies. The CPS mandate, however, was to help "rehabilitate families," not break them up, which meant that most of the time a child like Shanea was returned to the same broken home again and again and again.

When Robert presented Yulianna's confession to the boyfriend, he attacked Robert while other cops rushed into the interrogation room. A jury sentenced the boyfriend to life plus sixty. But it didn't placate Shanea's biological father, who killed the brother of the boyfriend because the brother helped dispose of Shanea's body. "An eye for an eye," said the Webb County sheriff. The prosecutor had no interest in taking the revenge killing to trial. What jury would convict?

As for Yulianna, she pleaded guilty to injury of a child. On the sentencing date, she was recovering from a cesarean section after giving birth to a third son. The judge sentenced her to twenty years, and sent the infant to foster care to join his brothers. With any luck she'd be out by the time her oldest son was Gabriel's age.

17

Who's the Next Top Drug Lord?

When Gabriel came out of jail in September 2005, people treated him differently. In Tampico, on the Gulf Coast's Miramar Playa, a hotel room waited when he showed up for a few days of vacation with Company men. In the clubs there, people murmured that he was one not to be messed with.

The Company's Laredo presence had grown in the three months Gabriel was away. There were more recruits; a new safe house on Hillside, a neighborhood by the public library; and a block of rented apartments in Lazteca, around the corner from his mother's house at 207 Lincoln. These places were stocked with food, weapons, cars—and more hit men, more American Wolf Boys who'd been recruited while Gabriel was away.

Something about these new recruits bothered him. They appeared to be "chukkies," wannabes, guys who'd never done shit, wouldn't be on point when it was "time to ride." Or the opposite: lunatics. One chukkie snorted so much coke that a crust of blood always ringed his nostrils. Another chukkie was cool, but his girl-friend was known to work for the other side, "the Chapos." If that secret ever got out, it would not go over well.

As the summer of 2005 faded, Gabriel and Meme Flores made their way back to Nuevo Laredo from the beach in Tampico, up Highway 85, over the mountains of southern Tamaulipas, and through the city of Monterrey. Driving in Meme's bulletproof Jeep Cherokee, Gabriel was edgy. If the contras appeared, protocol demanded that Gabriel, the subordinate, shoot it out, while Meme escaped. They both had .38 Supers strapped, eyes popped. Gabriel monitored radio frequencies to make sure the road ahead was clear, and answered calls on several cell phones plugged into the console. In the back of the Cherokee, a long-arm assault rifle—*una larga*—was attached to a tripod bolted to the floor. In his head he rehearsed the steps to unlock the *clavo,* the hidden compartment behind the dashboard, where more guns were stashed: 1) AC to high; 2) gear in neutral; 3) lock door; 4) pump brakes.

The Bruno Orozco debacle, and three months in county, had taught him that operating on the American side was more difficult than Mexico. He wanted to keep working for Meme, bringing him cars and weapons and maybe transporting small drug loads, but he'd decided he wanted out of the Company. He didn't want to do more jobs in Texas. He didn't want to go back to jail. During the four-hour ride to Nuevo Laredo, he tried to feel Meme out about the future.

"You could've been assigned to a hotter plaza like Monterrey or a city in Michoacán," Meme explained. "In those places you'd get in gun battles with the contras and the *federales* every day." Gabriel knew Meme was right. Since getting out of jail, Gabriel and friends from Lazteca had kept in touch with Wences. Wences would call to say "what's up" from some place like Michoacán, the southern state, and tell them about missions down there. The next day they'd see it in the paper and say, "Damn! That squirrel is flying high!" "You're assigned to the border," Meme said, "because you're the most trusted *sicario* for difficult jobs. The Company has plans for you. You've been singled out."

"Singled out?" Gabriel asked.

"Absorb everything," Meme said. "Be ready. It won't be long until you're sent to the six-month camp, and you become a commander."

Meme had been instrumental in Gabriel's development, taking him to Reynosa and Matamoros, teaching him how to operate. Meme vouched for him and oversaw his progress. And Meme was generous. Once, they'd been in a club when Gabriel complimented Meme's style. "That's a cool shirt, *güey*." And right there, as strippers swirled on poles, Meme took off his Versace shirt and traded it for Gabriel's old raggedy Guess shirt. Meme loved him. Plus, Meme was Catorce's favorite, his *consentido*, an adviser, and Catorce was the co-chief of the Zetas.

The most trusted for difficult jobs?

A commander?

Who's my man?

I'm the true one.

If Gabriel ever questioned the organization's loyalty, Meme's words changed his perspective. He felt something for Meme. It was stupid to think of him as a father. But Meme had saved Gabriel's life, showed him how to do business, and imparted confidence. So when Meme said being assigned to the border meant Gabriel was privileged, well, it made sense. He had met Meme while smuggling cars and weapons. Of self-made capos, underworld lore often had it that they started out in precisely such jobs, in precisely the way Gabriel started. *I remember when Osiel would get us cars! I remember when Miguel ran* mota *to Dallas for so-and-so!* You got what you set your mind to attain.

Maybe the chukkies weren't that bad, Gabriel thought. Wannabes, sure. But also brothers who could stand up and do jobs instead of you. He thought of his murder case. By the time his trial came around he'd most likely be in Mexico full-time, where he was untouchable.

As he and Meme neared Nuevo Laredo, Gabriel asked what running a plaza entailed. Meme thought about it—*a good question!*—and responded with several generalities. "Always be disciplined. Respect everybody. Compliment your *sicarios*. Don't degrade them."

Gabriel nodded. Surely there was more to running a plaza. But there would be time to learn.

They reincorporated in Nuevo Laredo, where everyone was watching the video.

LIKE ANY TRANSFORMATIONAL EVENT, A story about the video developed internally and filtered down through Company ranks. Five Zeta *sicarios* had gone to Acapulco with instructions to kill cops on the payroll of La Barbie and capture the plaza. They knew the rules: Don't go clubbing, don't go out at night, and never go out alone. Whether it was insubordination, or a youngster's inability to resist the seaside resort's nightlife, the traveling assassins went to a club, where their *norteño* looks marked them as outsiders in Acapulco's insular narco-community.

It was fifteen minutes before cops tipped off La Barbie: Los Zetas were in town to kill him. The next day, La Barbie's men raided their safe house and rounded up three of the assassins. While escaping, the fourth assassin dropped his cell phone in the backyard. The fifth was in town, using a pay phone to call his sister, when La Barbie's guys punched him in the stomach and hustled him into an SUV along with his wife and two-year-old stepdaughter, brought along to enjoy vacation. The escaped *sicario* drove through the night. When he delivered the news in Nuevo Laredo, Miguel Treviño called the lost cell phone, asked for La Barbie, and requested the return of his men: "I'll pay whatever you want."

"Nah," La Barbie said, "I have money."

"Okay, the plazas. Reynosa and Nuevo Laredo—Las que más quieres, las que por más peleas." *The ones you most want, the ones you fight for.*

La Barbie wasn't dumb enough to fall for that one. "La guerra es guerra," he said.

"Then let the family go."

La Barbie kept the wife and stepdaughter overnight. The next morning, he made the girl a bowl of cereal with a banana, and let her play in the pool. "Your husband said to tell you that he loves you," he told the new widow, and gave her a thousand pesos, about seventy bucks, to get home.

In the DVD video that had now surfaced, months later, four men, three of them shirtless, sat on the floor, bruised and bleeding, against a backdrop of black garbage bags taped to the wall. La Barbie, standing behind the camera, asked the captives to identify themselves and describe their jobs.

"I was in the army for eight years," said the first. "I have the contacts in the military to find out about the patrols." He explained that the Zetas were upset with the attorney general of Tamaulipas because he was taking bribes yet consenting to military operations against the Company. He also said Nuevo Laredo's newly elected police chief would be killed for raising too much attention—referring to the police chief who was assassinated the prior June, hours after taking the oath.

La Barbie moved on.

"I was in GAFE," said the second. "Now I'm a recruiter." The Zetas recruited people even if they weren't GAFE deserters, he said, and trained them in one of four camps—Nuevo Laredo, Monterrey, Miguel Alemán, or Ciudad Mier.

"I used to work as a hawk," said the third, meaning a spotter, someone who lurked in the plaza and looked for contras. "Then they put me on the caravans, picking up people with Miguel. After capturing someone, Miguel or Meme Flores says whether or not to take the captive to the *guiso*."

"What's the *guiso*?" La Barbie asked.

"It's when they grab someone, they get information about moving drugs or money, they get what they want, and then, after torturing him, they execute him. They take him to a ranch, they shoot him in the head, they throw him in a can, and they burn him with different fuels like diesel and gasoline."

La Barbie asked about a female radio reporter in Nuevo Laredo who'd recently turned up dead.

"Lupita Escamilla was responsible for writing the news, and making sure things didn't come out on the national level. But then she refused to continue working for them so they sent someone to kill her."

"And you, buddy?" La Barbie asked the fourth, a young man known as Pollo, whom Gabriel knew from childhood. But before Pollo could answer, a gun came into the camera frame and blew his head off. It was the first time Gabriel had seen a friend killed. The film cut off there, but presumably the others were shot the same way.

The Company put a million dollars on La Barbie's head. By most accounts, he had taken up residence in Acapulco, on Mexico's south coast, but some believed that he visited family frequently in Laredo.

Out of jail for one week, Meme's words still ringing in his head, Gabriel—having returned to the roches after finding religion in jail over the summer—decided he would do whatever it took to succeed in the Company, kill La Barbie, and become the next American drug lord.

IN SEPTEMBER, AROUND THE TIME Gabriel Cardona bailed out of jail, Angel Moreno's opinion about the possibilities of opening an OCDETF investigation of Zeta leadership changed. Moreno took a routine plea meeting with a busted American drug smuggler from Dallas.

Mario Alvarado's pink stash house on Topaz Trail, in north Laredo, had been busted following a routine crime-stopper's call. Alvarado had eighty pounds of weed stuffed in a couch, and a few kilos of coke hidden in a TV—personal-use quantities for a guy like Alvarado, but enough weight to warrant serious prison time. Looking to cut a deal, and reduce his sentence, the twenty-two-year-old Alvarado entertained Angel Moreno with an epic story of dealing directly with Zeta leadership for the past four years. Alvarado said he knew the Treviño brothers, Miguel and Omar, and their Zeta network personally. Alvarado said he hunted with them, did business with them; was even held hostage by them.

Moreno thought back to his summer lunch meeting with Robert Garcia, and began to wonder: Could he use that Gabriel Cardona kid and Mario Alvarado—unconnected but for their common link to the Zetas—as the basis for an OCDETF investigation? In theory, yes. But to get an OCDETF case approved, he needed at least one other federal agency to sign on. There were many possibilities: FBI, ATF, DEA, ICE. Every agency had a strong presence in Laredo, and Moreno knew all the bosses. He made the rounds, trying to build support.

The goal of an OCDETF investigation was to get big cartel bosses. But what did it mean for a drug lord to be "big"? The factors that formed the government's perception of "bigness" were the same factors that formed the public's perception: media coverage. The Treviños were not well known in the States, nor was Zeta leadership, composed, as it was, of obscure former special-force troops like Heriberto Lazcano and Efraín "Catorce" Teodoro Torres.

La Barbie, on the other hand, had been beefing up his PR campaign. He published newspaper editorials in Mexico claiming to be a legitimate businessman and imploring the Mexican government to eliminate the Zetas, whom he called "delinquents." Over the summer, Robert and Laredo PD had decided against publicizing the "Barbie Execution Video," as it was now known. But they did share it with some people from federal agencies—such as FBI, the agency in charge of investigating missing persons—to make sure there was no confusion about the growing threat. A FBI agent leaked the video, which somehow wound up at a small newspaper in Tacoma, Washington, in the hands of reporters who didn't know much about Mexican drug cartels and couldn't translate the Spanish. The Washington State reporters ran an Internet search for "Zetas," which turned up news stories by Alfredo Corchado, the Mexican-American journalist who ran the Mexico City bureau for the *Dallas Morning News*. They mailed the video to Corchado, who investigated the claims made in the video, wrote a story for the *Dallas Morning News,* and posted the video footage online. The Barbie Execution Video went viral, shown on a loop all over Mexican and American TV, and gave La Barbie a global reputation, erasing any doubts about what kind of business he was really involved in.

From his Laredo upbringing and earlier trafficking cases, American authorities knew La Barbie. Miguel Treviño's reputation was growing within Laredo law enforcement, as informants cycled through interview rooms and told stories about him, but many still believed he was a minor player. In reality, La Barbie was a successful smuggler and capable soldier, but a middling player, overall, in Mexico's narco-hierarchy, no more or less important than Miguel. Yet the gruesome video, the articles, the Laredo pedigree, and the blond preppy appearance all helped make La Barbie the new symbol of the war—in the eyes of the public, and therefore in the eyes of American government. Washington, D.C., wanted La Barbie. The DEA had a source inside La Barbie's circle; in fact, it turned out to be the same guy who gave Robert the video in the first place.

And so the agency heads declined Angel Moreno's OCDETF plan for the Zetas. Moreno had more power than the local agency bosses, but they had jurisdiction over their own offices. They respected Moreno. But some carried bitter memories of him undercutting their influence in the past—ordering around their agents, or going directly to their regional bosses in Houston. La Barbie, they said confidently, was the target.

AFTER RECEIVING THE DVD OF the Barbie Execution Video and watching it several times, Alfredo Corchado, the Mexico City bureau chief for the *Dallas Morning News,* travelled to Tamaulipas state to meet with José Luis Santiago Vasconcelos, a prosecutor who served as drug czar to President Vicente Fox. Vasconcelos, alleged in the video to be taking money from the Company, wasn't eager to be interviewed by Corchado, and canceled three times. Corchado finally scored the interview, but only after asking President Fox's administration to force Vasconcelos to meet with him.

Vicente Fox, a former broccoli farmer and Coca-Cola executive, became president of Mexico in 2000. Despite promises of change, he'd taken what many considered a lax approach to pursuing drug lords. American law enforcement sent tips to the Fox administration regarding key criminals in Mexico. But the tips went nowhere, or were shared with the criminals themselves. Corchado had interviewed Fox many times, and believed that Fox was simply unwilling to acknowledge the growing cartel menace. Fox didn't like how foreign coverage of cartels eclipsed the image of Mexico that he wanted to establish, that of a rising democracy.

"Total lies," said Vasconcelos when Corchado finally got in and forced him to watch the DVD, in which a Zeta hit man accused him of receiving bribes. "They will say any lies, especially when they're being tortured. This is nothing new." He told Corchado: "This isn't a story for you. Why don't you focus on tourism stories? They're safer."

18

All in the Gang

In early October 2005, Gabriel was back in Laredo, sitting in Nydia's Salon, when a short kid walked in. He wore sandals, black jeans, and a mesh muscle shirt. He sported whiskers—*catinflas*—and looked stoned, *grifo*. He'd grown an inch or two but still just barely exceeded five feet.

"Nada que ver!" Gabriel shouted across the narrow salon. *Ain't much to look at!*

"You haven't changed a bit," Bart said.

Prior to his own jail stint, Gabriel had been taking calls from his old friend Bart Reta, who was serving thirteen months in the Texas Youth Commission for an accumulation of charges, including marijuana possession and aggravated assault for the time he took a shotgun to seventh grade and beat it against the chest of a rival gang member.

In the ghettos that Gabriel and Bart came from, violence and volatility were taken for granted. In Gabriel's mind, a boy could be reckless, even cold, and still be "a good kid"—indeed, these were admirable qualities in the street. Gabriel thought of Bart as "a good kid," however, because Bart was extraordinarily loyal. He took the rap for others, and never backed out of a criminal enterprise.

Even Gabriel could see that Bart was odd, though. Bart not only disregarded the pain of others, he was incautious toward his own welfare. He thought everything was a joke. Getting arrested for aggravated assault, or drug possession—these setbacks caused him less anxiety than most people experience in rush-hour traffic. Taken away in cuffs, Bart always made his trademark sad puppy-dog face, then broke out laughing. "He could never be himself because he wanted to fit in," was how Gabriel described his friend, and blamed it on "the short-man complex." Behind the recklessness and the jokester façade, Bart carried the rage of a poor boy whose family couldn't feed him, of a short boy referred to as the Midget by friends, of a younger boy, now sixteen, who assiduously cultivated the approval of his gang elders, regardless of risk, and no matter the cost.

On the prison calls, during the months leading up to Bart's release from TYC in July 2005, Gabriel and Bart exchanged gossip. Who was locked up. Who was out. Gabriel said he was dating a *fresa* from United High. Bart said he'd been reading mythology and poetry, and even wrote some of his own verse. He could put a lot of emotion into his poetry, he boasted, and alter his voice to sound like anybody. In TYC, inmates fought every day, he told Gabriel. Bart said he manipulated others into fighting each other. He bragged of joining a California gang called Sur 13.

"Get off that *viaje*," Gabriel said: *Get off that trip*. "Sur 13 might be big in Califas, but it ain't shit in Texas."

This condescension was typical of their relationship; Gabriel pushed Bart's buttons, degraded him. It was understood, between them, that Gabriel wanted the best for Bart, wanted to help him, so long as it was clear who was boss, who was "the shit in the hood."

"Oh yeah?" Bart said. "You got something better?"

"Me and Wences have something big going," Gabriel explained. "When you get out, maybe you can get a lick on it."

Now, in Nydia's Salon, Gabriel told Nydia to put Bart's haircut on his tab.

Bart began going back and forth between the apartment Gabriel rented and Bart's girlfriend's house. Everyone knew Bart's girlfriend had been seeing another guy while Bart was inside TYC, that she had gotten pregnant and had the other guy's child. But in the hood it was taboo to live with a girl who already had babies, so, to avoid ridicule, Bart claimed the child was his.

One afternoon, a few days after they saw each other in Nydia's, Gabriel was driving around Lazteca when he spotted Bart riding a bike. He drove Bart to the Laredo mall, where they bought Lacoste and Versace shirts, Calvin Klein jeans, a belt, a watch, cologne, Polo boots, and a cell phone. Then Gabriel took Bart to Nuevo Laredo to meet some new people. Bart was an immediate hit with leadership, and Miguel decided to keep him in Mexico.

Just as Meme Flores had recruited Gabriel into the Company, Gabriel too became a scouter of talent, albeit a particularly well-placed scout: He was American. And just as Bart now sought the approval of Gabriel, Gabriel wanted to please his own "fathers" in the Company. Delivering a young *soldado* like Bart was a good start toward his advancement.

To understand what would drive Gabriel over the next six months, it was important to understand the difference between operating in Mexico versus operating in America. In Mexico, control came directly from the top of Company management. In Mexico, a *comandante de mando,* a low-level commander in charge of a small group, didn't choose his own employees, and was therefore less accountable to the top. But for a *comandante de mando* in the States—the promotion Gabriel now enjoyed—the trust was, in his view, "magnified," because he had no direct oversight, only far-flung bosses in Mexico. Gabriel took orders from Meme or Miguel. But in Texas, he recruited for his own *mando,* his team. Since he chose his partners and employees, he was more responsible for their actions than he would've been running a similar group in Mexico.

He liked the power and the pressure, and he loved the respect from his homies in Lazteca. Particularly when Gabriel's former boss came looking for work.

THE PRIOR JUNE, WHEN GABRIEL was arrested for the Bruno Orozco hit, the DEA busted Richard Jasso's drug warehouse in San Antonio. The trouble, for Richard, started when the DEA arrested Richard's Cuban buyer in Miami and, unknown to Richard, turned the Cuban into an informant. The Cuban had been a trustworthy client; so, when the Cuban told Richard that he'd recently been ripped off and needed more cocaine to pay the debt that he owed to Richard, Richard agreed and loaded up 227 kilos. The Cuban, wearing a DEA wire, picked it up. When the Cuban returned the following week with $6 million and an order for another four hundred kilos, Richard had been out partying the night before so he asked his brother-in-law to meet the Cuban at the warehouse. At the warehouse, Richard's brother-in-law found an arresting team of DEA agents.

Richard fled to Mexico, and his name came out in the ensuing indictment. Since he was supposed to be at the warehouse when it got busted, Richard's Mexican supplier, a Sinaloa affiliate, posed questions. The loss of 627 kilos, more than $10 million in coke, fell on Richard. It didn't help when his brother-in-law became a government snitch. But the supplier forgave Richard, then gave him

$200,000 to open up a new line of transport, and started him off with two "look" shipments of fifty kilos each. Trying to cut costs, Richard hired inexperienced drivers, and both loads were seized. Richard's prior successes now meant nothing.

The supplier offered Richard one last option: move to Monterrey, handle business from there, and earn back the lost money. Richard mulled it. An unknown Mexican city? Constant supervision? Leaving his family? It might've been smart or it might've been stupid. He could make money or he could turn up dead. He decided to return to Texas, where he sold off some old trucking equipment and used his last $15,000 to buy a load of cut-rate weed, which he moved to San Antonio but couldn't sell. He looked for transport work with people he'd partnered with in the past. But they knew he was hot. They knew about his brother-in-law, the snitch. They liked Richard, but they all claimed no longer to be working, and gave him their backs. In just a couple of tumultuous months, everything he built had vanished. He was twenty-one.

In truth, the transport business was getting tougher for everyone. The battle for Nuevo Laredo had driven up cocaine prices by 25 percent at the border, as more blood than ever had to be shed to move a brick through Mexico. But prices in Dallas, Atlanta, Chicago, and New York didn't adjust much for market fluctuations at the border. Runners like Richard, the middlemen, took the biggest hit in a down economy.

Richard had a wife and children. He needed money. He needed a fresh start.

Fortunes dwindling, he decided to approach his old associate, Gabriel. He heard Gabriel and some other boys from Lazteca, like Wences, had made inroads with the Company, handling enforcement work. Maybe Gabriel could bring Richard in on one of his killing crews. This kind of crossover was common in the border underworld: To survive, smugglers killed and killers smuggled.

Richard walked to the safe house on Jefferson Street, in Lazteca, knocked on the door, and requested a meeting with Gabriel in one of the back bedrooms. At first, Gabriel just stared at Richard, amazed he was asking for work. To Richard, it was clear that Gabriel, seeing how life had soured for his old boss, was a little, well, *glad*.

"We don't get paid nearly as much as you're used to," Gabriel said.

Richard nodded. He knew the Wolf Boys had no prospects for real financial gain. Gabriel lacked smuggling know-how; he couldn't take full advantage of his Zeta connections. But maybe Gabriel could still serve a purpose. If Gabriel could introduce Richard to people in the Company, Richard could establish "a direct connect" to the most powerful cartel. When that happened, *if* it happened, Richard would have to hope that his previous relationship with Sinaloa-allied suppliers would not be a problem.

Second chances were rare. But if Richard got one, his wife, who'd begun to show signs of betrayal, would believe in him again. The toys, the cars, the parties, the admiration and love—it would all rush back like a video game reset. And what would he have to do? Ride along on a few hits? Who cared. These people were going to die anyway. It was time to be about his business again.

Gabriel, in considering a partnership with Richard, had his own designs. To rise in the Zetas and get his own plaza in Mexico, he needed a partner who could advance the business of the cartel—someone who knew smuggling. From Gabriel's stint helping Richard on transport jobs, he'd learned how difficult that business was. Gabriel's only reservation was Richard's family. A good *sicario* was uncompromised. A man with wife and children was not a great candidate for an organization whose ethos boiled down to suicide missions. And still, this sense of a future, and this new respect from Richard—whom Gabriel felt had snubbed him when they were younger, when Richard was the big hustler and Gabriel an upstart—inspired Gabriel. He took Richard on.

LA BARBIE, MEANWHILE, MADE HIS own moves against Company leadership. In September, he requested a meeting with a prominent *pantera* named Laura "Black Widow" Molano. Black Widow dated the Zeta commander Iván Velásquez-Caballero, known by the nickname "Talivan." Talivan, who had started out as a personal cook and driver for Zeta chief Heriberto Lazcano, now co-ran the Nuevo Laredo plaza with Miguel. The Black Widow accompanied Talivan to meetings with municipal police in Nuevo Laredo, where Talivan made regular payments of $50,000. Whenever they slept, five armed men protected the perimeter. The Black Widow would often come out at night to fix them something to eat.

Now, summoning Black Widow through a Zeta traitor in Nuevo Laredo, La Barbie met her at his Acapulco house and offered her $1 million to set up Talivan to be killed. La Barbie tried to be persuasive. "Son unos mata niños, mata familias, y unos secuestradores," he argued. *They're child killers, family killers, and kidnappers.* La Barbie said he wished to end the war and return Nuevo Laredo to peace. Black Widow nodded. She knew that if she said no, she'd be killed. So she said yes. Then she went home to Talivan and told him about La Barbie's plot.

GABRIEL SEARCHED A WEBSITE THAT contained pictures from Laredo clubs. His uncle Raul insisted that La Barbie was hiding in plain sight, spending weekends at his parents' house in Laredo. Gabriel monitored the address. A Ford Expedition was parked in the driveway with its back to the garage. It looked bulletproof. There appeared to be a driver inside. Gabriel obsessed over the house, until

Miguel called and said: "Get off that *viaje*!" La Barbie was unreachable, for the moment. There was other work to be done.

The day before Thanksgiving, 2005, Gabriel wounded, but didn't kill, a Sinaloan enemy in Laredo. The next day, Laredo police went looking for him because he pulled a gun on some citizens after a minor traffic accident in a Laredo intersection. They arrested him at the Lazteca safe house on Jefferson Street. In the morning, an old Lazteca homie who now worked for him bailed him out for $31,000 (it was so easy!) and Gabriel joined other Wolf Boys at the Hillside safe house, where Bart, newly returned from the training camp in Mexico, was staying.

They began tracking the movements of a heavyweight smuggler in Laredo named Moises Garcia.

19

Brothers of the Black Hand

Hey," Gabriel was saying in a chauffeured SUV, speeding north toward the safe house on Hillside. "I can't believe you shot him just like that. You went right up to the window and shot him in the head."

"Yeah, I think I also shot the girl," Bart said. "I shot the guy right in the head. I don't think he survived."

The chauffeur, Richard Jasso's wife, snapped: "I don't want to know anything!"

She was eight years older than Richard, a decade older than Gabriel and Bart. She'd picked them up at a grocery store near Torta-Mex because none of the others were answering their calls. The boys laughed. She was an accomplice!

At the house on Hillside, Bart jumped on the couch like an excited child while they waited for the evening news to confirm the death of Moises Garcia. The boys razzed Bart. "Your first job! You're going to have nightmares!"

"Nah!" Bart said. He knew some were weak in the mind and could not carry it in their conscience, but he'd "sleep as peacefully as a fish."

BEFORE THE AMBULANCE TRANSPORTED HER from the parking lot of Torta-Mex to the Laredo Medical Center, the new widow told Robert Garcia that she and her family hadn't finished eating when her husband received a call asking him to return home. They were pulling out of the restaurant's parking lot when a white Ford SUV blocked their white Lexus at the exit. She was in the passenger seat. Her brother-in-law sat in back, beside her three-year-old son. A young male, she told Robert, got down from the SUV. He was a light-skinned Hispanic; cropped hair; short and stocky. She thought he was walking over to say hello to her husband, until he reached inside his jacket and began firing.

At the hospital, the widow, having absorbed two bullet fragments in her back and stomach, rated pain a nine. She was heavily sedated when Robert raced back in with suspect photos. A nurse advised him that now was not a good time.

MOISES GARCIA'S MOTHER GRIEVED, HAVING days earlier sat in the church pews during her granddaughter's baptism, processing the blessing of a new baby and the loss of a son. Now, on the shoulder of Zapata Highway, she sold five-dollar plates of chicken and rice to raise funds for the funeral.

Rene Garcia, her eldest son, just felt rage. There used to be a code among gangsters, rules: "Leave family out of it" was a big one. Rene and Moises—twenty-six and twenty-four, respectively—grew up in South Laredo. Their hood was called Santo Niño—"Saint Baby." Its criminal culture was more overt than most Laredo neighborhoods. Kids there often lived alone, running stash houses and *tienditas,* and fathering broods of their own. With two or three *tienditas* on every block, Laredo PD could set up on Saint Baby any night of the week and arrest a dozen personal-use buyers as they walked to their cars with fresh dime bags of marijuana ($10 worth) and $100 eight-balls of coke (3.5 grams).

In elementary school, Rene and Moises started a local gang, and graduated to the junior ranks of the Mexican Mafia—known as "La Eme," or the Black Hand—a Chicano gang that originated in California. "We are soldiers of Aztlán in the land of the Mexican," stated La Eme's constitution, referring to the mythical home of the Aztecs. "Our actions reflect the different forms of our struggle: economic, political, military, social, cultural. We are dedicated to any aspect of criminal interest. We will traffic in drugs, contracts for assassination, prostitution, robbery of high magnitude, and in anything else we can imagine." Ten percent of every member's "business or personal interest" went to back to La Eme. The gang's most fanatical members treated La Eme like a religion; they prayed to Aztec gods, spoke the ancient language of Nahuatl, and believed they were warriors.

Rene was proud of his younger brother, Moises, the star hustler who made trips to Dallas and, in the lottery-like slang of the smuggling business, "hit big with pounds and keys." As the years passed, they witnessed a civil war within La Eme's leadership; under the banner of discipline, the organization culled its own ranks. Splinter groups bore splinter groups. In the early 2000s, Moises did two years in a Nuevo Laredo prison for executing a fellow Eme member on the orders of a leader. In prison, Moises met Meme Flores. Through Meme, Moises expanded, and began doing business with the Company.

On December 8, 2005, when Moises was gunned down in the parking lot of Torta-Mex, his brother Rene, who was in the backseat, suspected that La Eme was behind it. There'd always been jealousy around Saint Baby, what with Moises coming up so fast in the business. And there was also a money problem: Moises had had successive drug deals go bad in Dallas, and his so-called *carnales,* his "brothers" in La Eme, refused to cover his debt to the Company.

Well, Rene now thought—pacing Zapata Highway while his mother bagged food and soda—his brother's fate was an organizational decision, up to the leadership of La Eme. But it was incumbent on the *carnales* to handle his bro's demise internally, rather than let another organization, outsiders, do it for you. To Rene, the assassination of his brother didn't feel like the work of La Eme. Not with Rene's sister-in-law, pregnant, in the front seat, and his three-year-old nephew sitting next to him in back. The *carnales* would never endanger innocent family members.

When the shooting happened, Rene hadn't seen an Eme member approach the car. Only a short guy emerging from a white Ford Expedition. Before Rene realized the black item the guy was pulling out of his pocket was not a phone but a gun, it was too late. Child locks kept him trapped in the backseat. All he could do was cover his nephew and scream until the shooter stopped.

Rene's sister-in-law survived and gave birth, the next week, to a baby girl.

Rumors came to Rene, including the name of the shooter: Bart Reta.

Rene wanted to get his sister-in-law a new car. But he was unable to sell his brother's bullet-riddled Lexus, associated as it now was with a notorious slaying. At the plate sale on Zapata Highway, an Eme leader—the Black Hand himself—showed up to make a contribution for Moises's funeral. The Black Hand hugged Rene's mom, then approached Rene and asked him what he needed.

"A car," Rene said.

The Black Hand offered to exchange his Trailblazer for the shot-up Lexus. Rene agreed and handed over the title and keys to the Lexus. But he received only the keys to the Black Hand's Trailblazer in return.

"How about the title?" Rene said. "My sister-in-law needs that."

"Forget her," said the Black Hand. "She'll be with another *carnal* soon. He can worry about it."

Rene nodded. "Why didn't you tell me?" he asked.

"Que?"

"That his number came up," Rene said, referring to his brother's death.

"It wasn't our call, *carnal*. He owed a lot of money to the *gente*."

The Black Hand discouraged Rene from doing anything rash. "You won't bring your brother back." He assured Rene that he himself intended to kill Miguel Treviño, but first he wanted Rene to accompany another Eme *carnal* across the river to retrieve $10,000 from the Zetas, along with some coke. The money, the Black Hand told Rene, was earmarked for a new smuggling operation. It would be stupid to cook Miguel Treviño before the *carnales* capitalized on the opportunity Treviño was offering them.

Rene—now locked in a fantasy of seeing Miguel Treviño and Bart Reta together, of gutting them clean and hanging their husks over International Bridge One with a *narcomanta* that read DON'T FUCK WITH THE FAMILY—was too dog-brained with fury to disbelieve the Black Hand's nonsense. "Okay," he said. "I'll go."

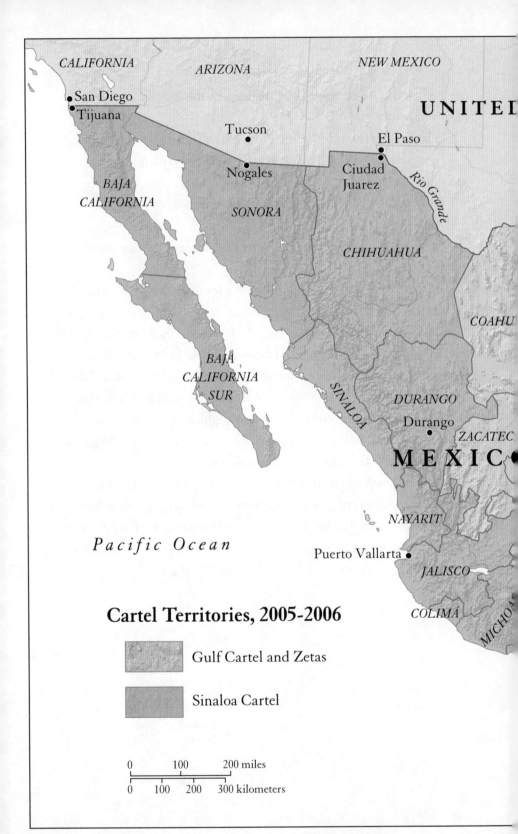

Cartel Territories, 2005-2006

20

Lesser Lords

The band's polka beats carried through the vaulted ceiling of the old ranch house in Valle Hermoso, a town just south of the border and fifty miles inland from the Gulf Coast, where a few hundred Company men gathered at property owned by Comandante Catorce to celebrate the holidays, and raffle off expensive gifts.

The musicians of Los Tucanes were effusive on this fine December evening. One singer, then another, took a turn at the band's biggest hits, or *corridos,* ballads that created a new iconography of the narco-world. Los Tucanes made the ballads convincing by acting them out, infusing each performance with a fierce, hard-edged humor. With his black mustache and piercing eyes, the leader of Los Tucanes married narco-chic to timeless Mexican machismo, to freedom fighters like Villa and Zapata. It was folk tradition kept alive in a world of cell phones, Italian sports cars, and huge tits spilling out of tight leather jackets.

The *corrido* celebrated modern Mexico's surreal juxtaposition: the extreme poverty and garish wealth, the elaborate courtesy and low-barbarian violence. The themes of the songs were smuggling, corruption, and betrayal. Another brave man killed. Another brother avenged. A spurned mistress caps her lover's bride. Women are murderous and deceitful. Poor boys, surrounded by menacing landowners, leave school to sell drugs because they are tired of picking fruit in the hills.

The print media, academics, and documentary filmmakers excoriated bands like Los Tucanes for endorsing mafiosi and pursuing opportunistic relationships with "armies of terror." Cartels were known to finance the promotion of new *corrido* bands in order to use them, eventually, as money-laundering fronts. The genre's defenders, however, claimed that the ballads were a chronicle of modern life, not an ad for it. "We are an effect of the drug traffic," the leader of Los Tucanes once told the music journalist Elijah Wald, "not a cause." There was a drug war going on; the violence and romance were what people were interested in. How were *corridos* any different than gangsta rap in the United States, or the old "murder ballads" of Johnny Cash and Woody Guthrie?

At the party, or *posada,* the Wolf Boys partied alongside *comandantes.* There were whole roasted chickens and goats; tamales; homemade tortillas; sprawling platters of salsas and jalapeño poppers; plus all the beer and whiskey and tequila one could drink. It was like the quinceañera parties that *fresas* threw in North Laredo, except that quinceañeras didn't serve piles of *lavadita*—"wash"—a coveted form of cocaine from which impurities had been removed.

Sixty new vehicles were being given away, compliments of the Company's "rip-off" fund—monies gained from extortion. Winners of the raffles simply appeared at a designated car dealership and claimed their prize, which had already been "paid for" and assigned for pickup. Houses and Hummers; bags of cash; jewelry; bales of weed and bricks of coke; watches and designer purses—they were all raffled off, and the *posada* raged on.

You could tell guests by their clothes. *Comandantes* paired Hugo Boss with ranchero accessories like fat belt buckles. *Sicarios* without rank dressed like *niños poppies,* Mexican preppies, in tight Lacoste shirts and faded jeans. American *sicarios* like Gabriel, Wences, Bart, and Richard opted for a more classic look: Versace shirts, khaki pants, burgundy or brown shoes, and a faded hairstyle. They had the look of confident, self-made young men. Their studied appearance also endowed them with that semblance common to upstarts in big organizations: eager sacrifices to a strange and powerful god. Boys going off to fight a war for someone else.

Los Tucanes played for hours. Everyone danced to the bleating notes of the *bajo sexto* and the hard-driving accordion breaks. The sound of the *corrido* grated against the sexier refinements of Anglo pop. Crass and rurally rooted, the genre was disrespected by trendsetting intellectuals, but not by Company men like Catorce and Miguel Treviño.

Even though Catorce hosted the party, Miguel financed the appearance of Los Tucanes, paying mid-six-figure rates for an evening of song. To have famous musicians singing of stories like his filled Miguel with emotion. For he could still feel pride; it was perhaps all he could feel—well, pride, and perhaps fear. The more power Miguel accrued: the more he worshipped respect: the more he feared losing it: the more he lost himself in work. Miguel didn't sleep well on the days when he didn't kill. He was no *panochón,* no pussy, but that didn't mean there weren't things that scared him.

The past year, 2005, was a great one for the Company, and a turning point in Miguel's life. It was the year he went from mere *comandante*—a soldier who oversaw enforcement, led raiding parties, and managed his own smuggling business on the side—to full-blown plaza boss, the Company's controller of an important territory, in charge of all illicit traffic that came through Nuevo Laredo. Miguel's string of successes changed him. Now in his mid-thirties, he shed some of his old modesty, ditching the jeans and T-shirts. On this night he wore orange ostrich boots, a shirt of white silk, black slacks, and a black trench coat—all Valentino. From a gold chain around his neck hung a gold grenade with "40"—his Zeta call sign—engraved on its pineapple shell. That necklace was standard issue for ranking Company men. But the gold-plated .38 Super—with a diamond-crusted "40" on the grip—was distinct. A bulletproof Porsche Cayenne was on order from the Company engineer.

But like a man on the rise in any highly competitive environment, Miguel—like Osiel Cárdenas before him, the old Gulf Cartel leader who created the Zetas—was prone to paranoia, the justified concern that the potential for treachery surrounded him, in the form of fellow Company men who would've loved to take his place. If Miguel was drawn to his younger *soldados,* the Wolf Boys like Wences and Gabriel, it might've been because they were still naïve enough to believe that a value system *did* exist, that loyalty toward one's boss was more than mere camouflage. Unlike his relationships with contemporaries, Miguel felt no jealousy coming from the boys, only reverence.

Miguel rarely drank, but at the party he drank eighteen-year-old Buchanan's whiskey from a giant bottle and called Wolf Boys over to do shots. When summoned for a shot, Wences mentioned that he might head out soon to go meet some girls somewhere else. Wences had been working with men for months; he longed for independence and female companionship away from the Company. "Sure," Miguel said. "But stay awhile longer. Then you can go."

Wolf Boys, observing the jealousy of older Company men toward Miguel, tended to assume that it was Miguel's success that engendered resentment. Look how smart he was. Who else worked that hard? But the older soldiers saw it differently. Miguel wasn't admired. He was a micromanaging dick who loved discipline for discipline's sake. If your woman called during the *operativo,* you better hope MT didn't call when you were on the phone with her because you'd get *tablazos*—spanked with a two-by-four with holes drilled in the business end for maximum batting speed, and not be able to sit down for a week. Even on *franco,* vacation, he expected you to call twice a day and answer when he called. If not, *tablazos.* What kind of vacation was that?

Miguel was generous with money, it was true, but only because he could afford to be. He made his attitude plain. He was the one who battled the incursion from the Sinaloans. He was the one who secured Nuevo Laredo. Miguel was all about Miguel. He cared nothing about the Company. Just look at the scheming bastard. At his own drooling envy of the Zeta Chiefs, Catorce and Lazcano. Lazcano trusted Miguel, and agreed to most of Miguel's suggestions regarding Company operations. A year earlier, Lazcano shattered the bones in his shooting hand, and could now barely work a weapon. He traveled by helicopter and with no fewer than seven bodyguards. Miguel would have the Chiefs eaten raw when the time was right, and his betrayals would destroy the organization.

"Todo va a ser de La Compañía!" Miguel hollered—*It will all belong to the Company!* He wanted the Company to run everything, he claimed publicly. Inwardly, he wanted to be king.

It had been five hundred years since Moctezuma the Younger's accession to the throne made the Aztecs the unchallenged masters of a tribute empire that controlled the Gulf Coast. The warlords of Tenochtitlan originated in the mythic northwest land of Aztlán—"the Place of Whiteness"—before migrating south and taking over the whole of middle earth. Like the Zetas, the Aztecs began as enforcers for an established power structure. The lord of Culhuacán, ruler of the old empire around present-day Mexico City, enlisted the Aztecs as mercenaries—just as Osiel and the Gulf Cartel formed the Zetas to handle violence—promising the Aztecs their freedom if they captured eight thousand Xochimilca enemies. The Aztec tribesmen carried out the slaughter, and delivered bags of severed ears to the throne as evidence. Later, after overtaking the lord of Culhuacán, the Aztec savages, rulers of a new empire on the muddy isle of Tenochtitlan, sacrificed their own so that spring would come, and offered children of the poor to Tlaloc, the rain god.

Aztec human sacrifice was perhaps no more extensive than comparable practices among ancient Syrians and Mesopotamians, or the barbaric Germans and Celtic Druids. If Miguel Treviño was destined for greatness in the cartel underworld, it was because he personified the extremes of these pre-moral cultures. If Miguel had an Aztec model, it was Xipe Totec, the skull-faced deity who threw bodies off pyramids and chewed on human limbs. Miguel, it was said, once removed a heart by reaching through the thorax of a beheaded corpse.

LATER DURING THE PARTY, TONY Tormenta, the brother of the imprisoned Gulf Cartel leader Osiel Cárdenas, took the stage and addressed the crowd, a mix of Company employees, both Zetas and Gulf Cartel members.

Tony Tormenta—who despite a healthy cocaine habit remained obese—gave the kind of rah-rah speech familiar to anyone who's worked in a corporate setting, where expansion and the bottom line are paramount. Tormenta said the Company was making progress. From its original territories in the Gulf states of Nuevo León, Tamaulipas, and Veracruz, the Company's control now reached west to Coahuila and even to part of Durango; into the central states of San Luis Potosí and Zacatecas; and to the crucial southeast states of Tabasco and Chiapas, where Mexico bordered Guatemala—a major gateway for traffic in cocaine and immigrants.

The Company's employee expansion reflected its success, Tormenta pointed out. When his brother Osiel created the Zetas in the late 1990s, the Gulf Cartel numbered fewer than 100 people. Now, from leadership to lookouts, the Company, Gulf Cartel and Zetas combined, employed about 10,000; and that number would double over the next five years. The Company also had a strong social conscience, a love of Mexico, Tormenta said. This goodwill took the form of cash to the poor; millions sent to fund-raisers; and trailers overflowing with toys on Christmas. The U.S. military had its Toys for Tots program. The Company had its Día del Niño. The Company men smiled. They all knew the rewarding feeling of giving a poor person a gift, how an old man would mutter "Bendito sea el señor" as he walked away. Miguel would often approach beggars on the street and ask them why they were poor, then take them to Soriana, the chain of Mexican grocery stores, and fill a pickup truck with food.

Tormenta continued: The coming year of 2006 would bring more blood. But their cause was just. The war was born of the other side's greed. It was Chapo Guzmán and the Sinaloa Cartel—through La Barbie and the Beltrán-Leyvas and other smuggling clans aligned against the Company—who had started the war by offering rewards, a going rate, for dead Company men. The Company's soldiers, Tormenta said, would be deployed widely—to Reynosa and Monterrey—and even to plazas in the far-off Yucatán Peninsula. Some would be sent as far south as Santa Elena, the Colombian port city, and one or two as far north as Boston. All work, he concluded, would be rewarded, and, if need be, each Company man's family would be compensated in the event of his death.

The men in the audience straightened and nodded like stoics. By the time Company men achieved *comandante* status—or something above a mere hit man—most were old enough to know how the cartel life ended. Gabriel's godfather, Meme Flores, characterized the gleeful fatalism of the Company man when he inhaled coke and tequila and screamed, "A coger y a mamar que el mundo se va acabar!" *Let's fuck and suck because the world is about to end!* But in January 2006, at nineteen, Gabriel was still young enough to believe it would last forever, that each violent engagement was something more than an isolated project. He saw the vacations and bonuses, the gifts to the poor and the trailers of toys on Día del Niño. Such perks conveyed the sense that some Company committee set loyal Wolf Boys on a path, coaxed along by pay raises and the promise of management.

Gabriel looked around the *posada*. Refugees of officialdom surrounded him. Politicians and cops. Artists and models. The accountant from whom Gabriel collected his Company salary had once been a federal prosecutor. The son of Nuevo Laredo's new mayor sipped tequila a few feet away. Celebrities escorted cartel leaders: through an agent, *comandantes* paid five thousand dollars a night for the company of Latin singers and actresses. He thought of the parties he used to read about in *Vibe* magazine. He thought of Tupac, and of Suge Knight's infamous attorney who made all problems disappear. This Company life really was no different.

Something had happened in the three months since Gabriel got out of jail. He'd followed orders, did his time, and came back out. Prison is where the Company lost some recruits, but he not only continued, he *expanded*. He brought in Richard, who was liked. And he brought in Bart, a much-loved Wolf Boy. Little Bart! If you wanted him to do something, all you had to do was tell him not to do it! Gabriel was proud of Bart, and felt no threat. Gabriel already had "credit" from the *comandantes*. He "jumped at the front of the barrel" when others held back. People listened to him.

Gabriel reflected on his path to this point. As a new recruit he'd worked hard in the training camp, then bounced around from plaza to plaza and helped out restlessly, voluntarily, until the *comandantes* saw his dedication and started giving him more important jobs. He learned the radio codes. Nuevo Laredo was Nectar Lima. Miguel Alemán was Metro Alfa. Mexico City—*el distrito federal*—was Delta Fox. Reynosa was 9-6. "Nothing new" was 3-4. "I'm waiting" was 3-1. "Army" was 8-0. *Puros guachos* were the military you had to watch out for, soldiers who hadn't been bribed. *Papeles,* paper, meant money. *Nacional,* national, was marijuana. *Extranjero,* foreigner, was cocaine. *Puntos* were safe houses, but could also mean targets for assassination. *Chapulines,* grasshoppers, were traitors. Devices, birds, and calves were kilos. Your stack, or post, was your crew. ("Look, *güey,* my stack is all tangled up.")

Gabriel knew how to be around the Chiefs, how to answer questions with to-the-point responses. In public settings, especially if a *comandante* was out with his family, Gabriel nodded discreetly but left them to their space, unlike other *sicarios* who kissed ass. He also learned to recognize resentment from midlevel managers who weren't keen on a younger talent. Once, when he had to abort a mission because the *puros guachos* interfered, a *comandante* disparaged him in Miguel's presence. Gabriel scoffed. The guy was dicksucking Miguel! But Gabriel respected rank. He simply said that he knew what he had to do and would do it.

A soldier could piss away his rank by avoiding missions or crapping out on the *operativo*. He could misbehave on *franco,* dry shooting or killing without permission. And then there was the pitfall of any poor kid who came into money and reputation: unruly family who "ripped a load" from the wrong person, hit on the wrong woman, or threw their notorious relation's name around too liberally.

Gabriel's uncle Raul, his mother's youngest brother, fell into this last category. Much of the time Raul was in jail for crossing weed or illegal immigrants, or for violating probation when his urinalysis inevitably came back dirty. Raul was always getting in bar fights, then dropping Gabriel's name when he got picked up by the police.

"If you don't cut that shit out you're going to get in trouble!" Gabriel would tell him. Raul waved these warnings off: "But you rule Nuevo Laredo!"

It was true. As a favored soldier of Meme and Miguel, during a moment in time when the Company appeared to be effectively fighting off enemies and controlling the border, Gabriel was tantamount to the law. He could run free, swagger, lord over, *fuck with*. And that status conferred power on his entourage. At clubs like Eclipse and 57th Street, the VIP area was always reserved for the Wolf Boys. Even if the tables were taken, people left without being asked whenever Gabriel walked through the door. He even had his own driver, a subservient boy from Lazteca called Chapa. When Chapa was locked up in a Nuevo Laredo jail, Gabriel's older brother, Luis, also a member of Gabriel's entourage, barged into the police department, shouted out Gabriel's Zeta code, and demanded that Chapa be released.

Such demonstrations of power were routine, and, admittedly, they set a poor example for Uncle Raul. But what could be done? Raul was like a brother, and Gabriel loved him. Whenever Uncle Raul hit big with a load of drugs or illegal aliens, he gave everything he made to family. So when Raul came charging home from another bar scrap and demanded a gun, Gabriel instructed everyone to deny him one. They gave him a phone instead and told him to call them whenever he ran into trouble.

Gabriel loved the power, most certainly. But he didn't like what he did for a living. Years earlier, the youngster from Lazteca had run out clean and come back hard. He ran out with a pacifist's heart, calcified by the communal code of vengeance. The after-school fights, the club scene, the border itself—these were the doorways through which white halls led to the darkness beyond. And now? Yes, he was cold. One of the Company's prized cold ones. A *frío*. But no sadist. He would never shoot a cat, as Bart did when they were kids. He would never swerve out of the way to hit a sleeping dog, as Miguel did in Mexico. How do you think that made him feel? A dog lover! And yet when it came to killing, Gabriel could remain unshaken in the face of any engagement. He did so with the help of the roches, but also by focusing on the execution of a plan rather than the elimination of a human target. In his mind he was not a doer of acts but an agent of business, an accountant of fates already inked. As Gabriel told Robert Garcia, back in June, after the murder of Bruno Orozco, "One knows what one gets into." He saw himself as a soldier in a war, knew his enemies saw themselves in a similar light, and accepted whatever fate befell him. This mentality made torture and beatings easier on his mind: If the situation were reversed, and Gabriel was kidnapped, his enemy would take no pity on him. Sure, it was an underworld principle—supposedly—to try to spare a target's family whenever possible. But Gabriel didn't feel much guilt over Bart having shot Moises Garcia's wife by accident. She was married to a well-known smuggler and killer. What did she expect?

This code earned Gabriel success, and now, within the Company, he didn't doubt where he stood. "I'm clear on my circle," Miguel would tell him with a nod, a way of saying he knew his associates were trustworthy and that Gabriel was part of that circle. He felt a destiny, merging with Miguel's, toward some exalted corporate realm that Richard and Wences lacked the sacrificial will to penetrate. "I'll let you take this one," the other Wolf Boys would often say to Gabriel on jobs, as if doing him a favor, then mumble something about having kids, a family.

Among the Wolf Boys, only Richard declined to openly exalt Gabriel. To Richard, Gabriel chose wrong by connecting himself so closely to Meme. Any reasonable person saw that Meme was not of Miguel's ilk. He just didn't have the right stuff for leadership. Take the house where Miguel kept his wife and daughters: well cared for but discreet. Then look at "El Castillo," the name of Meme's palace in La Amalia. With its big columns and lookout towers, El Castillo was the garish theme park of lesser lords. Meme was from the school of Die-Young-And-Look-Beautiful-In-The-Casket. Like other *comandantes* who would never become top capos, Meme was more soldier-in-the-field than general-at-his-desk. A loyal gunslinger, sure, and respected, but not, in Richard's words, "a business-wise individual." In Richard's opinion, Meme was too friendly with younger guys like Gabriel because he hadn't earned the respect of his peers.

Now, as the *posada* carried into the early-morning hours, Gabriel and Richard drank whiskey with Miguel.

Richard, his nose packed with *lavadita,* blithely mentioned that he'd seen Miguel's ex-girlfriend Elsa Sepulveda with a Laredo doper named Mike Lopez, a successful smuggler who transported drugs for the Zetas. This loose talk annoyed Gabriel. Everyone knew of Miguel's jealousy. A month earlier, Miguel had barged into another ex-girlfriend's wedding and danced with the bride. And everyone remembered Yvette Martinez and Brenda Cisneros, the Martin High students who worked as gofers for Miguel. When Yvette and Brenda started talking to a former Company man, a bodyguard who defected to Sinaloa, Miguel gave the girls tickets to a Paulina Rubio concert from which they never returned. As for his ex-girlfriend Elsa Sepulveda, the beautiful daughter of a Nuevo Laredo cop, Miguel was so humiliated when she broke it off that he threw a grenade at her house. He coveted intelligence about his girlfriends, present and past, as if the vicissitudes of romantic drama were business itself.

Gabriel wondered: Was Richard trying to win Miguel's favor by passing info that should've gone to Gabriel first? When Richard joined the Wolf Boys, Gabriel introduced him to Miguel and told him to tell Miguel everything he knew about logistics. *Tell him about the trucks. The warehouses. The front company. Go ahead, tell him.* Conversations followed, and their candor surprised Gabriel. Richard told Miguel that, prior to his San Antonio warehouse getting busted by the feds, he'd been moving drugs for a Sinaloa supplier. Gabriel expected that Richard would hide this former association with the enemy. It was even more surprising to Gabriel, however, when Miguel just shrugged it off. Miguel told Richard to request a loan when he was ready to get a new line of trucks running. Miguel and Richard, it seemed, shared some sophisticated approach to business, a mature understanding.

Still, Gabriel felt secure in his "chosen path." A young man from poverty who landed in this higher-status milieu, he possessed the requisite anxiety and anger that fueled an obsession with detail. Such conscientious managers were the lifeblood of companies, of capitalism itself. As a middle manager located in one of the Company's crucial international territories—Laredo, Texas—Gabriel was now both point man for Laredo jobs, and fall guy when things went wrong. He relished the responsibility, though it created pressures he did not yet understand.

Miguel called a *pantera* to ask if it was true: Was Elsa Sepulveda with Mike Lopez?

Richard and Gabriel could hear the woman's voice break on the other end. Miguel clicked the phone shut, pulled the golden .38 from his belt, spun around, and brandished it in different directions, laughing, as if trying out ways he might kill Mike Lopez, or have him killed.

Miguel glanced at Gabriel.

It didn't matter that Mike Lopez was an American who lived in Texas. Miguel had enforcers on that side as well.

21

A Boner for Bart

South Padre Island?" Ronnie asked. "Now? It's the middle of the week!"

A prepper by nature, Ronnie Garcia needed time to prepare for a trip, to write lists of what to take and consider all options for transport and lodging. So when Robert announced, last minute, that they were going to South Padre Island for a long weekend, and that Trey would come along, Ronnie was pissy from the moment they got in the car. She was even pissier four hours later when they checked into a roach motel and she realized she forgot her sunscreen and bathing suit. Robert yanked her along South Padre's main strip, in and out of beach shops that sold bikinis, seemingly oblivious, after fifteen years of marriage, that a big girl like Ronnie didn't *do* bikinis.

As 2005 turned to 2006, the Moises Garcia murder case, in the parking lot of Torta-Mex, had been going cold when Robert reported to Frost Street, the scene of another execution-style killing. Piecing together information, it appeared as though Noe Flores, the half brother of a Laredo doper named Mike Lopez, was killed in a case of mistaken identity. Lopez, Robert learned, had been dating an ex-girlfriend of Miguel Treviño. At the scene, a female witness identified her old Martin High classmate Gabriel Cardona as the shooter.

Gabriel Cardona: Robert hadn't seen the kid since the previous summer, after he was arrested for the Bruno Orozco murder.

Robert presumed there was a good chance that Gabriel fled across the border. So he gave U.S. Customs a photo of Gabriel with instructions to call if the kid tried to cross back into Texas via the bridge. He also kept Gabriel's arrest warrants filed at Laredo PD only, and declined to file them at the Office of the Webb County Clerk, the record holder for the county courts, because Robert heard through a source that Gabriel had a contact working at the clerk's office. Now, if Gabriel called the clerk's office to check whether there were any outstanding warrants for him—whether it was safe to return to Laredo from Mexico—his record would come up clean.

Robert also requested "tower dumps." Laredo had about two hundred cell phone towers, divided largely among three service providers: AT&T, Sprint, and Verizon. He found each provider's closest tower to Frost Street, and subpoenaed all the cell phone information that hit those towers around the time of the Noe Flores murder. A really smart criminal didn't bring a cell phone to a crime, but most criminals weren't really smart. Since cell providers purged their tower data every thirty days, it was better to request the data and not use it than need it and not have it.

Robert and his partner, Chuckie, located the abandoned car used in the murder, a gray Nissan Sentra. They found a receipt for cell phone minutes, which led to a used-car dealer, which in turn led to the car dealer's cell phone, which led to a Wolf Boy's cell number. With that cell number, Robert subpoenaed phone records and "cell site" information. Cell site information told Robert which towers that particular phone "hit"—during calls—on the night of the murder, and at what times. The phone bill led to a Laredo tattoo artist.

Robert's visit shook the proprietor of Chester's Tattoos. In his cell phone, the tattoo artist had a listing for "Bart"—a kid, he said, on which the tattoo artist had recently begun to render a large shoulder tattoo of a demon. Bart, the tattoo artist said nervously, had left halfway through the tattoo and planned to return soon to have it finished.

"Why do you call him 'Bart'?" Robert asked.

"That's what his friends call him, because he's short and looks like Bart Simpson."

The tattoo artist said he had a family. He didn't want any trouble. He didn't know who the kids were. Robert gave the tattoo artist his Laredo PD card, hoping that news of his investigation would leak back to Cardona and whoever he was working with—and it did. When Bart came in the following day to have his tattoo finished, the tattoo artist passed on Robert's card. A day later, Bart called Robert from Mexico.

"This is Bart. Are you looking for me?"

"Hey, Bart," Robert said. "I have been looking for you. I need to—"

"Look, you need to quit the investigations for these murders or I'm going to kill you and your family. You don't know who you're messing with. Understand?" Then Bart hung up.

Robert slammed the phone down. *How dare these kids!* Then he thought: murders? He'd only been investigating them for the Noe Flores murder. What else had they done? He went back and looked at the case file from the Moises Garcia murder in the parking lot of Torta-Mex. Both Rene Garcia, the brother of Moises, and Diana Garcia, the wife, had ID'd the shooter as a short guy with buzzed hair and a mole above his lip.

A few days later, the threat from the cartel began to feel more real. An Arizona cop contacted Robert and sent over a recording of an informant interview: *"I got offered something real big in Laredo. I don't know if he's head of homicide? Head of narcotics? But his name is Robert Garcia. The Zetas want him gone. I guess he busted some guy named Cardona? Gabriel Cardona?"* Miguel Treviño, the informant said, had pictures, a home address, and info about Robert's schedule.

Laredo Chief of Police Agustin Dovalina listened to the recording and mulled the threats. "Take your wife on vacation while we run this through Internal Affairs," he told Robert.

Now when Robert returned from South Padre Island, PD issued him an off-duty weapon and put around-the-clock surveillance on his home. He could no longer keep the threats secret from Ronnie.

Ronnie had served her country, too. She accepted Robert's career and its risks. But a little danger was one thing. Being held prisoner in her own home, and town, quite another. Eric was out of the house; he graduated in 2005 and enrolled in a school for motorcycle mechanics in Phoenix. But Trey, now a sixteen-year-old jock, was no longer allowed to play hockey because the arena was across town and practice was late at night. At first, Ronnie managed to hold it together. There was no use in heightening an already-elevated stress level. And there *was* stress.

On some days, the Wolf Boys made Robert more tolerant of his own sons' imperfections. He used to yell at Trey and Eric when they neglected the lawn, or played too many video games. His new perspective: Who gave a shit? But he could also go the other way. Coming home on some days, crazy with adrenaline and sleeplessness, snapping at everyone and everything, Robert would head straight to Trey's bedroom, and, if any part was messy, flip his stuff like a SWAT team before heading back to work. Ronnie tolerated it for a while, then snapped one day and chased him out to the driveway: "You're fuckin shittin' me, right?!"

For fifteen years Robert had served this city. And for what? A bullshit war. And for who? Absent fathers, women beaters. For the same immigrants who tried to break into the Garcias' family home back in Eagle Pass until Robert's father studded the walls with broken bottles. For delinquent American-born kids who claimed to be Mexican when they didn't know the first thing about Mexico. For the Mexican Mafia gangsters, and the ignorant solidarity they claimed with Aztec culture. At stash-house busts in Santo Niño, when the pregnant teenagers filed out barefoot and bursting, Robert and his buddies shook their heads and called it "job security." He felt shame because they were his people. He felt spite because he was a wetback, too.

As a young cop he took pride in making drug arrests and busting criminals, but after a while the cycle of crime and dysfunction in the city had begun to make his struggle as a cop feel futile. And now here was something more than little drive-by shootings and robberies: a battle between two cartels, spilling into Texas.

The spillover was real. Since 2004, the FBI had investigated nearly one hundred cases of U.S. citizens going missing in Nuevo Laredo—and those were just the *reported* disappearances. The most famous among them were Yvette Martinez and Brenda Cisneros. Supposedly they dated Miguel Treviño, or did errands for him, and then somehow crossed him by stealing drugs or dating an enemy. Yvette Martinez's stepfather went big in the press. He started a website called Laredo Missing to chronicle all the disappearances of Americans. *People* magazine profiled him ("Who Is Stealing Laredo's Young?"). In Laredo homes, cops and federal agents were finding assembly lines for building automatic weapons and improvised explosive devices. In law enforcement, the mood was both ecstatic and grave. *Something's happening! Bombs and shit!* The cartels that Robert once lectured about at the Laredo police academy were now here. The reality of the spillover gave his path a heft it never had.

And there was something else that motivated him, something that had always bothered him as a Mexican who loved his country and could no longer return to it: The cartels and their violence lay at the root of everything Robert hated. And not just because they ruined Mexico, but because they tarnished the entire image of the country. Was he really related to these fratricidal people? The decapitations; ripping faces off. It was worse than any Middle East terror organization. Where did it come from?

"This shit pisses me off," Robert would tell Chuckie, his homicide partner. "I take it personal, dude. I really do."

Chuckie, also born in Mexico before immigrating to Eagle Pass, took the cartel violence personally as well. Unlike Robert, however, Chuckie never received any personal threats, and he declined PD's offer to have squad cars watch his house. The cars, he believed, brought more bad attention than they were worth in actual security.

Ronnie knew what angered her husband. The Garcia family, like most in Laredo, used to go across to Nuevo Laredo regularly to shop, eat dinner, and drink in the bars. They took the boys on trips to their father's country. Whether for a wedding, birthday, funeral, or any other reason to see family, the Garcias returned to Piedras Negras several times a year. Now, because of the violence, they couldn't go across, and that was a shame. But if Ronnie sympathized, she still couldn't grasp the extent of Robert's obsession with these investigations. In her opinion, he hadn't been the same since that terrible murder case, the prior year, with the dead girl at Lake Casa Blanca, and that case had nothing to do with the cartels.

It certainly wasn't the money that drove him. Laredo PD was one of the most highly paid police departments in the state of Texas, but policing, even in Laredo, was still poorly compensated relative to the hours and the risk of the job. Overtime was decent. But busts or no busts, Robert made what he made: about $60,000 in base salary. In a few years—unless he became a chief, which would never happen because he wasn't political enough, couldn't sit in an office, and pissed too many people off—his PD salary would top out at $65,000. PD wasn't like a federal agency, where the college boys got bonuses for big busts. In PD, there was no bonus for solved cases. Robert got awards that entitled him to some sideways promotion, more managerial responsibilities, more awards, and then the same pension as everyone else. "What do I need more money for?" Robert would joke. "I like mowing my own lawn." His obsession wasn't explainable in terms of money. Ronnie could live with that, but not with these threats. The distance Robert's work put between them rended the relationship again, maybe this time for good.

In his man cave, sipping whiskey and going over PD reports while squad cars watched his house, Robert shook his head. Those boys had done a pretty good Mental Fuck on him.

But the threats only hardened his resolve.

He felt an exhilarating combination of pride and fear. It was one thing to be threatened by the Wolf Boys, another to be in the crosshairs of the big man himself. It meant he was doing his job right, and, in his own sick way—he told no one at the time—he "got a boner out of it."

He kept the off-duty gun next to his bed. One night, in the wee hours, he nearly shot Trey's best friend in the head when the kid woke up and used the wrong bathroom.

22

The Varieties of Power

The cartel war meant different things to different people. For some it brought problems, for others opportunity.

The American ambassador, Tony Garza, had no interest in criticizing the Mexican government, but he couldn't shy away from speaking out when safety was at stake. The State Department warned Americans not to visit northern Mexico. "As friends and neighbors, we should be honest about the rapidly deteriorating situation along the border, and the near lawlessness in some parts," Garza had said in a statement back in June 2005, after the Nuevo Laredo police chief was murdered on his first day in office.

As for Laredo, the mayor's mandate was clear: deny. She insisted the war was *not* spilling over into her charming Texas town. Like a restaurant that advertised "Clean Food," Laredo's beleaguered tourism board would plaster "Laredo Is Safe" across buildings and billboards.

But not all bureaucrats and law enforcement officials in Laredo shared the same agenda. Laredo's sheriff still warned that terror-ists could arrive at any moment. The sheriff wasn't stupid. Ever since 9/11, the word *narco* turned few heads in Washington. *Narco-terrorism* was a different matter. Local law enforcement used national security threats to argue for bigger budgets. Spillover vio-lence, and the perception of chaos at the border, also gave political challengers an opportunity to criticize incumbents for their failure to maintain the peace. As for the journalistic community, reporters could always use a good story, and peacefulness didn't create good stories.

For its part, the U.S. government was eager to minimize the spill-over narrative. Unlike the state of Texas, which defined spillover as *any* cartel-related violence, regardless of the victim, the federal defi-nition excluded "trafficker-on-trafficker" violence. This approach conveniently ignored, or glossed over, the reality that many traffick-ers involved in the spillover, such as Gabriel Cardona, were Amer-icans. But the federal definition meant that most cartel violence in the United States could be categorized, at least at the federal level, as non-spillover.

At bottom, spillover violence, and how it was defined, came down to money. Which was why Laredo Chief of Police Agustin Dovalina was happy to expand *his* definition: it meant more money for his department. Between lieutenants, sergeants, patrol officers, investigators, and administrative people, Chief Dovalina had about five hundred employees spread among: drugs; crimes against prop-erty; auto theft; crimes against people (homicide, aggravated assault, armed robbery); sexual offenses (child abuse and child pornography; and adult crimes); and juvenile crimes.

Dovalina's police force represented about 10 percent of all Webb County law enforcement, and competition among agencies for fed-eral funding was fierce. At the municipal, county, and state levels, Dovalina competed with the Sheriff's Department, the constables, the Alcoholic Beverage Commission, the Department of Public Safety, Food Stamps, and Child Protective Services. At the federal level, he had DEA, Border Patrol, Homeland Security, FBI, ATF, ICE, Justice, and the Internal Revenue Service.

Every year, in the spring, Chief Dovalina went to Washington, D.C., for the big national police conference. Upon arrival, he always visited the stingy bastards over in the Department of Justice, the ones in charge of doling out COPS grants—federal money allotted for local PDs under Community Oriented Policing Services. In reality, COPS grants never amounted to much; if Dovalina was lucky, one year of every four he came home with a pittance. He often felt shorted by the federal government. And even now, with violence on the rise, he didn't feel the federal government gave him what he deserved.

So recently, when two of Dovalina's PD underlings—a lieutenant in charge of the stolen-property division, and a sergeant assigned to the narcotics division—came to his office and said the Mexican Mafia wanted to launder money through its slot machine casinos, the *maquinitas,* by programming the slot machines to pay out above the legal limit of five dollars, Dovalina listened to the proposition. The Mexican Mafia would compensate the Laredo Police Department to look the other way, close down a competitor, and help keep the heat off.

Dovalina considered it; he wanted a new set of golf clubs. He agreed to the kickback scheme.

If Dovalina felt irreverent, it wasn't only because he felt shorted on government funding. The cartel war gave Dovalina some power. His counterparts in Nuevo Laredo law enforcement came across the bridge seeking supplies such as body armor. "Of course," Dovalina would say over lunch. And who knew? Maybe those supplies would reach crime-fighting cops in Nuevo Laredo. Probably not. But they would contribute to the war, a conflict about which Dovalina had few emotions, save that it was bad. One side or the other would win. His own battle would go on.

MIGUEL TREVIÑO'S BATTLE CONTINUED.

In church, he sat next to his mother and simmered. Mrs. Treviño knew her sons' business and wept: Fito, her sweet boy who only loved to hunt, just twenty-six years old, had been sitting outside reading the newspaper when Sinaloan assassins shot him four times in the face, once in the chest, and once in each hand, then dumped his body by a swing in a park. The church in Valle Hermoso was sealed off for the closed-casket funeral.

Miguel's little brother had been murdered, and Miguel was infuriated that the incident had been reported on TV. It was the ultimate disrespect from the press, whose activities Miguel financed. Miguel had applied Catorce's management model to Nuevo Laredo, and put local crime journalists, from *El Mañana* to *El Diario,* on a pay schedule. But these journalistic relationships, Miguel learned, were always in flux. The Company offered the publisher of *El Mañana,* for instance, a deal: His newspaper would become their mouthpiece, and the publisher would agree to no longer investigate drug trafficking. The *El Mañana* publisher worried about the arrangement. Agreeing to be the Company's mouthpiece was the same as signing his death sentence. If the Company didn't kill him, the other side would. But the publisher was not stupid, and he agreed to the second condition. From then on, a Company spokesman would communicate, through a crime reporter, which stories about crime could run in the paper. Arrangements such as these worked, most of the time, but reporters were untrustworthy. They took money from the Company. Then they took money from the other side. And soon they became *orejas,* ears, carrying information back and forth between criminal groups.

In 2005, Miguel had had to make an example of Guadalupe "Lupita" Escamilla, a radio host who was supposed to make sure that certain news didn't come out on the national level, which meant not reporting it at the local level. Lupita, it was rumored, had demanded a raise for her work as a Zeta mouthpiece, and tried to influence the Company by airing material contrary to its wishes. She was warned. She did it again. In January the Company put a few rounds of bullets in the side of her house. When that didn't shut her up, the Company set her car on fire. In March, the final warning was given, and in April she was gone.

And now Miguel had to contend with this fucker from Televisa, Juaquín López-Dóriga, the famous TV news anchor in Nuevo Laredo. That morning, López-Dóriga reported that a man was reading a newspaper outside a café when he was killed. He didn't say "Fito" on TV, but, to Miguel, it was the principle that mattered, the disrespect. López-Dóriga, Miguel had decided that morning, had to go. It hadn't helped Miguel's temper when he received a call from his ex-girlfriend Elsa Sepulveda, in which she taunted him for having lost his brother, and for killing the wrong guy in Laredo.

Now, at Fito's funeral, sitting next to his mother, Miguel had second thoughts. Maybe it was his own love for his family, his wish to protect them from another loss. He also remembered a recent meeting in Monterrey, when he and Catorce and Lazcano met with the head of SIEDO—Mexico's federal organized-crime unit. "Just keep the violence down," the man had said, "and for godsakes keep it out of the news!"

If López-Dóriga, a high-profile TV anchor, died, it would not go unreported. No, it would go wide in the news. Miguel would catch a reprimand from Catorce and Lazcano, possibly a fatal one. The Chiefs already accused him of being too reactive.

Miguel hugged his mother, then got the attention of Meme Flores and shook his head: *no*.

Meme called Bart Reta and waved him off the job. Miguel accepted condolences, and headed back to work.

ON THE MEXICAN SIDE, WHERE Gabriel had been for most of January 2006, the Wolf Boys worked, and attended another Company party. Whereas Gabriel had once loathed doing jobs in Texas, he was now eager to get back. In the States, he was a more valued Company employee. In Mexico, he was just one of dozens of Wolf Boys willing to work.

At the Company party, in a raffle, Bart won a Mercedes C55 AMG, valued at $70,000. He gave it to Gabriel because Bart already had a bulletproof BMW M3, customized by the Company engineer.

Bart was being sent on big commission jobs, making a lot of money, and buying designer clothes and watches and video games by the bagful. He could only wear so much Valentino and Versace at one time; much of his booty went unused and unopened. He felt indebted to Gabriel for the older boy's generosity in bringing him into this world. In a life where "home" was an abstract concept, a car was one's biggest statement of identity. The Mercedes was a kind present, and an exceedingly difficult one for Gabriel to accept.

Their competitive relationship stretched back to their football days in Lazteca, when Bart was the tough little dude who loved to get tackled and Gabriel hoped to do the tackling. Their brief and brilliant trajectory, entailing large shifts in experience, was ripe for internal tension. How delicate was their system of reciprocity. How easily the Wolf Boys were irked when the unstated terms of their goodwill shifted beneath them.

Gabriel still felt he had the upper hand in his circle of Wolf Boys. He had more experience. He was the leader. But he also wondered: Why was Bart going on more missions with Miguel? Why was Bart making more money?

Money, in their world, was the strongest kind of power. One expressed that power through benevolence. On a personal and communal level, the powerful paid it forward. A cared-for constituency, a happy family: These ends justified the means. Gabriel made a weekly salary of $500, and earned about $10,000 per hit—sometimes more. He gave most of it to his brothers, Christina, his mother, aunts, and friends. He paid for everything at clubs. Having money to waste was the ultimate mark of success, and many needy enablers surrounded him.

His mother, La Gaby, made extra cash by buying used cars and having her second husband fix them at his garage. A couple of years earlier, gone on the roches and furious over being kicked out of the house after La Gaby found his prized Mini-14 rifle in the closet, Gabriel took a baseball bat to a Malibu she hoped to renovate and sell. But now, thanks to him, she could buy several used Malibus and fix them up. In middle school, Gabriel had felt unequal to the girls he liked because he couldn't buy them things. Now he loved seeing Christina wear new clothes thanks to him, and his younger brothers enjoy luxuries like video games and snacks at school. He loved seeing his mother and aunts "out their gutter"—becoming debt-free—because of him. La Gaby made the usual squawks. *Where did this come from? Leave that lifestyle!* But she never turned the money down. That only happened in movies.

At one point in Gabriel's young life, La Gaby had hopes for her second boy, as she did for all her boys. But each dream, one after the next, grew far-fetched, and a painful and familiar distance divided her from her sons. She knew the signs. They all did. La Gaby and her friends on Lincoln Street could forecast delinquency just as mothers on Park Avenue intuited Ivy League admission. A faded haircut was ominous, bald worse. It started with tattoos, sagging pants, staying out late at parties. La Gaby saw the woman down the block put a pool table in her driveway so the kids had somewhere to gather at night. Smart, she thought, and bought an old computer, hoping it would help keep her boys inside. A computer, she'd heard, was what kids needed to succeed nowadays. And still she wondered where her car went, where her son was. And still she found bullets and random gun parts in the closet.

The tumble from where he was to where he ended up was quick, the transformation almost instant: alternatives, boot camp, TYC. La Gaby shrugged, breathed. It was all she could do. What could she do? La Gaby's new man was about to "throw" another twelve months behind bars on another trafficking case. IRS notices piled up; a final warning came: The younger boy sold his work papers to an immigrant.

She yelled loudly. She really did. But now Gabriel could give her in a week what she made in six months. The money was beyond what any brother, boyfriend, or husband ever generated from drugs, immigrants, or money laundering.

Gabriel stopped by the house in all-black clothes, staying only long enough to drink a glass of water, as if somebody was after him: "I'm a soldier, Mom." He came back a month later, his body thickened by the weights: "I'm a commander, Mom."

"A commander of what?" she said. "Someone's going to come to the house and kill me because of you!"

"Here's ten g's. Rent a new house."

"Dios te lo oiga," she said—*God will deal with you*—and then pocketed the cash and backed away.

AS THE WINTER OF 2006 wore on, ambition consuming him, jealousy and suspicion began to take hold in Gabriel, in spite of (or because of) his power and status in the Company. He often stayed in hotels now, and Christina occasionally came to Mexico and stayed with him. A male classmate from United High kept calling the phone that Gabriel had given her. Each time the phone rang he grabbed her from behind, made her answer it, then took the phone away to hear what the guy said, then put it back to her ear and told her how to respond.

"Hola, Christina."

"Hola."

"Qué pasa?"

"Nada."

"Tienes plans today?"

"Pienso que no."

"Want to meet?"

"Porque?"

"To grab a bite to eat?"

"Comiendo o cojiendo?" Gabriel would have Christina ask. *Eating or fucking?* Because the words sounded the same. And then Gabriel ripped the phone away to hear the answer.

But if he was jealous over Christina, he was also distant from her. He followed the example of his Company elders by keeping Christina on the perimeter. He visited her when he could but excluded her from much of his life. He was busy. But he was also a thug, and there was nothing good for her about going out in public with his kind.

From her vantage, all Christina saw was love slipping away, a relationship reverting from serious to casual.

"Why haven't I met your mom?" she asked.

"The house is old."

"I don't care. Take me."

"But the paint is peeling."

"Take me."

Gabriel never took Christina to 207 Lincoln Street; Christina had only met his brothers. But he did frequently mention "mi padrino Cero Dos"—*my godfather Zero Two*—referring to the call sign for Meme Flores. To her, it was as if he wanted to impress her with his connections *and* be secretive at the same time.

Christina, nearly seventeen, tried to remain ignorant, as her own mother had done with regard to her father's illicit activities. Gabriel had spent the previous summer in jail. But the specifics were unclear. He was the driver on the Bruno Orozco hit. Wences pulled the trigger. There was a rumor about what happened a few days before Orozco. Gabriel supposedly rang the doorbell of a Sinaloa-allied gangster named Pompoño, then shot Pompoño's thirteen-year-old son by mistake. But people said lots of nonsense in Laredo.

Growing up among the churchgoing devout, Christina had been a vehicle of faith. *Believe in a better life, and love unconditionally.* But that vehicle was now parked on a steep incline. She was desperate for the affection and attention she never got from her own father. The world just disappeared when she was with her guy. Gabriel was gentle in bed, not rough. But sometimes he couldn't get erect. He'd be "all downer," and say: "Sorry love, a friend slipped something in my drink." And when he said it a third time, and a fourth time, Christina thought: This one does pills. And so they'd just embrace until he had to run off again.

But during those brief interludes, as he sank into that droop-eyed haze, he confided private thoughts. "Soy un joto para matar," he said. *I'm a fag to kill.* The pills weren't just for recreation; they were necessary, and their necessity worried him. He loved the money and power. But was he a true Wolf Boy, a real Company man?

Yes, he still believed he was, and he would soon prove it.

23

I'm a Good Soldier!

After crossing the border on foot with one of his Mexican Mafia brothers, his *carnal,* a black Suburban with an assault rifle holstered in PVC pipe screwed to the center console picked up Rene Garcia and the *carnal* and drove them to a horse ranch on the outskirts of Nuevo Laredo, where three dozen Zeta soldiers milled around eight more black Suburbans. In the middle, Miguel Treviño relaxed in the passenger seat of a white Porsche SUV, door open, his foot on the rail, as he flipped through a binder of pictures.

Minutes later, Miguel emerged from the Porsche and announced that it was time to eat. Several men left and returned with a truck full of sodas and *parilladas,* platters of Mexican barbecue. Everyone ate off the cars like a tailgate party. Afterward, Miguel told Rene and the *carnal* to get in the back of the Porsche. Don't worry, he said, he paid $200,000 to bulletproof the vehicle.

They didn't get far before they stopped on the side of the road to consult with a group of Zeta soldiers returning from a raid. One soldier had taken nonlethal gunfire and was bleeding through bandages. Miguel instructed that he be brought to the Company hospital.

When they arrived at a second ranch, Miguel returned his attention to Rene and the *carnal*.

Rene didn't know the purpose of this trip. He'd come along on the instructions of the Mexican Mafia leader in Laredo, the Black Hand. Now he was face-to-face with the man who ordered the death of his brother, Moises, in the parking lot of Torta-Mex. Rene's *carnal* spoke up: He said they'd been sent by the Black Hand to collect $10,000 and 200 kilos of cocaine.

Miguel asked the *carnal,* "So you're now in charge of the *cuadros?*"—referring to "bricks," or kilos, of coke.

"Yes," said the *carnal*.

Miguel sent for the $10,000, but told the *carnal* that he could give only 40 kilos of coke, not 200.

Rene began to understand what was behind the plot to murder his brother. Seeking to advance his station, the Black Hand probably gave up Rene's brother, who'd been stealing from Miguel. The $10,000 was either compensation for setting up Moises, or funding for further murder operations in Laredo. In addition to the money, Miguel was going to front the Black Hand "a test load" of cocaine, but wanted to limit his initial exposure to $400,000 worth of coke (40 kilos) rather than $2 million (200 kilos).

Miguel turned to Rene and asked, "And you're in charge of the *quiebres?*"—the killings.

Rene didn't know what Miguel was talking about. So Rene said yes, because Miguel gave off a distinct sense of: *I'll kill you now, just give me reason.* It must be easy, he thought, to be as confident as Miguel when you're surrounded by bodyguards and a city of soldiers at your command. But Rene decided he would do whatever was asked of him until he had the chance to kill Miguel, and then kill Bart Reta, the ones responsible for his brother's death.

Miguel returned to his binder and flipped through pages of photos. "Forty of them," he mumbled, referring to the people in Laredo he wanted killed. He reeled off a few names: Mike Lopez, Chuy Resendez, Mackey Flores. "Do you know them?" Miguel asked Rene.

"No," Rene said.

"Do you know Moises Garcia?" Miguel asked.

Was Miguel mocking him? Rene wondered.

"No," Rene said.

"Really? But wasn't he with the Mexican Mafia?"

DUST, DUST, DUST: IT CAME in through the windows, a soft invasion of dissolution filling the vehicle as they motored from Guerrero to Reynosa, part of a three-truck convoy in early February. Miguel in front, Gabriel and Bart in back, both of the Wolf Boys *todo pildoro*—high on roches.

The Company permitted alcohol and cocaine. Marijuana was okay, but never on the job and *never* in front of Miguel. Pills, heroin, and meth were forbidden. Not every Wolf Boy required roches to kill; about one of every five assassins used the pills. Bart didn't need roches to mute his conscience. He didn't have much of one to begin with. But Gabriel relied on them, now averaging more than ten a day—an astounding intake for a pill said to be ten times as strong as Valium. The drug, combined with a can or two of Red Bull in the morning, rendered him focused and energized, then touchy as he came down. His tolerance stellar, Gabriel could conceal his roche habit around the *comandantes*. Bart? Not so much.

Sober, Bart was *huevado,* ballsy; he volunteered for everything.

The pills brought out an even more concentrated version of the Midget's "short-man's complex." Bart became twice as eager to be accepted by the big boys, "to jump at the front of the barrel."

I'm a good soldier!

That should never be doubted!

I'll lay it down for La Compañía *anytime!*

Partway to Reynosa, Bart blurted out, "Give me *piñas*! An AR! I'll do the mission!"

Miguel laughed and looked at them in the rearview mirror. "Slow down. What mission?"

"Any mission!" Bart said.

Miguel turned around: "Andas pildoro o qué pedo?" *Are you pilled up or what the fuck?**

"Nah," Bart said, as if such a thing were impossible. "Me?"

Gabriel, able to act natural in spite of the roches, said to Bart: "No andas de mentiroso, güey." *Don't be lying, dude.*

Miguel turned to Gabriel and asked: "Tú también?" *You, too?*

"Yo no chingo con ese mugrero," Gabriel said. *I don't fuck with that shit.*

Bart looked like he was about to shit his pants. Why was Gabriel ratting him out in front of Miguel?

Miguel told the driver of the truck to turn around. He dropped both boys back off in Guerrero, then left.

Standing in a cloud of dust, Bart was on the verge of tears. "I want to talk to you," he said to Gabriel. "Why are you doing that to me?"

"Doing what?"

---

* In border slang, *pedo*—literally, fart—means "trouble," or "problems." To the question "Qué pedo?"—"What's the matter?"—someone might respond, "No hay pedo. Ya está todo controlado," meaning: "There's no trouble. Everything is under control."

"Talking that shit!"

Gabriel pulled out his gun and pointed it at Bart. "You started it by acting stupid. Talking nonsense to MT." Bart stood at attention—no emotion, no fear—waiting to see what Gabriel would do. "You're the one to deal with your dumb comments," Gabriel said. "You're the one to be self-blamed."

When the boys were younger, and had been arrested for small-time crimes, they assured themselves that, because they never snitched then, they never would. But now, who knew? Minor arrests formed a bond. As bigger arrests loomed, that bond would be tested. Growing up, the boys always heard about drug lords who "fell on a *cuatro*"—were set up. In the end, Gabriel knew that everyone was betrayed. *Everyone*. But he also knew that you couldn't be paranoid all the time. If you were, you should go flip burgers for a living.

"But you shouldn't be treating me like that," Bart said, "because we're homies." He gave Gabriel his sad puppy-dog face. "I love you, *güey*. I'll lay it on the line for you!"

Bart and Gabriel made up, but the whole episode put both of them in a terrible mood. Later that day, back in Nuevo Laredo, Bart shot at someone randomly because he didn't like the way the person looked at him. As a consequence for the unsanctioned shooting, the Mexican Military Police raided the Nuevo Laredo house where the boys had been staying, and confiscated Gabriel's new Mercedes.

Gabriel went straight to the Military Police's base, identified himself as "Forty's people," and demanded to speak to the chief of police. The chief came out and denied knowledge of the car, treating Gabriel like an idiot. Gabriel dialed Miguel and put his phone on speaker.

"This is Miguel Treviño. I gave him that car."

The chief laughed. He didn't believe it was Miguel.

"It's Miguel! That car was picked up by you!"

The chief went white.

"Look, you son of a bitch! Give that car back or you'll know who I am personally!"

Out came the Mercedes. The two policemen stationed at the base's entrance opened the gate and nodded to Gabriel as he drove away.

Cruising through Nuevo Laredo, he heard the ring of a bell coming around a corner: the hotdog guy. He remembered when he and Luis, as little kids dressed in their Sunday best, American clothes, would buy a bunch of one-dollar hotdogs for themselves and their Mexican cousins, telling the guy to pile on beans, chopped onions, and tomatoes until their plates overflowed with condiments. Then they'd run to the famous *elote* stand, Granolandia, and buy ears of boiled corn smothered in mayonnaise, cheese, and chili pepper. Gabriel's Mexican aunts earned around eighty dollars a week, some of it paid in grocery store coupons, *bonos*. By American standards, he was poor; but in Mexico, because he was from America, he never felt poor.

He thought of Laredo. He wanted to go back there, where he was needed, to finish what he started and prove himself worthy of greater roles in the Company.

It had become known as "Forty's list of forty"—the people in Laredo whom Miguel and the Company wanted dead; the final "sweeping" of enemies that, once completed, would secure the Laredo border crossing and the coveted I-35 smuggling corridor. Miguel spoke of his list like some grand project he planned to soon put in motion. He mentioned the list often to Gabriel, his most active *sicario* on the U.S. side of the border. "We'll hold off a little longer, until the heat over there cools, and then we'll go to work," Miguel had told him, referencing Robert Garcia's investigation of the boys following the murder of Noe Flores on Frost Street in early January.

When Gabriel joined the Company, Meme and Miguel told him he would enjoy perfect privileges in the warrior house, and he did.

If he got caught or landed in jail they'd come for him, and they did. If he worked hard and handled business, they said, he'd come up in the Company, and now that was happening, too. Any Wolf Boy who made himself instrumental in this final sweep, Gabriel believed, was guaranteed a Mexican plaza of his own, and the title of a bona fide *comandante*.

He'd waited in Mexico long enough.

Now, as he drove north through Nuevo Laredo and back into his birth country, the sky snapping off into darkness, he resembled a fantastic insect stuck at the center of a huge vibrating web, or some rodeo bull pulling against opposing ropes while being rigged for a rider. What they didn't tell him, what he couldn't have known, was that the American legal system, for all its flaws, was a patient one. It waited.

PART IV

Prophecy

"Rivalry" is a densely textured relationship, building opposition out of similarity, and solidarity out of the intimacy of shared ambition and mutual envy.

—*AZTECS*, INGA CLENDINNEN

24

Last Meal

D o you need the phone?"

"Yes."

"Who are you calling?"

"My brother."

Robert Garcia slid Gabriel's cell across the table. "Tell him you'll call him later."

"Hey," Gabriel said when Luis picked up. "I need you to call my brother Mike and tell him I'm arrested. Do you have his radio code?" Robert knew of Gabriel's three brothers. There was no Mike. "They're charging me with two murders, but I don't know anything. They say there's a witness. I think it's all bullshit. Tell my brother Mike it will be a $2 million bond ... yeah ... tell him to send $200,000. He'll pay it. You just keep collecting what's mine, every Monday."

On February 5, 2006, Gabriel had driven back to Laredo, but he hadn't returned to Texas heedlessly. A few days earlier, he'd asked a friend to call a cousin who worked in the Webb County clerk's office and inquire about warrants pending for each person in his crew. Gabriel had none, he was told, so he thought it would be fine to come across. Robert's gambit worked and Gabriel was arrested at the border.

Eight months had passed since their last meeting. Gabriel had put on ten pounds of bulk, his back pushing against the seams of an untucked button-down, and he walked with a new swagger. His hair, which he wore shorter now, revealed the old scars of shotgun fragments. He behaved not as a young man facing heavy time on multiple murder charges but as one engaged in an elaborate game. The kid, looking at millions in bail, was concerned about getting his five hundred dollars per week in salary from the Company. The open mention of "brother Mike." The confidence that the money would arrive. Robert decided to play to that ego.

"Last summer you told me about the murders you committed across," Robert said. "Or was that bullshit?"

"No, they were true. I like to do them across because there is no problem across."

"You said you had help from the police?"

"They set them up for you. Those guys have everything under control."

"Were those deaths reported? Or did they disappear the bodies?"

"All the ones I've done they disappeared."

"What do you use over there?"

"ARs," Gabriel said, referring to AR-15 assault rifles. "They're faster."

"Why don't you use ARs here?"

"Because over here it's more difficult with the law," Gabriel said, referring to America's heightened penalties for using assault weapons in crimes.

Robert raised an eyebrow, leaned back, crossed his arms, and regarded Gabriel impassively. It was the posture of a nonjudgmental therapist acknowledging the gravity of his patient's disclosure. Without changing tone, Robert transitioned: "So, the Torta-Mex murder, you said you didn't participate. And this one, on Frost Street, tell me what happened."

Gabriel denied any involvement with the murders of Moises Garcia at Torta-Mex, or Noe Flores on Frost Street. Robert said he had an eyewitness on the Flores murder, enough to get two more warrants on Gabriel—one for murder and one for "engaging in organized criminal activity." An eyewitness was weak, Gabriel knew, but enough to hold him. He needed to provide a story. So he continued in a general way about Zeta operations on the U.S. side. Some hits had been done under the instruction of Miguel Treviño, he said, but he didn't know which ones. There were other groups in Laredo working under other people.

Here it was, Robert thought: swirling nuggets of truth into his bowl of bullshit. Good, just keep him talking.

But then something happened that Robert didn't expect. Once Gabriel got going on the story of the Noe Flores murder—the one he'd supposedly heard about through others—it was as if he couldn't help himself. So authentic was his understanding of the case, the details so real, that his mixed-in lies tended to stand out against the truth, and vice versa.

A man named "El Señor," he explained, had ordered the job. At first, Bart and his crew were confused about how to carry it out. But then girls who worked with El Señor ran into the target, Mike Lopez, while partying at a Laredo club called Cocktails. The girls called El Señor, then followed Mike Lopez home. Bart drove the hit squad across town in a gray Nissan. The girls' job was to lure Lopez out of his house. But in the confusion on Frost Street, the shooter got mixed up and killed Noe Flores instead.

"Who was the shooter?" Robert asked.

Gabriel said that a guy named Joseph Allen shot Noe Flores with a .40-caliber handgun. It was the same guy, he said, who killed Moises Garcia with a 9 mm at Torta-Mex back in December.

Joseph Allen was a real person. He was wanted for another murder—and it just so happened that he looked like Gabriel, a coincidence Gabriel emphasized. It explained the eyewitness. Robert pondered his notes and nodded. *Ah, Joseph Allen. It all makes perfect sense now.*

"Who was the eyewitness?" Gabriel asked.

Robert steered him back toward Frost Street.

The hit squad, Gabriel continued, dumped the Nissan at a grocery store around the corner. Later, it came out on the news that it was not Mike Lopez they killed. That had seemed like a problem, at first, Gabriel said, but then El Señor said it was no problem. Mike Lopez was going to die anyway.

"There was a pack of cigarettes in the abandoned vehicle," Robert said. "Who smoked?"

"They all smoke. But supposedly they belonged to Bart."

"There was a cap left behind, too. What kind of cap was it?"

"A camouflage cap."

"Whose?"

"Bart's."

"What's the deal with Pablo, Polo, and David?" Robert asked, referring to other Wolf Boys in Laredo, those chukkies that Gabriel called "the B team." The chukkies had been arrested for a botched hit at a Laredo Wal-Mart a few days earlier, and had implicated Gabriel in the Noe Flores murder. "Were they also in charge of murders?"

"Yes," Gabriel said.

"But they never did anything? What, they weren't any good?"

"They were afraid."

"How about Chapa?"

Gabriel's driver, Chapa, had been brought in for questioning a few weeks earlier, caught coming back across in the white Expedition used in the Moises Garcia hit.

"We don't tell him anything," Gabriel said, then asked to use the phone again. With Robert sitting right there, he called "brother Mike."

"No, brother, I was going to tell you, I am detained. . . . No, on the other side. They're accusing me of a murder I had nothing to do with. . . . Yeah, I was with my girl when they got me. . . . No, the others remained on the other side. Yeah, *they* did listen. But you know how it is with my girl. . . . I'm just asking for some help if you can. If not, no problem."

Over the past year Robert had interviewed more than a dozen cartel informants. This kid was deeper in the underworld than any of them. When Gabriel asked to make two more calls, Robert told him to go ahead, to take his time.

Gabriel called Luis again: "I just told Mike of my bond. He told me he warned me not to come across. He got angry and didn't want to talk to me anymore. But he said he would pay. He'll release the money. Just tell the midget to call Mike and confirm that everything's cool. . . . Okay . . . And add some minutes to the Verizon phone so I can call you from county." Then Gabriel called Christina back: "He'll get me out. . . . Yeah, my brother Mike. It'll be $2 million. Can you believe that? . . . Where are you going? Your house? . . . Okay, I'll call later. . . . Love you too. Bye."

Robert wanted to come across as friendly, fatherly, not antagonistic. He didn't want that cartel lawyer, David Almaraz, interfering with his investigation. He said: "Okay, this is what's going to happen. We obtained the warrant because the others accused you. And because you were ID'd. You are part of the group. That you can't argue about. But I'm not going to screw you over with something you didn't do, okay?"

Gabriel nodded. He was a son of God, a man of principle. He appreciated the fair treatment.

"But I need access to you," Robert continued. "I know you're going to speak with your attorney, which is your right. Tell him that you're speaking with us. Maybe later I can show you a photo of that guy"—Joseph Allen—"to verify it's him. If we can verify that you weren't there, then maybe we can drop all the charges. I'll continue to investigate. But tell me something: Where are these guys if I need to find them? Bart and these other assholes?"

"Across. But it would be very hard. They'll shoot it out. They're trained."

"Bart is trained?" Robert asked. "But he was arrested and came out of TYC last summer, right?"

"Yes, but three or four years ago he was already with them. He came back here and was arrested with me. I was sent to county and released. He was sent to TYC."

In early 2006, Bart was sixteen and a half years old. Joining the Zetas "three or four years" earlier would've made him twelve or thirteen on entry. At that point, by all accounts, he was still menacing middle schoolers, fantasizing about Navy SEALs, and pledging allegiance to the Sieteros. But Gabriel's story about Bart already having become a Company man before going to TYC—a story invented from Gabriel's guilt over having fingered Bart for the Flores murder—made an irresistible addition to border myth. The prepubescent cartel assassin! Even Robert's bullshit sensor melted down.

But Robert had other reasons to believe, or to pretend to believe, whatever Gabriel said. As he continued the investigations, he hoped, eventually, to turn Gabriel into a cooperating witness—someone who would identify the others involved in the murders, and provide more information about Miguel Treviño, who, by February 2006, was now considered a "high-priority target" by Angel Moreno, DEA, FBI, and the rest of American law enforcement.

WHILE MIGUEL PLANNED HIS FINAL assault on Laredo enemies, the murder of his brother, Fito, sent him on a killing spree in search of his brother's assailant.

Now a tattered couch sat in an open field. Miguel told Wences Tovar to walk the handcuffed men over to it. Miguel would be back in a moment.

An hour earlier, Wences had been taking *franco* in a Nuevo Laredo hotel when Miguel pulled up in a Ford F-150 and told him to come down. Wences crowded into the backseat of the extended cab, next to three bound men: two brothers and their father.

Omar, Miguel's brother, was in the front seat. They drove to the Company ranch near China, a town in the neighboring state of Nuevo León. When Wences understood that one of the two bound brothers had confessed to killing Fito Treviño, he thought: I would not want to be you guys.

Now, Wences brought the three bound men to the couch in the middle of the field, and told them to scoot over so he could sit down. It would be a while until Miguel and Omar returned. Wences disappeared into the task of rolling a joint, until the familiar scream of a maiming interrupted him, and something wet slapped against his face.

A severed ear.

Miguel stood at the other end of the couch, next to the man who killed Fito. Miguel wore black jeans and a Tommy Hilfiger shirt. His knife was smeared with blood. Tucked between his torso and the knife-wielding arm was a container of potato salad, from which he speared bites with a plastic fork. "If I ever see you doing that shit around me again," Miguel told Wences through a mouthful of potatoes, "you'll be next."

Wences tossed the joint aside and stood up. He didn't want to look away. Miguel hated that. So he looked at the wound of the guy who had killed his boss's brother. Every time an ear was cut, Wences was always surprised by how small the inside was. Just two tiny holes in the head.

The killer requested that his brother and father be spared. "They weren't involved," he said.

"Was *my* brother involved?" Miguel asked. "No, he wasn't. So now you're going to watch *them* die."

Miguel radioed a doctor. He wanted this affair to be slow. Then he heated his *cuchillo* over a flame and soldered the ear wound shut hastily while his brother's killer screamed, then vomited.

Omar looked impatient.

Of all Treviño siblings, Omar was closest to Fito, and most upset by his death. Going slowly didn't work for Omar. He pulled the father, a huge man, off the couch and shot him in the face with an AR-15, emptying dozens of rounds into the nose, cheeks, chin, eyes, and forehead. Upon the gouge of each bullet, the man's face sucked further backward until the head was flat on the ground like a rubber mask, pancake-thin. Wences forced himself to watch.

Miguel, his right hand on his .38, his left leg shaking, looked around. "Where's that doctor?"

Spurred on by his brother Omar, Miguel let his impatience get the better of him as well. He shot the brother of his brother's killer in the legs. This shooting went on for five magazines. He loaded a sixth magazine and shot the brother in the cranium at a glancing angle, revealing brain. He holstered his gun, walked to a nearby mesquite tree, and cut a spoonlike sliver of bark. He squatted by the head of the dead brother, scooped out a serving of gray matter, and handed the spoon to his brother's killer.

Was Miguel messed up? Wences wondered, but then thought: Nah. How could Miguel be so intelligent if he was also messed up in the head? Sure, it was true that Miguel cut bodies open a lot, and seemed to enjoy it. But so did doctors and medical examiners.

"How does it taste?" Miguel asked, having fed his brother's assassin several servings of brain.

"Like chicken," he said.

This flourish of defiance elicited a smile from Miguel before he shot the young man in the head and walked away.

Wences, lingering in the shadows of early evening, stared at the father's decimated head, a wet mush of holes into which flies now swarmed. The endless, anxious making of the self, the endless striving, and then the reversal: the sudden, massive, physical assault for some possibly involuntary dereliction. The threat was always there, as was the evidence of its reality. When Wences closed his eyes, the flattened face remained like an afterimage, and he tripped, imagining his own family. What if someone told a lie about *him* to Miguel? he wondered. Was this everyone's fate?

"Vámonos!" Miguel shouted, and the caravan departed to another ranch. Elsa Sepulveda, Miguel's ex, had been found.

THE *AGUILERA*—LITERALLY, THE NEST—WAS A house of discipline, a place to store Company men who disobeyed orders, as well as immigrants, contras, and other collateral. Wences followed Miguel inside. They passed middle-aged women who asked for food and bathroom privileges, children who asked to go home. Miguel walked to a girl tied to a chair in the corner. He ripped the tape from her eyes and mouth.

When he saw her face he became furious.

He called over the soldier who brought her there, and threw pictures of Elsa Sepulveda on the floor. How was it possible that the soldier confused Elsa for this person? The soldier apologized and attempted to prostrate himself. Miguel laughed. The only thing he hated more than incompetence was a sorry-ass *panochón*. He shook his left leg, threw his head back, sighted down his nose, then pulled his .38, said "Ya mamastes"—"You're gone"—and shot the soldier in the head. He told the woman on the floor, whoever it was, that she was coming with them. He told Wences to drive the Porsche Cayenne.

Outside, the woman tried to open the door of the Porsche, before Wences unlocked it, and received a shock from the armoring system.

Wences deactivated the security and they all got in. It was night. As they returned to the China ranch, Miguel spoke to the woman in shockingly frank and emotional terms about his relationship with Elsa Sepulveda. He spoke of how humiliating it was when she left him, of how that humiliation deepened when he found out she was cheating on him. When she called to taunt him over the death of Fito, that was the last straw.

At the China ranch, Miguel ordered the white tiger.

The cage arrived.

Bodyguards emerged from a chicken coop carrying the naked, lifeless bodies of the three men murdered that afternoon, the scalp of one torn away. The starving tiger, released from its cage while a bodyguard controlled it with a leash, devoured the arms and legs while Miguel laughed. He told the woman—a friend of Elsa's, apparently—that they'd stolen the tiger from a circus. He vowed to do the same to Elsa, if he ever found her.

They departed the ranch.

Near the border, Miguel and Wences turned the woman over to a man they called El Licenciado, a lawyer for Miguel who would take her to the bridge and see she made it back to Texas.* El Licenciado told Miguel that the family of the men killed that afternoon requested the bodies for a proper burial. Miguel laughed and asked for the phone. His brother, he told the family, had no proper burial, and neither would they. He said the bodies had been thrown on the side of the road. He didn't remember where. Maybe they were eaten.

---

* The moniker "Licenciado"—a graduate or licensed person—suggests a kind of fake respect for lawyers and politicians in Mexico's corrupt elite, those educated people who do business with criminals. Their power, writes journalist Alfredo Corchado, is a symptom of impunity that has "roots in power structures dating back to the days of the Aztecs, which were molded to the modern age by the PRI."

25

Heroes and Liars

In late January 2006, two young DEA agents contacted Angel
Moreno to say they had an informant who claimed to be connected to Miguel Treviño. The informant—"Rocky"—was a
former Zeta employee who'd come out of a long hospital stay after
being beaten nearly to death by Omar Treviño. The DEA agents
were confident they could use Rocky to make big cases against high-
level guys in the Company.

It was one of the greatest aspects of the system, and one of the
worst: the incredible discretion given to someone like Angel Moreno.
For agents looking to make a case, Moreno was the guy they had to
come to, go through, for a simple reason: In court, before the actual
judge, the federal prosecutor was the face of the American government. Arguably, Moreno had more influence over a criminal's future
than any judge. Who got charged; when; how many times and for
how much; and whether a mandatory minimum sentence got tossed
in—these decisions were all up to Moreno. He liked to say he did

more for defendants' rights *before* they got charged than any defense attorney did afterward.

Prosecutors at the border entertained two kinds of drug cases: "reactive" and "proactive." The reactive ones were simple. Border Patrol busted a guy coming across the border with a load of dope, and called DEA or ICE—agencies with arresting powers. An agent drove to the bridge, or the checkpoint, made the arrest, and interviewed the smuggler about his network. Could the guy lead to bigger fish? Was he willing to cooperate in exchange for a sentence reduction? Then the prosecutor opened a case, and the negotiations began.

The proactive cases were the ones where agents pitched the prosecutor: *Joe Blow doesn't have a job but he owns lots of trucks. We have good information that he's moving coke. We want a search warrant.* The agents submitted an affidavit, and the prosecutor opened a case.

Moreno handled pitches for a subset of proactive cases: Agents who wanted to submit a case for OCDETF designation and funding came to him. Each agent had his or her own pitching style. Some agents, often the newer ones, wanted to come in and tell Moreno the whole story with a PowerPoint presentation, and Moreno would sit there thinking, Thanks, but I can read. But he always tried to listen and act interested. As a boss, stifling enthusiasm got you nowhere.

J. J. Gomez and Chris Diaz had everything short of a Power-Point presentation when they came into Moreno's conference room talking about the promise of Rocky—their new informant, or confidential source. J. J. Gomez was a twenty-six-year-old local boy who went to Martin High seven years ahead of Gabriel Cardona. He played the drums in school and liked to study. He thought the barrio gangs were childish. He was more scared of his mother. On summer weekends, his father took him and his brother to a construction site, where temperatures reached 115 degrees in July and August. The lesson: Do everything you can to avoid this fate. At Martin, J.J.

remembered, there were the good people and the bad people and you knew the screwups. They walked tough in the hallways and talked shit to teachers. They hung out across the border, had cars and chicks. Many students in J.J.'s class were the Gabriel Cardona type, and now they were dead.

The second DEA agent, Chris Diaz, was a twenty-nine-year-old former cop from Virginia who spoke gringo Spanish. Chris knew the streets. His father was a Mexican who grew up in East Los Angeles. Chris was tall, lumbering, and wore a long goatee—an undercover look. His devotion to DEA was evident by his very presence in the Laredo office, a hardship post to all but the most ambitious outsider.

In federal circles, particularly in the U.S. attorney's office, newer agents like Chris Diaz and J. J. Gomez were known as "FNGs," Fucking New Guys. FNGs, Moreno believed, rarely had a clue what they were doing. He didn't know that Diaz and Gomez had eight years of DEA experience between them, nor that they'd been investigating cartel activity in Laredo since 2003. As for this "Rocky," any new informant was risky. But after Rocky helped the FNGs set up two successive Zeta drug busts by the river, Moreno reconsidered his assessment of Diaz and Gomez and took a closer look at the case—and so did the DEA boss.

A couple of months earlier, the agencies had been set on La Barbie, the size of La Barbie's public profile correlating to the value of his hide. But in December 2005, the DEA's La Barbie informant walked away. It turned out he'd been playing both sides all along. Now, in retrospect—as was often the case with informants—what had come before made sense. When the informant first appeared, back in June, he gave the "Barbie Execution Video" to Robert Garcia, who held it for a while and then shared it with agents at DEA and FBI. La Barbie never sent the video to the *Dallas Morning News,* as was reported. A FBI agent leaked it. La Barbie's face wasn't even in the video. La Barbie's purpose hadn't been to build his reputation but to have independent news organizations broadcast the other side's depravity.

Tell us about the guiso, *and burning people with different fuels.*

Tell us about that journalist you killed.

With voluntary informants (and even with involuntary informants, the ones you had a charge against), it was impossible to tell if they were genuine. Often, the supposed informant had nothing, and simply wanted to get paid by the government. Or he was there on the orders of a capo to extract (or deliver) intelligence (or misinformation) and then disappear. Even if you got a case out of it—even if you got a guilty plea or a conviction—you never knew whether you had been played. Cops and criminals called the war on drugs "the game," but that was a misnomer. In games, opponents were delineated and a winner emerged.

Informants were a consequence of an escalating war. As each new interdiction strategy was countered systematically by a new evasion technique, the war relied increasingly on paid snitches. In Mexico, criminals paid cops. In the States, cops paid criminals. In Laredo, aspiring informants networked with drug agents, called the office, and stopped by all day long, pitching business like hopped-up entrepreneurs:

AGENT: How can I help you?

SNITCH: I want to start school again and do Job Corps. I need to report to my probation officer. I owe about four hundred dollars.

AGENT: What's the fine for?

SNITCH: I was caught at school with clonazepam for my anxiety. I'm eighteen but I've lived a forty-year life. Do I have regrets? No, because it made me the man I am today.

AGENT: Okay. How can you help me?

SNITCH: I can help you take down heroin and coke. Can you talk to my PO?

AGENT: The faster you work the faster you get paid. Tell me the addresses of the houses. I hope it's not ones we already have.

SNITCH: You don't have these, trust me. They're not addresses. They're deliveries.

AGENT: Delivery guys?

SNITCH: Yeah. I used to be a heroin addict, so they trust me.

AGENT: Who are they?

SNITCH: Family friends. Cousins. The biggest heroin dealers in Laredo. They were the ones who hooked me, so fuck them. I constructed their house.

AGENT: Like you actually built it?

SNITCH: I painted it. Look, the only reason I'm doing this is for my girl and my child. I've seen friends die of overdoses. I love my city too much to see it go down this fast.

AGENT: Do you have the delivery numbers?

SNITCH: No, they're in my phone and I broke my phone.

AGENT: [Looking at snitch's phone] What phone is that?

SNITCH: My girl's.

AGENT: And you mentioned some bad cops earlier?

SNITCH: I've sold to them. I'm not gonna mention names.

AGENT: Why not? You're already here.

SNITCH: [phone rings] Hello? . . . yes . . . Ma'am, can I call you back? [to agent] Sorry, I'm trying to get meds for my ADHD. But let me see how this works first. It's all about trust. You can't find trust nowadays. That's why I wish I was born in the seventies and eighties. . . .

To use snitches, and not get used by them, you had to understand their motivations. First, there was the "regular informant" who just wanted to get paid. This informant was a person who perhaps sold real estate or banking services, and who'd never been arrested. Regular informants stood at a distance from crime, were generally trustworthy, but provided the least information. Second, there was the "political informant"—a foreign official who had to be approved at the highest level of DEA. They were a black box; you could only guess at their true allegiances.

Third was the "restricted informant," the most common type of snitch. This informant was a criminal who wanted money or revenge, or who wanted to move out his competitor. Or it was someone who had soured on the underworld and felt as though he should've been law enforcement all along. It could be a drug-addled liar who woke up one morning and decided it would be fun to play cop, wear the badge, fantasize. Restricted informants could make huge cases, and were always difficult partners. They went back on their word, and played both sides. When you finally made a plan and went undercover, the informant invariably changed the plan at the last minute and blew the operation if you didn't get him out of the way fast enough. One of every twenty was a decent informant, but it could take multiple meetings to assess. To employ them, you had to provide endless paperwork on their criminal pasts.

History of coke?

Heroin?

Domestic abuse?

Assault?

Well, we'll have to massage that for the paperwork.

If the case went to trial, and the informant got called to testify, the defense attorney would try to use the informant's criminal history to impeach his testimony. It rarely mattered, however. Jurors assumed informants were liars.

The economics of the border complicated the spy game. The best informants could earn six figures over a snitching career, but the majority were lucky to make a few thousand dollars. So, without a personal vendetta driving an informant, or some black-market prerogative, the meager snitching salary often proved insufficient against the lure of criminal paydays and the risk of community banishment, or worse.

Rocky, however, was ready to work. He wanted revenge for the time he was mistaken for a traitor and beaten by Omar Treviño. Rocky maintained a healthy coke habit, chattered incessantly, was highly manipulative, and beat his wife from time to time. But at least he had no murder raps, at least not on this side. If he delivered as promised, he'd earn his snitching salary.

After he proved himself by helping DEA set up two drug busts at the river, Zeta leadership asked Rocky to service a new hit squad in Laredo. On the wire that Rocky now wore, the DEA agents, Diaz and Gomez, learned that Miguel had dispatched two hit men to make the loudest statement yet: a *Scarface*-style massacre at Agave Azul, the hot Laredo nightclub owned by La Barbie.

THE BLACK HAND, THE LEADER of the Mexican Mafia in Laredo, was supposed to use Miguel's $10,000 to rent a safe house in Laredo for one of Miguel's hit squads. But the Black Hand spent the money, which was why he asked Rene Garcia, still looking to avenge his brother Moises's death, to check Miguel's hit men into Laredo's El Cortez Motel, then serve as their concierge and chauffeur.

"We need to kill a lot of people so we can make our point here," one hit man said in the presence of Rocky, who was working with Rene to service the hit men. *"So they can know who the Zetas are!"* They snorted *lavadita* at the motel, and vowed to use grenades if the cops showed up.

Rene, working as co-concierge with Rocky, took the hit men to the mall and to bars. He helped procure guns, drugs, and prostitutes. One hit man told Rene that he looked like Moises Garcia, and asked if they were brothers. "No," Rene said. He had to play it cool long enough to meet Bart Reta, then cook the fool where he stood.

But Rene would never get his chance.

When Rocky was sent out on another errand, Diaz and Gomez ordered local police, led by Robert, to raid the motel and make "wall-off arrests" in order to conceal federal participation.*

In just two months, Rene went from witnessing his brother's murder, to seeking revenge, to being arrested for aiding the organization responsible. It was a bizarre path whose logic somehow made perfect sense in Laredo.

FOR MORENO, THE BIGGER CASE was saddling up nicely. Rocky was legit. The DEA pledged support for Moreno's OCDETF case.

A trial unfolded in his mind. He'd use info obtained from Zeta minions to indict the leadership. At trial, when the defense attorney pointed out that the only witnesses were killers, Moreno would pull out a line he hadn't used in years. He'd tell the jury that you can't have angels as witnesses for crimes committed in hell.

He smiled at the thought of it, and recalled his favorite Christopher Walken movie, *The Prophecy,* in which one character says: "Did you ever notice how in the Bible, whenever God needed to punish someone, or make an example, or whenever God needed a killing, he sent an angel? Did you ever wonder what that creature must be like? A whole existence spent praising your God, but always with one wing dipped in blood? Would you ever really want to see an angel?"

---

* When making an arrest, federal agents often use local cops to "wall it off." Bigger fish are less likely to be scared away if they think their subordinates have been busted by local law enforcement. Signs of federal involvement can tank the larger investigation.

Moreno submitted the OCDETF proposal under "Operation Prophecy," and signed the request for a federal war chest.

COPS FILE CHARGES. PROSECUTORS REVIEW warrants for probable cause. And judges decide bail. But in Laredo, drug dealers drive luxury cars with ads on the windows supporting their favorite judge. A Mercedes says, "Elect Ricardo Rangel for Justice of the Peace." Rangel was convicted of federal bribery charges. A Jaguar says, "Elect Manuel Flores for District Judge." One of Flores's sons provided the weapon in a triple homicide; another was indicted for shooting someone with a gun given to him by his mother.

In Texas, the prosecutor could ask the court to deny bail in cases of multiple homicides, or cases of murder-for-hire. But that never happened in Gabriel's situation. Instead, a justice of the peace reduced his bail on the "engaging in organized crime" charge to $50,000, and his bail on the murder charge for Noe Flores to $150,000. When Gabriel went before Judge Manuel Flores (no relation) on the Orozco murder, Flores set bail at $2 million, putting Gabriel's total bail at $2.2 million, 10 percent of which—the amount it would cost to "bond out"—was $220,000.

The Zetas wouldn't pay that.

When David Almaraz, one of Laredo's prosecutors-turned-cartel-lawyers, convinced Judge Flores to call a bail-reduction hearing, no one at Laredo PD was notified. A different state prosecutor appeared than had appeared at the first hearing. Almaraz said he and the new prosecutor agreed to $200,000 for the Orozco charges, putting Gabriel's total bail at $600,000, meaning it would cost only $60,000 to bond out.

Texas had become a stock market for killers. Miguel Treviño didn't like Gabriel at $220,000, but loved him at $60,000. So on March 20, 2006, a jail guard at Webb County screamed "Cardona!

Con todo y chivas!"—an old saying meaning "Grab all your stuff," literally: "Everything including the goats."

A nineteen-year-old Zeta killer tied to multiple murders on this side, and more in Mexico, walked out of jail for the third time in six months.

CHRIS DIAZ, J. J. GOMEZ, and Robert Garcia met for lunch at Danny's, a popular chain of Laredo diners specializing in classic Mexican fare. They traded information about the cartels—but didn't share everything.

For instance, Diaz and Gomez didn't tell Robert that Chuy Resendez was a former Zeta; nor that Chuy, now a Sinaloa-allied smuggler in Laredo who worked with La Barbie, was a "source of information" for DEA. Back in the 1990s, before the Zetas moved in, the old gunslingers—independent smugglers—were well known around Laredo and Nuevo Laredo. People feared and respected Chuy Resendez—including Miguel and Omar Treviño, who grew up with Chuy in Nuevo Laredo, stealing cars and trafficking drugs together. When Miguel assumed control of the Nuevo Laredo plaza for the Zetas, he tried to charge his old friend Chuy a smuggling tax. "Come on, *güey*," Chuy said. "We grew up together. We're buddies." But Miguel insisted: Chuy could pay the tax or get *borrado del mapa*. Chuy refused to fold. In 2003, when Miguel sent Zeta hit men to Chuy's Nuevo Laredo house, Chuy was ready with grenades and AK-47s. He killed all of Miguel's men, then "jumped the river," partnered with La Barbie and the Sinaloa Cartel, set up a new smuggling operation near Laredo, and began passing intelligence about the Zetas to two young DEA agents: Chris Diaz and J. J. Gomez.

While his relationship with DEA appeared to benefit Chuy's bottom line, it didn't always protect him. The Zetas hunted Chuy, and nearly killed him, recently, at the Laredo Wal-Mart. They had

Chuy on the run. In murdering Bruno Orozco, another Zeta traitor, in June 2005, Wences Tovar and Gabriel Cardona removed one
of Chuy's best sources for Zeta intelligence, thereby diminishing
Chuy's value to DEA.

The cop and the agents ate and talked. From the parking lot,
Gabriel watched them.

"I'M HERE," ROCKY TOLD THE *comandante* after walking across the
bridge from the United States to Mexico.

*"Okay, I couldn't come get you. But go around the block. There's
going to be a guy in a silver Jetta waiting for you."*

Rocky was nervous he'd be killed, and for good reason: He'd
been present at two drug busts at the river, and at the bust of the hit
men at the Cortez Motel, and all three times he walked away without being arrested.

There was a guy around the corner in a silver Jetta. The guy put a
gun to Rocky's head while he searched him. "Everything's okay," the
guy told Rocky. He mentioned that the Company had a long list of
targets in Laredo, then handed Rocky $5,500 and asked him to set up
a new safe house in Laredo, a large house for a new group of assassins.

Rocky returned to Laredo on foot with the money, and critical
new intelligence: The Zetas had a long hit list of people in Laredo.
Who was on the list? Rocky didn't know. But there seemed to be
dozens of targets.

Robert Garcia, Chris Diaz, and J. J. Gomez met with Angel
Moreno. If you wanted to kill one guy, or attack a nightclub, you ordered it done and your hit men fled back to Mexico. But several hit men
and several targets? A safe house? They were planning on a slaughter.

This new information altered Moreno's thinking: Operation
Prophecy was no longer just about an OCDETF investigation, and
building a case against capos in Mexico. Moreno, the agents, and Robert

needed to try to identify some or all of the targets on the hit list so they could foil the murders before they happened. Simply arresting hit men didn't mean stopping the murders; if a cartel wanted someone dead, it would keep putting out a contract until the job was done.

Moreno proposed a plan: wiring a safe house for sound and video, and then using Rocky to lure Zetas into the house, where the government would monitor their movements and record their phone calls with Zeta leadership in Mexico, trying to find out who was on the hit list and gathering as much evidence as possible against top Zeta leaders before kicking down the door. Moreno, the agents, and Robert mulled it. It could be insane, or it could be brilliant.

Letting assassins roam Laredo while the government watched? It was definitely without precedent.

What if people died while agents watched from the wire room? What if the assassins asked Rocky to get them guns? Could the government provide criminals with weapons? *Absolutely not,* ATF said. *Well . . . maybe under certain circumstances. Maybe if the guns were nonfunctioning.* Actually, they didn't know. What if the assassins asked Rocky for drugs? Could the government provide drugs? Probably not, but DEA could watch the criminals consume their own drugs without shutting the operation down. More questions came up. What would air and ground support cost per day? What if there was a shoot-out around the safe house? Would there be an extraction plan for neighbors? Did they need to alert the neighbors? *Just ignore those kids across the street . . . they're assassins.*

Moreno called a meeting of every agency boss in Laredo and described the plan.

"If it works, we'll all be heroes," he told the room. "If it doesn't, I'll get indicted."

The agency heads stared at Moreno with grudging respect. They were all federal bosses. But Moreno, as prosecutor, had the power to make charging decisions and authorize investigations. Every boss had his or her share of war stories about bitter face-offs with Moreno—usually over a wiretap or a subpoena that he wouldn't submit to the court, usually because the affidavit wasn't sound. The disgruntled DEA agent, for instance, would kick it up to his local boss. The local boss would call Moreno and say, "You need to push this forward. Our legal counsel says the affidavit has enough." And Moreno would say, "Yeah, but your legal counsel doesn't rely on it in court when the case goes to trial. I do." And then the local boss would kick it up to the regional boss in Houston, and the regional boss would call Moreno: "You need to do this now. Time's wasting." And Moreno'd say, "Have you read the affidavit? No? Well read it, then call me." And then instead of taking five minutes to read the affidavit, the DEA's regional boss would call the Department of Justice's regional office in Houston and demand to speak with the drug chief, only to be told that the drug chief was Moreno. Then the regional boss would call the head of the DOJ's Criminal Division, then Washington, and up and up and up.

Prosecutors like Moreno tended to have a different relationship with the more esoteric federal agencies. Fish & Wildlife, for instance, would get pretty excited, and be extremely thankful, when a prosecutor took on a case that would land the agency in the headlines. But the bigger agencies, the ones Moreno dealt with every day—DEA, FBI, ATF, Homeland Security—they were the worst, and Moreno had no patience for their bullshit. If Operation Prophecy succeeded, the younger agents would get bumped up a pay grade, to GS-13 or journeyman status. But if it failed—or even if it succeeded while a minor part went wrong—they would not share in the ignominy. The weight would fall on Moreno alone. He knew a fellow AUSA who was prosecuted for advancing himself cash on his government ATM card. A dumb move, granted, but an infraction for which an agent might've caught, at most, a reprimand. If an agent pissed off a judge, or screwed up testimony, it was hardly mentioned. But if a judge bad-talked a prosecutor, that prosecutor had better self-report before it became news. When Moreno took a hard line, agents wondered why he was being an asshole, and he just thought: not compared with what they do to us. This arrangement was the prosecutor's trade-off, and part of the reason why the American legal system largely worked. Complete power came with complete responsibility.

Moreno amassed the resources of nine federal, state, and local agencies, including DEA, FBI, ICE, ATF, the U.S. Marshals Service, Border Patrol, and Laredo PD. The DEA bosses were gung ho about the investigation and committed to seeing it through. Rocky, after all, was their informant. But the other agency heads clashed over a complex, high-stakes operation. They wanted the case but they didn't. It was their case one day, when the outlook was good, then not, the next, when the investigation hit a bump. If it succeeded, every alpha dog wanted credit. If it didn't, no one wanted liability. This, Moreno knew from experience, was the essence of a multi-agency OCDETF investigation.

Diaz and Gomez worked hard. It was their case, and they owned it. They reviewed Fourth Amendment law to find out what could and couldn't be recorded in the safe house. Diaz wrote the Title III warrants for the wiretaps. Robert got guns from the Laredo PD evidence room, took them to the shooting range, and filed down the firing pins just enough so that the guns clicked when the trigger was tested but didn't actually spit rounds. His drive and controlling approach to work pissed a lot of people off; those who hadn't worked with him before came around to the same opinion as those who had: asshole. But Robert was used to this dynamic in team situations, and didn't stop moving long enough to process the gossip. Far as he was concerned, the same rule applied. Lead, follow, or get out of my way.

IN LATE MARCH 2006, THE Prophecy team was still getting the legal aspects of surveillance squared away when Zeta leadership called

Rocky and asked if the safe house was ready. It was painful to put the criminals off, to risk losing the operation, but bureaucrats moved at a glacial pace. Diaz and Gomez told Rocky to ask for a couple more days.

By April 1, when the wiretap warrants were signed by the judge and everything was set to go, Rocky's phone had turned cold. Miguel Treviño had grown impatient. Zeta leadership turned to a different concierge. A new cell was setting up somewhere in Laredo, a massacre was coming, and the agents of Operation Prophecy were helpless to do anything about it.

26

Career Moments

After finishing a midnight workout on the weight set he bought for the Hillside house, Gabriel sat on the balcony with an AR-15 across his lap and a *corta,* a handgun, in his belt. He smoked weed by converting an orange into a pipe, carving out a bowl on top and poking a hole through the middle.

The marijuana opened and focused his mind.

What is this game, he wondered, snapping people as if they were flies?

And then he was outside his head. He watched himself pull out the *corta,* release the clip, roll a bullet between his fingers. He thought: I possess an AR. I possess a *corta.* I have a Versace shirt and a roll of cash in my pocket. Lines by Tupac Shakur ran through his head.

He thought about the book he read in jail during February and March. It was an investigation of the murders of Tupac and Biggie Smalls, aka Notorious B.I.G. Gabriel turned ten on the day Tupac, twenty-five, died in 1996. Tupac and his producer, Suge Knight, were in Vegas, driving from the Mike Tyson fight to a party, when a Cadillac screeched to a stop in front of Suge's BMW. The rear window came down, and .40-caliber bullets tore open the "Thug Life" tattoo on Tupac's torso as he tried to scramble for cover in the backseat. Six months later, a twenty-four-year-old Biggie Smalls—Tupac's East Coast rival in the 1990s hip-hop scene—was also killed in a drive-by.

Gabriel had always believed that Tupac and Biggie died in a gang war between West Coast and East Coast rappers, Bloods versus Crips.

This book told a different story. In this account, Tupac was in the midst of a tricky comeback when he was murdered. The year before his death, Tupac sat in a New York prison, settling into a fifty-two-month sentence for the sexual assault of a groupie. By then, he'd put out two bestselling albums, and starred opposite Janet Jackson in *Poetic Justice*. He'd also been arrested eight times, escaped conviction in the shooting of two off-duty police officers, and cheated death when he was shot in the lobby of a Manhattan music studio. Plaintiffs tried to sue Tupac in civil court, blaming his lyrics for the shooting of a Texas trooper, and for the paralysis of a woman hit by a bullet during one of his concerts. Of Tupac's many assault cases, one charged him for attacking the filmmakers of *Menace II Society* when he felt they were casting him as a sucker.

Imprisoned, finally, for sexual assault, Tupac felt ready for a change.

He'd helped build gangsta rap into a bazillion-dollar business with crossover appeal. All those white suburban kids living vicariously through his ghetto rhymes. Yet, financially, Tupac was ruined. Thug life ate his earnings in legal fees. If that life was real, he began thinking in prison, let someone else represent it.

Suge Knight, the book said, visited Tupac in prison. Tupac's problems made him more attractive to Suge. If Tupac agreed to join

Suge's music label, Death Row Records, Suge said, he could spring Tupac. One week later, Tupac was released from prison.

If Tupac was the warrior-poet, Suge was the general, buying and intimidating his way to impunity. Within the hip-hop castle, however, they were competitors vying for the same subjects, a core ghetto audience that demanded crime and sex from their rap-industry stars, in art as in life. But they also did socially minded activities. Suge hosted Mother's Day celebrations and sponsored Christmas toy giveaways, Gabriel read. And Tupac had his own milk-and-honey stuff, such as his ode to mothers in the song "Dear Mama." In another song, "I Ain't Mad at Cha," Tupac encouraged kids to ignore negativity and rise above the hood. But take away those assaults, the cop shootings, that prison time: Without all that crazy shit to woo the illest, Tupac, like South Park Mexican, would've had no stage, would've been no nigger for the times.

The bad, Gabriel decided, made the good possible.

When he came out of prison and joined Death Row, Tupac's idea was to maintain a friendship with Suge but slowly separate his business from Death Row and start his own label, Makaveli Records, the name inspired by his prison reading of Machiavelli's *The Prince*. Unwinding the business relationship with Suge was difficult. That prospect faded when Tupac's first album on the Death Row label, *All Eyez on Me*, earned $10 million in its first week, second only—at the time—to *The Beatles Anthology* as the best commercial opening in history. But, Gabriel read, Tupac remained determined to cut loose. He relied more on his East Coast attorney, a Harvard professor, and fired Death Row's lawyer.

The Tyson fight in Vegas was ten days later.

The book maintained that everything about Tupac's murder was strange. In a typical drive-by, the shooter's car pulled up alongside the victim's car, such that both passenger and driver were in the line of fire. It also made the getaway easier. But the Cadillac pulled in *front* of Suge's BMW. The shooter had a frontal shot at Tupac, and *only* Tupac. The murder appeared, at first, to be retaliation for an attack Tupac made on a Crips gang member earlier that night, as Tupac and Suge were leaving the Tyson fight. The book suggested that Suge staged the altercation to create the appearance of a motive.

Blood in, blood out, Gabriel thought.

Well, he didn't admire Tupac any less. But Gabriel's own code was different. If he used to think of himself as independent, he'd matured into a soldier, a Company man—more than a mere Wolf Boy—and now he lived by the principles of duty and loyalty. *Por y sobre la verga.* For and about the idea. Anything within the business was nothing more than business. Do the job and make yourself valuable, he had always told himself. And he did. Big brother Mike would be there, he had assured himself, and he was right.

The law kept letting him out, the Company kept paying for it. What clearer validation could there be?

His leadership skills were impeccable. With those Wolf Boys beneath him in the hierarchy, he was generous but stern. He respected authority. He listened first, then spoke. He knew the organization. He knew who controlled each plaza in Mexico. He knew, for instance, that Cancún was up for grabs, and that he was a contender to run it. Mexico would be easier. A beachside plaza of his own. He and Christina living like royalty among a crew of his closest homies.

He slept.

The next day, Richard and another Wolf Boy came by with news. Alfonso "Poncho" Aviles, a sixteen-year-old whom Gabriel remembered from school, had joined the Sinaloa Cartel and was recruiting other kids from Laredo.

Gabriel called Meme, who said, "Find out who he works with and what he does."

Gabriel, Richard, and the third Wolf Boy, who knew Poncho, went to Poncho's house and passed themselves off as fellow

Sinaloans. Poncho mentioned the names of a few prospective recruits, then a suspicious relative came outside and the Wolf Boys left. A few minutes later, Poncho called. He said he knew that they were really working with Forty, and that if he ever saw them again, it wasn't going to be nice.

No, Gabriel agreed: It wasn't.

THE SIX WEEKS GABRIEL SPENT in jail during February and March were not a waste. They were a write-off. He met a young man named Pantera, who was in jail because his brother-in-law, Chuy Resendez, betrayed him. The Sinaloa-allied Chuy controlled the trafficking routes through Rio Bravo, the Texas border town just east of Laredo.

Chuy would be a hard kill, a trophy for any rising Company man. Cooking Chuy would all but guarantee Gabriel's promotion. So when Pantera made bail, a week after Gabriel made bail, Gabriel and Richard asked Pantera to get a picture of Chuy. Richard blew the picture up on a Xerox machine, and the three of them drove across to meet with Miguel.

Surrounded by ten gunmen wearing bulletproof vests and armed with AR-15s, Miguel greeted Gabriel, Richard, and Pantera, and invited them into his Porsche Cayenne.

"Okay," Miguel said. "How much is it going to be?" He looked back at Gabriel and Richard, awaiting a number. When Gabriel didn't speak, Richard said: "Fifty for us and forty for Pantera?"

Miguel agreed: $50,000 would be split between Gabriel and Richard, and $40,000 would be paid to Pantera for setting up Chuy. Pantera would alert the Wolf Boys when Chuy was in town, tell them where he stayed, and who he was going to visit.

As Richard and Gabriel exited the Porsche, Miguel said, "Hey, Gaby. There's another group over there trying to locate Chuy. Meet up with them, use them however you want. You run it, but stay back. Me entiendes?" *Understand?*

"Sí, Comandante," Gabriel said, and ran off.

Later that day, they met the six other Zeta assassins in a park in Siete Viejo to coordinate their protocol. Then Gabriel, with Pantera, went out scouting for Chuy in the Dodge Ram while Richard and several Wolf Boys from "the B team," the "chukkies," waited at a safe house. Pantera and Gabriel relayed Chuy's movements to Richard and the others: Chuy's truck was on Highway 83. Richard and the Wolf Boys ran out to a green Chevrolet pickup and sped away from the safe house.

Armed with a 9 mm, Richard lay down in the bed of the pickup, between two boys with AK-47s. The driver spotted Resendez's truck on 83, pulled next to it, then pulled ahead. When the boy in the passenger seat of the pickup began to shoot, Richard and the two in back popped up like skeletons from a grave and shredded Chuy's Suburban with more than ninety rounds. Chuy's truck slowed, then coasted away, crossed lanes, and stopped when it hit a wrong-way sign.

Later that day, Sunday night, Gabriel and Richard showered, picked up Richard's wife, and went cruising on San Bernardo Avenue.

On Monday, Miguel and Meme invited Gabriel and Richard to Nuevo Laredo for lunch. It was Gabriel's biggest commission yet: $50,000 to be split between him and Richard. Gabriel would take $30,000 and Richard would get $20,000.

At the meeting with Miguel, they bantered about business. Two months after Fito's death, Miguel still bemoaned the loss of his little brother. "It wasn't fair," he kept saying. "Fito wasn't involved." Gabriel sympathized. But Richard thought: How many innocent people have *you* killed, Miguel? Weren't *you* the one who started all this family stuff? Killing children no older than ten?

Miguel wanted to know if they'd located Robert Garcia yet.

Gabriel said he knew Robert's schedule, where he lived, even where his son played hockey; knew his Jeep and had memorized the license plate. He also knew, but didn't say, that killing an American cop got you sent "straight to the chair."

The detective, Miguel said, was worth $500,000.

J. J. GOMEZ AND CHRIS Diaz fumed.

They'd made a lot of promises to a lot of people. Funding was laid out. Angel Moreno backed them. As far as confidential sources, they didn't consider the death of Chuy Resendez a major loss. They had several sources within the Zetas; Rocky was the closest one to the cartel's top commanders. But if Operation Prophecy failed now, because *their* informant got locked out, well, Diaz and Gomez would be Fucking New Guys forever. They berated Rocky.

"We're not losing our careers over this!"

"Get them in the fucking house!"

Calm under pressure, Rocky ran scenarios through his head, discarding those that seemed likely to end with him being tortured and killed. He thought back to the day when his body lay broken in a Nuevo Laredo stash house, and Omar Treviño was seconds away from putting a bullet in his head. On that day, it was Iván Velásquez-Caballero, the Zeta leader known as Talivan, who saved Rocky's life.

So, on the morning of Saturday, April 8, 2006, Rocky called Talivan. He mentioned that he was waiting to hear from a commander about a safe house, and wondered if Talivan had heard anything about it. Thirty minutes later, Rocky's phone rang. The commander told him to meet two guys in the parking lot of Best Buy, just east of I-35.

And just like that, Operation Prophecy was back. The federal, state, and local agencies mobilized. The DEA techs booted up the wire room at the main DEA office, on Shiloh Drive, and rechecked all the wire equipment that had been installed at the safe house on Orange Blossom Loop, a quiet suburban street on Laredo's north side. DEA planes were reserved if needed. Four marked PD squad cars would be on standby, plus a dozen unmarked units. Two SWAT teams, one from PD and one from the sheriff's office, would alternate eight-hour shifts, hanging out in a DEA conference room set up with cots and food. A DEA tractor-trailer, rigged with cameras and microphones, would handle mobile surveillance of the house and the hit men.

At 2 p.m. on Saturday, Diaz and Gomez followed Rocky to the meeting at Best Buy, but couldn't get close enough to see the two guys that Rocky gave the keys to.

Rocky escorted the assassins to the safe house, a white-brick rambler on Orange Blossom Loop, nestled inconspicuously in suburbia.

Back in the wire room, at the DEA office on Shiloh Drive, less than a mile away, three screens displayed three camera feeds. The first camera, installed above the safe house garage and facing outward, showed the house's driveway and the street in front of it. The second screen showed the kitchen, with a white Formica island in the middle, cabinets above it, and a breakfast nook with a small table overlooking the lawn and the house next door. The third screen showed the furniture-free living room. Microphones picked up everything, except in the bathroom and bedrooms. The cell phone of everyone in the safe house would also soon be tapped.

As Operation Prophecy got under way, there was no reason to think Gabriel Cardona figured in the sting. Such were the vagaries of Laredo's bail protocol that no one even knew Gabriel had walked out of jail three weeks earlier. From the wire room, Robert and the agents watched the assassins enter their new pad and settle in.

"Holy shit!" Robert said. "That's the guy I've been arresting all year!"

27

Catch That Pussy

S hit, Rocky thought, where *are* they?

After getting the keys from Rocky at Best Buy, and going to inspect the house on Orange Blossom Loop, Gabriel told Rocky, "We'll come back later." Then Gabriel and Richard drove to Mexico, and Team Prophecy lost contact with them.

Now midnight approached, and Rocky, dressed in a striped button-down shirt and baggy shorts, paced the living room of the empty safe house. Rocky's primary role in Operation Prophecy was to keep the Wolf Boys in sight, and try to report their movements before they moved—duties he'd already messed up. He could almost hear Diaz and Gomez screaming at him from the wire room: *Fucking call them! Find out where they are!*

Rocky called Gabriel, and tried to sound casual. "Qué onda, güey?" *What's up, dude?*

"Nothing," Gabriel said. "What's up with you?"

"Nothing. I'm just here at the house. You haven't told me to do anything."

"Well, we're already working. We're gonna do a job, *güey*. But we already have the group ready."

"What do I do?"

"Well, nothing. We already have everything. Everything's very well organized."

"All right," Rocky said. "I'll be here." He wanted to ask, "Where's the job?" but restrained himself from a question that might sound suspicious coming from a mere concierge.

Gabriel hung up.

Then Gabriel called back. "Listen, *güey*. There is a mission for you. The job we're on is like this: There's a blue Hummer parked outside Cosmos. A blue Hummer. Outside Cosmos. We need someone watching for the *vato* who's gonna be walking toward the Hummer. You watch for him." Gabriel explained that as soon as Rocky spotted the *vato*, the guy, approaching the blue Hummer, he was supposed to call the Wolf Boy doing the job. "I'll give you his number. You call and say, 'Hey! The *vato* is getting into his truck! The *vato* is getting into his truck!'"

"All right," Rocky said, heading outside to his car so he could speed over to Cosmos Bar & Grill. "Trae juguete?"—did he bring a toy?

"He already has a toy," Gabriel confirmed. "He already has a toy."

"GUN," ROBERT TOLD THE WIRE room. "Toy means gun."

Robert headed down to the DEA parking lot. The console of his Jeep Cherokee was full of radios, one each from FBI, DEA, and Laredo PD. He ordered ten unmarked units stationed near the safe house to head toward Cosmos Bar & Grill. Then he drove there.

There were two driveways in and out of the Cosmos lot, an unmarked unit parked near each. Another unit located the blue Hummer, parked nearby. A six-man SWAT team stationed itself in an armored vehicle a quarter mile away, behind some water tanks. Robert hid himself in a lot across the street, behind a standalone Sprint store: headlights off, AC on. He listened to his three radios.

Within two minutes, an unmarked unit reported that it spotted men who fit the descriptions of the *sicarios* from the safe house.

"How about Cardona?" Robert asked.

"Negative. Don't see him yet."

Outside Robert's car, traffic cruised by. Cosmos was part of the nightclub strip in central Laredo—including Tonic and District and F-Bar. Lots of SUVs and pickup trucks came and went.

Every second vehicle in Laredo was a pickup.

A pickup came by that moved more slowly than the others. The blue Dodge Ram held up traffic, oblivious to the cars accumulating behind it. The driver of the Ram rubbernecked at Cosmos but didn't pull into the lot.

Instead, the driver of the Ram pulled into a lot kitty-corner to the one Robert was in, and parked near a bank, backing into the spot so the nose of the Ram pointed at Cosmos. The driver was young, looked about twenty, wore a black Polo golf shirt and khakis.

"I got him," Robert said.

Gabriel was on his phone, using the push-button walkie-talkie function. A slight delay, then the wire room relayed Gabriel's call back to Robert.

"Mackey is the one we're going to kill," Gabriel told Rocky, who was now parked near Cosmos as well. *"Before Mackey gets into his truck, you call J.P. and you tell him, 'There goes Mackey, there goes Mackey! He's the one wearing such and such!'"*

"J.P. is the only one I'm supposed to call? Just him?"

258

"Yes, just him. He'll do the job, and then another guy will be waiting around the corner for the getaway."

Okay, Robert thought, they had enough on this attempted murder: *Mackey is the one we're going to kill.*

Robert ordered two marked cop cars to pull into the Cosmos lot, flash their lights, and sit there. The squad cars would spook Cardona, make him cancel the job.

The squad cars pulled into the Cosmos lot and flashed their light. Gabriel didn't move.

Robert watched Gabriel watch the cop cars. Gabriel got back on his radio.

The wire room relayed the call to Robert. Gabriel wanted his crew to stay in place until Mackey left Cosmos. They would let Mackey get into his blue Hummer, let him drive away, then follow him. They would each take turns tailing him for a little while, then drop back and let the other take the lead, like cyclists in a peloton. They would do so, Gabriel instructed, until Mackey got somewhere isolated, alone. And then Gabriel would kill Mackey himself.

Sixty minutes passed. The nightclub cleared out. It was 2 a.m.

The owner of the blue Hummer pushed through the doors. His eyes took a moment to adjust to the halogen lamps in the parking lot. He climbed into the Hummer. When he turned the ignition, Robert issued an order to the squad cars: "Pull Mackey over as soon as he hits the road."

The wire room conveyed another conversation to Robert.

"What's up, güey?" Gabriel asked. *"Where's the Hummer going?"*

"He's coming out through the north side," Rocky said. *"The north side. He's leaving the lot. But, um, there are two cop cars behind him."*

"The north side? Like he's heading toward Del Mar?"

"Yeah, yeah, yeah. The north side. But be careful, man. The cop cars are right behind him."

"Okay, I'm headed over there."

"*He's parked!*" Rocky said. "*The police pulled him over!*"

"*Qué onda?!*"

"*Pinche puto!*" Rocky said. "*This culero is very lucky.*"

"*Let's wait and see if they let him leave.*"

"*All right. I'm watching everything. It looks like they're arresting the guy! It looks like they're handcuffing him, like they're gonna take the puto away. Do you think he was drunk or what?*"

A TOW TRUCK CAME AND hauled the Hummer away. The Wolf Boys departed.

Robert walked across the street to the squad car, and looked in back. The man inside was not Mackey. He was a local dentist who looked a little like Mackey and owned a blue Hummer that looked just like Mackey's. The dentist was apoplectic over why his car was being towed while he sat in a police cruiser. Robert said some hit men almost killed him. "We arrested you to protect you."

"It's my fucking wife, isn't it?!" the dentist screamed. The dentist's wife had nothing to do with it, Robert assured him. "She must have hired them! I know it! We're going through a divorce. She wants me dead!"

BACK IN THE WIRE ROOM, the main members of Team Prophecy collapsed on the couches, highly emotional after the close call: *What the fuck just happened?*

For them, the only thing worse than getting "burned"—having the bad guys find out about the investigation, and split—was getting someone killed. Operation Prophecy, they realized now, would be no typical wiretap investigation, where you could use your informant to wield some control over the criminals' actions. The boys had their own agenda, and would do whatever they wanted.

Team Prophecy decided to keep the operation going, so they could record conversations between Gabriel and Company leaders in Mexico, and so Rocky could find out who else was on the hit list. They would have to be in a reactive mode constantly. Only twelve hours had passed since they gave Cardona the keys to the safe house. How long could they keep up with these kids?

THAT NIGHT, GABRIEL AND RICHARD went looking for an old and familiar target on Miguel's list, Mike Lopez, at Taco Palenque, where many in Laredo went after the bars closed, but they couldn't find him. Driving north on I-35, Richard noticed they were being followed by an unmarked car, a white Ford Explorer. Richard sped away. The Explorer followed. Richard exited the highway, made a U-turn beneath the underpass, and got on I-35 heading south. He stepped on it, exited at Saunders Street, called ahead to a friend who lived nearby, asked him to open his front gate, and a few minutes later Richard and Gabriel pulled into a driveway and shut off their lights.

"Lost them," Gabriel said.

The Explorer drove by slowly.

"Fuck!" Richard said.

"The FBI must be investigating the kids," Gabriel said, referring to Poncho Aviles and the other Laredo teen, both Sinaloans, whom Gabriel and Richard kidnapped from a Nuevo Laredo nightclub a week earlier. Gabriel shrugged it off. Those murders were done on the other side, he assured Richard, so it didn't matter.

Still, the tail made Richard skittish. "We're calling too much attention to ourselves," Richard said. He wanted to call it a night and go to Nuevo Laredo while the heat cooled.

"You catching that pussy, man," Gabriel said. "Let's do this job."

Gabriel and Richard had never differed so openly. The argument's subtext was clear. During their younger years in Lazteca, Richard had the money and the power. He was the boss. Now the roles had reversed. Deep down, Richard was angry at himself. Six months earlier, he got into the killings for what seemed liked a good reason: to meet Miguel Treviño and get back to smuggling.

In recent months, Richard and Miguel had had many conversations about Richard getting back into logistics with a start-up grant and all the cocaine he could move. Miguel trusted Richard because Richard was with Gabriel. Every time they saw each other, Miguel asked if Richard was ready to start a new smuggling operation. Richard always invented an excuse. The real reason being that the assassin's power to instill fear had sapped his ambition to work hard and make real money again. Fear, over the long term, might be a weaker power than money, but in some ways it was a more addictive one. It was one thing to have money and be able to get out of a jam with Mexican authorities. But you still had to go by their rules. Because enemies might have *more* money, and therefore more power over the cops. Whereas the power of fear meant running off cops without paying them. The privilege to humiliate had seduced Richard, and he'd lost his way.

"We're looking for a fucking ghost," Richard said. "I'm done for today."

Then Gabriel's phone rang. It was Meme Flores calling from Mexico. Meme explained that there were two young Company men in Nuevo Laredo who were taking their weekly salaries but never doing jobs. They needed to be disciplined. Could Gabriel handle it? In an endless war, the enforcer's work was never done. Yes, Gabriel said, he could do it.

"Okay," he told Richard, "you get your wish. Take us across."

Later, Richard stayed in Mexico to continue partying. Gabriel returned to the safe house on Orange Blossom Loop in the predawn hours. It had been a long night. He slept.

SUNDAY PASSED WITHOUT ACTIVITY. ON Monday, the third day in the safe house, Robert watched the boys. None of the bedrooms had cameras. But he could imagine Gabriel sleeping on the deluxe air mattress bought at Wal-Mart. While plainclothes officers followed them through the aisles earlier that day, the boys bought bedding, kitchen utensils, and a triangular cabinet for the old TV—the singular living room item furnished by the U.S. government.

At noon, the Wolf Boys woke up and Gabriel went into his neat-freak mode, putting each associate on a task: clean the kitchen, the bathroom, find a mower and cut the lawn, assemble the TV stand. This place was going to be a "straight house," he told them, not a dump. They would all learn to respect what they'd been given. He unwrapped the kitchen utensils, filled a drawer, went to the garage, and came back with an armful of Martha Stewart towels, new white ones with stripes, some of which he hung on the rack and the rest he distributed around to the other Wolf Boys.

Now, in his bedroom—where Robert could hear but not see—Gabriel tried to make up with Christina on the phone.

"Are you busy or what?" she asked.

He could hear his underlings working away in the garage. "I'm cleaning the car," Gabriel said into the phone. "What's up, love?"

"I was checking in because you haven't called."

"All right."

An uncomfortable silence.

"Help me be strong, Gabriel," she finally said with a heave. "I don't have anyone else. You don't understand how I feel when you don't call me! It just feels so . . . terrible!"

Gabriel's renewed dedication to his Company work, specifically this killing spree in Texas, put major stress on their relationship. She'd call him about plans and he'd say, "You don't understand! I'm working!" "But you said we were going to be together!" "Fine! I'll come get you!" And Gabriel would come get her, and they'd go somewhere for fast food and Gabriel would bitch at her to reorganize the pickles on his burger, to lay them out evenly so that there was one pickle for each bite.

She could no longer claim ignorance of his work. Not since the recent night he returned from Mexico and removed his black Versace shirt, which hung so attractively over the late-adolescent bulk. She noticed it was splattered red. A rumor floated: Two kids from Laredo were taken from the Eclipse night club in Nuevo Laredo, beaten, and stewed in the *guiso*. Shacked up at another hotel, Gabriel asked Christina if she wanted a new car. She said she'd love a new car. She could have any car she wanted, he said, so long as she helped him deliver La Barbie's head in a box. "What the fuck, Gabriel!" she yelled. "What?" he shrugged. She clucked her tongue against the roof of her mouth, what she did when she was sad. They could be good together, strong, she thought, but the Company was coming between them, and she was tired of it.

"You know sometimes I can't call," Gabriel now told her on the wiretapped phone. "I've been busy. And if you don't believe me, just look at Chuy Resendez."

She breathed deeply, exasperated. "I know. I don't want to know." She said someone was offering a thousand dollars for information about the murder. "I understand you're busy, Gabriel. But when you love somebody, like really love them, you try to make at least a little bit of time to call. At least a little bit of time. I fucking love you!"

They agreed to meet for dinner in two days. She said be careful. They hung up.

IN THE WIRE ROOM, DIAZ and Gomez rolled on the floor. Robert chuckled. They could almost empathize. The kid would do life because his girlfriend was lonely.

28

Twilight

A Big Gulp sat on the kitchen island, in the house on Orange Blossom Loop, and each boy sipped from it as they milled around and constructed the TV stand purchased at Wal-Mart.

Gabriel pulled up his shirt and showed off a new back tattoo of Santa Muerte, the Goddess of Death: a hooded skull holding a scythe and globe. The scythe symbolized the cutting of negative energies. As a harvesting tool it also stood for prosperity. The skull represented death's dominion over the earth, while the globe meant both power and oblivion, the tomb to which they all would return. During Gabriel's most recent stint in the Webb County jail, he'd become a Santa Muerte devotee. When he first arrived at the jail in early February, the guards housed him in a segregated unit. He prayed to Santa Muerte. The next day, the guards moved him to the tanks. He prayed to her again, this time for the lawyer to come, then discovered that David Almaraz was on his way. He prayed for a bond reduction and got it. Now the boys took turns rubbing the tattoo. They agreed it was cool.

Gabriel sat on the living room floor, his back against the wall, and chatted with Rocky.

"Qué onda?" Rocky asked. *What's up?*

"Esperando que cruzen los dos sicarios . . . entonces Checo," Gabriel replied: *Waiting for the two hit men to cross over . . . then Checo.*

"Checo?" Rocky confirmed for the benefit of the wire room.

"Sí."

"En qué area vive?" Rocky asked: *What area does he live in?*

Gabriel said: "Hmm, chingado, no sé." *Hmm, shit, I don't know.* "Todavía a no me dicen. Nomás me dijeron, 'Consigue los muebles, y los sicarios listos, y los fierros.'" *They still haven't told me. They just told me, "Get the vehicles and the hit men ready, and the guns."*

Gabriel mentioned other targets, including Mike Lopez, and said there were a total of forty targets, several of whom had already been killed.

Rocky nodded, then said: "Si quieres, yo me puedo encargar de ubicar la gente. Tú nomás me dices va a hacer éste y éste y éste." *If you want, I can take charge of locating the people. You just tell me it's going to be this one, and this one, and this one.*

"Simon," Gabriel said: *Right on.*

"Porque no puedes salir muchas veces, hijo," Rocky added: *Because you can't go out too much, son.*

"Yo sé. Pero con Checo ahorita ya está en corto. No hay pedo." *I know. But right now Checo is about to happen. There's no problem.*

Rocky asked how Checo would be killed, and Gabriel explained: "Mike dijo: 'Como tu pienses . . . Mientras ustedes lo hagan bien.'" *Mike said: "However you want . . . As long as you guys do it well."* Gabriel said that because he'd heard Checo was very trusting, he thought that whoever killed Checo could simply yell Checo's name—"Hey, Checo!"—then walk up to his car and shoot him.

Rocky asked what cars Gabriel needed. Gabriel said he needed a used car that cost around five thousand dollars—a car with front-wheel drive and an eight-cylinder engine. An Alero, Gabriel said, would be a good car for doing hits because bystanders often confuse Aleros with Mustangs. Rocky suggested a car that doesn't call attention to itself, something "chiquito y tranquilo pero bueno y efectivo"—*small and calm, but good and effective.* Rocky suggested putting bumper stickers on it, maybe political stickers or kids' stickers, as cover.

Gabriel's phone rang. He stood up, answered the call, and paced. He spoke to Wolf Boy associates based in another Laredo safe house about locating a target named Tiofo.

ROBERT SCRIBBLED DOWN ALL THE names Gabriel mentioned, including "Tiofo," and wondered: How did he know Tiofo? *Ah, yes!* A hit man for La Barbie, Tiofo had given Robert the Barbie Execution Video the previous summer.

Robert sent out a list of the targets to Laredo PD, with instructions to contact the targets and their families. It was a start. But what about the other targets on the list? There were forty?

LATER THAT DAY, GABRIEL TRIED to put together a small cocaine deal. Between gifts to his family and friends, and his Company-related work expenses, which often weren't reimbursed, the money from the Chuy Resendez job was already gone. Gabriel had sent his buddy, a minor Wolf Boy named Camacho, to pick up ten ounces of coke from a Laredo dealer. First Camacho called to say that the scale had run out of battery power and blah blah blah. Then Camacho called and said it was only just over four ounces.

"What do you mean four?" Gabriel asked. "Why are you saying that?"

"Four ounces, dude."

"Four?"

"It's like four plus a little, but I hope—"

"I'm not going to work with you anymore if you are going to be doing this shit. Now, we came up with ten ounces. So don't come with that shit that there are four. As a matter of fact, I'm going to call him right now, and if he gives me his word that there were ten—"

"No, man, wait! I mean there are nine and three-eighths. Almost ten. I was saying four because I already have five for you in another glass I already weighed."

Gabriel shook his head. Did these *pendejos* think they were smarter than him? "All right, call me later so I know how much it is exactly."

Camacho laughed. "You almost had a heart attack, dude."

"All right."

"You were going to kill me."

When the coke arrived, Gabriel wanted his driver, Chapa, to mule it to Dallas on a bus. A buyer would give $5,000 for ten ounces, a $3,000 profit. They discussed how Chapa could hide the coke during an eight-hour bus ride.

"Stuff it down my pants?"

"Nah."

"Between the seat cushions?"

"I know," Gabriel said, grabbing the Big Gulp. "You wrap it up really tight, like *water*tight, and hide the coke in the Coke. That way, when they pull the bus over for checks, you can just carry the cup out and keep sipping."

The boys liked it. Had Richard been there, he would've rolled his eyes. Ten ounces? That was personal use. Why risk a case for such a small score? Shit, even DEA would laugh at that.

IN THE WIRE ROOM, ROBERT smirked. If he were a doper, he'd rent a house in Laredo under a false name, furnish it, fill the furniture with drugs, then hire a moving company to take the furniture to an apartment in New York. He never heard of anyone doing it. Maybe it would work.

He took a break while Diaz and Gomez jotted notes on the drug stuff. Conspiracy to traffic. More charges. More years.

Behind them, hanging on the wall, was a whiteboard with a couple dozen photos attached. On top was Miguel Treviño. Below were members of Gabriel's crew—some of them flunkies, like Chapa, some of them bona fide Wolf Boys. Robert had drawn lines from Gabriel, in the middle of the board, to various Zeta superiors. In addition to foiling the hits, the goal in the coming days would be to use wiretaps to bolster connections within the hierarchy, and come away with enough evidence not simply to put Gabriel away for good but to indict the top of the hierarchy as well.

On the morning of the fourth day, Robert woke to the ping of a new call on the wire. He knew the voice on the other end. When a guy threatened your family, you never forgot his voice.

"I just started here and already several people got whacked," Bart reported to Gabriel. "It's like, 'Hey, kill that guy,' and *poom*!"

Bart was in Mexico traveling with Miguel's *escolta*. Bart said he was resting, playing video games on Xbox 360, and smoking weed while he tended to a nasty wound. During a raid the previous day, he had shot himself in the leg with an armor-piercing bullet.

"We were like seven cars armored. I was in a nice green Marquis. We were cruising around and then we arrived at the house. I got off and went inside through the back. I had *piñas,* the whole shit. They were all on the ground. It was awesome. Bang! Bang! Then the rats came. I took off in a hurry. My leg felt hot. I looked down. It's one of those holes where I'm missing flesh from my leg!" Bart laughed hysterically. "I'm missing flesh from my leg, dude. That says it all!"

Gabriel said: "I'm going to go there and you'll see the sweeping I'm going to make. In the meantime I'm going to continue here a little longer. By the way, have you seen Richard over there?"

"Negative."

"He's been gone two days. If he doesn't come back he's a deserter." There was a pause. "The good thing is that I haven't done anything, dude. We have heat. But things are calm right now because we are just hiding. Once we go out, that's it: bang, bang, bang. We do the action. I don't do anything. I direct on the radio. 'The guy's here.' 'He's there.' 'Get off and shoot him down.' Richard and the one from Dallas, J.P., they are going to be doing the killing. I know those are sure shots."

Gabriel and Bart filled each other in on their living situations. Gabriel said his room was smaller than the others, but fancier. "What do I need a big room for if I don't have much furniture?"

They talked about guns, bullets, and vests. They discussed the virtues of the FN Herstal, the gun that many Company men had been given. The flat trajectory of the 5.7x28 mm bullet all but guaranteed a hit in close-quarter scenarios, plus it had a low recoil. Bart yawned. He said it freaked him out, what a .50-caliber bullet did to someone's head.

Bart asked about the status of a debt that Gabriel owed him. Gabriel was supposed to repay the debt out of the Chuy Resendez money. He explained: "Shit, dude. I spent it. There were fifty. I gave twenty to Richard. I had thirty left. I spent four, five, six, seven, eight on the Mercedes—for a grill, bumper, fan, fog lights, and a new paint job. From the remaining twenty-two I gave one thousand to Chapa and one to my little brother. So that's twenty. From those twenty I bought two thousand worth of clothes. That's eighteen. I spent on hotels. That's fourteen. Of those fourteen I gave ten to my mother. I have four left. From those four I used two to buy the ten ounces. So let's say for now that I only have two thousand."

Bart was suspicious that Gabriel was holding out on him but accepted the explanation. Gabriel asked if Bart heard about the Sinaloan teens, Poncho Aviles and Inez Villareal, whom Richard and Gabriel kidnapped from the Eclipse nightclub.

"Nah. Where did you cook them?"

"That house on Kilometer 14. You should've seen Poncho. He was crying like a faggot. 'No, man, I'm your friend.' 'What friend, you son of a bitch, shut your mouth.' And *poom*! I grabbed a fucking bottle and *slash*! I slitted his whole fucking belly. I grabbed a little cup and filled it with blood and *poom*! I dedicated it to my holy death, to my Santa Muerte. And then I went to the other faggot and *slash*!" Gabriel said he believed the FBI was getting involved, but that wasn't a problem because the murders were done on the other side.

The conversation shifted to Company leadership. Bart said Miguel and Omar turned up at the safe house where Bart was healing and showed everyone an updated hit list, including more people they believed were involved in the killing of Fito. Gabriel and Bart complained about Miguel, about how he didn't always respect them but always came back later calling them "brother" when he wanted something.

"Ask El Comandante if you can come back here," Gabriel said. "Tell him I've got the next *punto* lined up," referring to the Sinaloan smuggler known as Checo. "If you want, you can help."

ROBERT, HIS EYES RAW FROM lack of sleep, walked to the whiteboard, stepping over burger wrappers and pizza boxes. He uncapped a marker, drew lines from Miguel Treviño to Omar Treviño to Meme Flores and other Company brass mentioned by code in the call. The lines between the Wolf Boys and their Mexican bosses were firming up.

But there was a problem: Miguel's hit list contained forty targets, possibly more. Operation Prophecy would never learn them all through wiretaps alone. From now on, it would be a constant cost-benefit analysis: How much was more information about the cartel and their targets worth against the risk of letting Gabriel and his crew run around Laredo? Cosmos had been a too-close call; they didn't need another one.

What they wanted, most, was a conversation between Gabriel and Miguel, and on the fourth day in the safe house—Tuesday, April 11—they got it.

"WHAT'S GOING ON, MAN?" MIGUEL asked Gabriel over the phone.

"I bought the two vehicles on the other side," Gabriel said, referring to cars he bought in Mexico. "One is a green Malibu, the other a white Marquis."

"And who is it going to be?" Miguel asked, referring to who would kill the next target, Checo. *Who's my man?*

"I'm one *sicario* short," Gabriel said, referring to Richard, who hadn't yet returned from Mexico. "But if you want, we can do Checo right now."

"Let me see," Miguel said: *Show me what you've got.*

"Okay. Once I put together the *cuadro*"—the team—"I'll call you to let you know that we are on our way there."

GABRIEL HEADED OUT TO PICK up Christina from school and have an early dinner. At Applebee's, he apologized for not calling more. "I do love you," he said, "it's just work."

"I know. I don't want to talk about that anymore." They ordered orange sodas and waited for their sandwiches. She mentioned she'd heard people refer to him as "Comandante Gaby."

This information delighted Gabriel. It could only mean that Miguel was talking about Gabriel coming up in the Company.

His phone rang. A Wolf Boy at the safe house reported that two guys had just knocked on the door: "One tall. One short and chubby. The short one was dark-skinned, had glasses. I think it might have been Robert!"

"Don't worry," Gabriel assured him. "It wasn't Robert. The cops have no idea where I am." The men waited, knocked again, waited some more, knocked a third time, then walked away.

The associate confirmed it wasn't Robert. "I think they were actually real estate men because they were wearing ties and long-sleeve shirts."

It was a nice April day. Gabriel and Christina drove to Lake Casa Blanca, and took a stroll in the park that surrounded the lake just south of the TAMIU campus, where University president Ray Keck lectured on *One Hundred Years of Solitude* in the original Spanish, and Isaiah Berlin's view of Machiavelli. The teen lovers walked in and out of the reedy peninsulas that jutted into the water. Gabriel told her about how he and his Lazteca hoodies, whenever they got some money, used to come to the lake, back in the day, rent *lanchitas,* little airboats, and make carne asada. Nostalgic, they shared a shivery kiss.

"Don't worry," she said, "I haven't told anybody. I play dumb. I don't even want to know." She sighed, clucked her tongue. "I like fighting together, Gabriel. But the Zetas are starting to hurt."

"I know, my love. But I have to keep helping him. What can I do? There is nothing I can do with this man. That's the way it is, Christina."

The reeds blew against their jeans. He told her he had a new place and wanted to bring her to live there.

When he dropped her off at home, he gave her five hundred dollars. He'd call soon and tell her when to pack. They hugged. "Tighter," she said.

A COUPLE OF HOURS LATER, when Gabriel and Richard finally spoke on the phone, Gabriel said he'd been looking for Richard for a long time. "I hope I'm not disturbing you," Gabriel said sarcastically.

"I'm here at La Quinta," Richard said, referring to the Laredo hotel where he'd been entertaining weekend girls.

"Well, they called and . . . Checo."

"All right," Richard said, and told Gabriel he'd come back to the safe house. On his way, he stopped for a quick dinner at Subway, and, while eating, saw one of the Orange Blossom crew drive by in the white Marquis. The Marquis, Richard saw, was being followed by a white Explorer. He called Gabriel about the tail, but Gabriel told Richard that he was being paranoid. "Man, you catching that pussy again."

At the safe house, with Richard finally back, the Wolf Boys circulated in and out of the kitchen, swinging their arms, touching their toes. Two of them wiped the cars down. The cars had fake tags, paper dealer plates filled out with random sequences of numbers and letters.

Stalking the house with quick steps, the Wolf Boys readied themselves for the evening's work.

In slacks and a new white Polo shirt, Gabriel stood in the kitchen and squared up his newest recruit. The kid, J.P., had come from Dallas with no clothes, so Gabriel lent him a *Scarface* T-shirt. He gave the kid a last-minute tutorial: "You walk up to him and just *poom!* *En la cabezota*. But with both hands. In the crown, *poom!* You'll fuck him up. Otherwise, *poom! poom! poom! poom!* Four in the chest. And then *en la cabezota,* to make sure."

They were young and vigorous, fiery in their belief of success.

"It's time to take care of business!" Gabriel yelled to the group, clapping encouragement.

Everything was ready. This was it. This was the beginning of something.

CHRISTINA WENT TO THE MALL with the five hundred dollars, bought shirts and shoes and earrings, then went home to take a nap. She dreamed of packing a suitcase and joining him for a new life. A life in which promises were kept and men didn't disappear. A life in which people respected faith and worked hard to get closer to God.

Awaking in twilight, she called his phone, like pinching herself, to make sure it was real. No one answered.

ROBERT CONSIDERED THE OPTIONS. THEY had hoped to keep the wire going for longer, but the kids were too active.

Well, he had what he needed. They all did. So as dusk settled, he dispatched a SWAT team to Orange Blossom Loop, then headed for the parking lot a minute before the wire room's main screen whited out in an incandescent blaze.

A COMMOTION OUTSIDE, BOOTS, LOUD voices, a slamming: BANG!

In the kitchen, Richard and Gabriel met eyes: Richard shaking his head in disappointment—*I told you so*—Gabriel in disbelief.

A stun grenade came through the front door. The concussive blast disturbed the fluid in Gabriel's ears. He wobbled. A bright flash bleached the photoreceptors in his eyes, making vision impossible for three seconds. *One. Two. Three.* He was facedown on the carpet, hands cuffed behind him. He thought he might die. He thought he might get out of it. The world of possibility was vast.

Then he heard that familiar voice. "How you doing, Gaby?" And he knew his outcomes had been reduced to one.

SHE CALLED AGAIN AND AGAIN but no one answered. There was a knock at her front door. Robert Garcia had two uniformed cops and a van idling. He told her that she needed to come to the station.

"But I don't know anything," she said.

He smiled. "Just look at what you're wearing," he said, referring to the clothes bought with Gabriel's murder money.

"What?" she said, looking down at herself. "They're new."

"They're covered in blood."

"TÍO?" GABRIEL SAID INTO THE phone, having called Miguel.

"Call back later," someone, not Miguel, replied. "He's busy."

"The thing is, they caught me," Gabriel said. "I don't know if they're going to lock me in. I just want to let you know."

"Who's going to lock you in?"

"The law. I'm here in the office of the law. They came and told me, 'Here, this is your radio, use it however you want. Your right is to call your relatives so they know what's up.' They raided our house. They're saying we did what happened to Chuy."

"They're just blaming you for that?"

"They haven't told me yet. The freakin' lawyer won't answer. He's got his phone turned off. They brought in my woman and they were putting pressure on her . . . like over and over . . . they wanted her to say I did that. I went rascal on them, man. I gave them a tough time."

"Listen, *güey*. Fuck them."

"They're investigating Rocky and the other buddies, too. I don't know if the others are going to say something. I was standing up to the FBI and telling them to go fuck themselves. So they put me in a room alone."

"Let them check you out. Those faggots are always making mistakes."

"Yeah. No. I'm just letting you know. But it's no problem. I'm going to call the attorney so he can get me out of here. But let Uncle Mike know. Just let my friend over there know, okay?"

PART V

Frozen in Time

For the warrior, fame was the immediate point of it all . . .
the glances of the women, the adulation of the children, the
careful respect of one-time peers.

—*AZTECS,* INGA CLENDINNEN

29

Legend of Laredo

In the office of the law, Gabriel tried a new tactic: When talking could've helped him, he said nothing, and cut no deal. Fear and prudence trumped pride. Motivated by a wish to protect his family from the Company, he decided not to contest his case, nor cut his sentence by snitching on the Zetas, and instead be the stand-up guy that Angel Moreno had rarely seen in twenty years as a prosecutor.

For his alleged roles in the murders of Bruno Orozco, Moises Garcia, Noe Flores, Chuy Resendez, and Chuy's nephew, he pleaded guilty. His three fifty-year sentences and two eighty-year sentences would all run concurrently, meaning he'd serve a total of eighty years in state prison.

As for his wiretapped confession to the murder-by-beating of the two American teens in Nuevo Laredo—Poncho Aviles and Inez Villareal—it didn't matter that no bodies or evidence had been collected, nor even that the murders occurred in Mexico. Though there were many options for charging Gabriel, Moreno let him plead guilty to one charge: a new post-9/11 federal law intended to be used against Americans who enlisted with a terrorist group and went abroad to fight. It covered the murder of an American by an American on foreign soil.

Moreno's federal indictment in Operation Prophecy named more than thirty defendants, including Miguel and Omar Treviño, Rene Garcia, and even the Black Hand, the Mexican Mafia leader.

When Gabriel and Richard appeared for their 2008 arraignment in federal court, Gabriel, having decided to plead guilty, balked a little before the judge. "I didn't know I was giving up my right to appeal in the plea bargain," he told Judge Micaela Alvarez. Judge Alvarez explained that if he didn't want to give up his right to appeal, then it was the government's right—Moreno's right—to pull the plea agreement and head to trial. Gabriel relented: "I'll go ahead and give up my right to appeal."

Judge Alvarez wanted to make sure he understood what giving up his appeal meant. "Let's say I sentence you to life, which is a possibility," she said. "You're sitting in prison. You're thinking, My lawyer didn't do a good job for me. My lawyer should've fought harder. If you file a notice of appeal—it's kind of funny to say; people still file them even though they gave up their right—the first thing the government is going to do is say, 'Hey, wait a minute, he gave up his right.' And the Fifth Circuit"—the federal court of appeals—"will say, 'Yeah, he gave up his right.' Now, the other thing I talked about, the 2255. Let's say you're sitting in prison. You're talking to prisoners. And they say, 'You know what, there is something you can file called a 2255'"—a so-called collateral attack that can be filed by a defendant within a year of sentencing. "I look at it. I say I explained all of this to him. I told him he wouldn't be able to do this. Do you understand?"

"Yes, ma'am."

Moreno then read aloud the facts that the government intended to prove if the case went to trial: the disappearances of Poncho Aviles and Inez Villareal; their murder by torture; Gabriel's admission on the seventeen-minute phone call with Bart.

When Moreno was done, Judge Alvarez asked Gabriel: "Are there any actions here attributed to you that you would say you did not engage in?"

"No, everything is correct," Gabriel said. He denied only the statements attributed to him in which he allegedly talked about third parties. He wished not to be on the record as having discussed Miguel Treviño, Meme Flores, or any other Company leader.

Gabriel's sentencing date came seven months later. At the sentencing hearing, when Judge Alvarez asked if any victims wished to address the court, the mother of fourteen-year-old Inez Villareal stepped forward. She could've been speaking for thousands of Laredo mothers when she explained how she lost a year of work looking for her son, and was about to lose her house and car as well. She addressed Gabriel directly: "I am going to tell you this, son, because I know your mother is going through the pain that I am. But the stronger sorrow is mine, because your mother knows where you are. I ask you, even if you want me to ask on my knees, if you know where my son is buried, please tell the judge."

The judge thanked her, told Gabriel to give his attorney any information he had about the whereabouts of Inez Villareal, and then asked if he had anything to say on his own behalf.

The young man who once aspired to be an attorney said: "I apologize to the government of the United States and to the community of Laredo for having participated in these kind of crimes. And just give me the least amount of sentence that you can. That's all. Thank you."

Gabriel's lawyer in the federal case, Jeff Czar, urged the judge to give Gabriel "some hope in terms of a light at the end of the tunnel." Czar argued that Gabriel's personality was "a strong one," but disagreed that he supervised other parties. "There's nothing that shows us that his intelligence is such that he was somehow brighter or smarter than the rest of that group." Czar said drugs played an aggravating role; that Gabriel was a high school dropout and lived on the streets most of his life. "The history and characteristics of my client are not good. There's nothing I can do about that in the report. There's no way to doctor it up." The facts being tossed about, true or not, had, he claimed, turned his client into an "urban legend."

Angel Moreno replied.

Since the arrests of Gabriel and his crew, three years earlier, Laredo's murder rate dropped to less than half of what it was when they were operating, Moreno argued. He emphasized Gabriel's leadership role, and that he had direct contact with cartel heads in Mexico. "He was the one that was calling the shots." Although Gabriel was young, he was no younger than the men and women who served our country in war. He was arrested several times. Regrettably, he was always released on bond. But he had plenty of opportunity to stop. "As to whether this case has become a legend, your honor, I would say ninety percent of what's in the report came directly from him. His statements. His admissions. The interceptions of the calls. The videos. Maybe, in his head, it was romantic to be part of this group and engaged in these activities. If it's become a legend, it's become a legend because the defendant has elected to make it so."

The judge conceded that Gabriel "was not in charge of the entire organization," but said the record clearly reflected that he was "in charge at least of his own particular group." Whether a problem of environment, DNA, or drugs—or because he lived in a fantasy world where he thought committing these murders glorified him— the judge concluded that, bilingual though he may be, she and Gabriel did not speak the same language, "the language of humanity." She said: "Very frankly, I see nothing in this report to indicate that you have any consideration for your fellow human beings." For the safety of Laredo, for the safety of the entire United States, a sentence of life imprisonment, she held, was warranted. He was lucky, she said. In her opinion he deserved the death penalty.

THERE WERE STILL MANY ARRAIGNMENTS to come on the Operation Prophecy indictment. But, observing Gabriel's sentencing from the back benches, Robert was disappointed. The media feted Laredo law enforcement for the case. Narrating a TV documentary about Gabriel and Bart, an actor from *The Sopranos* called Robert "the Sherlock Holmes of the Tex-Mex border." But Robert had hoped Gabriel would contest the federal charge and take the case to trial. He wanted the snitches to be paraded onto the witness stand, the curtain pulled back on the gruesome reign of Miguel Treviño, a man who was only a few years into his ascent in the Company when he told Gabriel and Wences that he'd killed more than eight hundred people.

Back in 2006, three months after Operation Prophecy stepped on the safe house, there had been hope of a big Zeta trial in Laredo. In Mexico, Bart Reta had defied Zeta orders and attacked a night club in Monterrey, killing four and wounding others. Without Company protection, he landed in the hands of Mexican authorities. When they arrested Bart, they raided his house and found $275,000 in cash, a bulletproof BMW M3, a diamond ring valued at $25,000, and about $50,000 of new Versace clothes. Psychological evaluations judged Bart's condition as "personality dissociative disorder," and concluded that he was not only unstable but a security threat to whichever institution housed him.

Each country had different extradition requirements. If Moreno wanted to extradite someone from Canada, he sent a small envelope of papers. Mexico was at the other end of the spectrum: Their system demanded a truckload of paperwork. Extradition took years, or didn't happen at all. But Mexico offered up Bart without a single document filed—and Bart was eager to get out of Mexico. If he stayed, he faced the wrath of the Zetas. In Texas, he believed authorities had only weak evidence linking him to the murders of Moises Garcia and Noe Flores. So, on the day after Bart turned seventeen—July 28, 2006—Robert met the mythic killer in the middle of the night on a tarmac at the San Antonio airport. Handcuffed and shackled, Bart grinned widely and recited the license plate number of Robert's undercover car.

For several days in the interrogation room—over Bart's requested meal of Wendy's spicy chicken sandwiches, and bottles of Big Red with cups of crushed ice—Bart told Robert stories from his time in the Company. Killing made him feel like James Bond and Superman, he said. He was basically a detective, just like Robert. He had a job, like any man, and he was good at his job. He never showed emotions. One minute you were having fun, kicking it like brothers, and the next minute he was putting a bullet to your head. No, it wasn't normal. He knew that. And yes, at first he did it for the money. But after a while it got addictive. He couldn't stop. He used to get a high out of it. It got to the point where if he didn't kill someone that day he wasn't satisfied. Taking the gun away, he said, was "like taking candy from a baby." Shit, he was so gone he could've killed his own father and felt nothing.

Their blood-soaked chatter assumed a weird, affable normality. Robert and Bart spoke nonchalantly of live humans fed to tigers and burned in oil drums; of hacking and torture; of the camps. Miguel Treviño was a smart man, Bart believed, and ruthless. Miguel trusted Bart like a son, molded him into an assassin. Bart even wanted to purchase two white tigers so he could be like Mike. And yes, it was true, absolutely, what Gabriel had said: Bart was nothing but thirteen when he joined up. Miguel practically raised him, sent him to a special-force military camp where he always got the highest scores in guns, explosives, hand-to-hand combat, how to move as a ghost. Then he was sent to different places around the nation, to unknown places—the only evidence of his being there a trail of dead bodies.

Robert had interviewed dozens of killers. They all went straight to the excuses, the justifications. But for whatever bullshit Bart fed Robert, he was the first murderer who came right out and said that he killed not because he was from poverty or because his mother didn't hold him enough as a baby. He killed because he liked to kill. Robert's feelings for Bart were complicated. Sure, the kid had wanted to whack his ass, had even threatened his family, but Robert liked him. He actually liked the kid.

Bart's candor was certainly part of his charm, but so perhaps was his naïveté. Surprised to discover that his forthrightness in the debriefings would curry no favor with the state court on the murder charges for Moises Garcia and Noe Flores, Bart was also deeply hurt when Robert told him that Gabriel gave him up on the Flores murder. Bart wondered: How could his brother do that? Robert pretended to empathize, playing up the betrayal until Bart decided to challenge his case and go to trial.

The following summer, all of downtown Laredo was secured during Bart's state trial, with squad cars parked at every intersection near the courthouse. Robert took the stand and explained the investigation of the Flores murder, how the cell phone trail led to the tattoo artist. The tattoo artist, fearing for his family, took the witness stand and pleaded with the judge to send him home. When Christina took the stand, she was so scared that she refused to confirm anything she'd said in her deposition a day earlier. The Lord, per Isaiah 3:16, had laid bare her secret parts, taken away the bracelets, scarves, and perfume. Due to her involvement in the case, she was fired from her job at a bank. In Bart's trial, however, neither the tattoo artist nor Christina was necessary. The evidence against Bart was heavy. On the third day of trial, he decided to end it and plead guilty.

"I hope you take the time in prison to reflect on your life," the judge told Bart as he announced a sentence of seventy years. "It's a young life."

IT WAS UNCLEAR HOW MANY people on Miguel's List of 40 avoided being killed. Interviews and debriefings helped Laredo PD identify many targets on the list. Mike Lopez, the Laredo smuggler who slept with Miguel's ex-girlfriend, ignored law enforcement's advice to leave Laredo; in 2007, a gang member from the Texas Syndicate murdered Lopez while he was standing in front of a Laredo bar that he had just opened.

New informants cycled through Robert's office, and he learned some interesting facts. Miguel had been wrong about the next president being "on lock": The Company bet on the wrong horse. The Company now wanted to execute President-elect Felipe Calderón for refusing the bribe. Company brass believed Calderón favored the Sinaloa Cartel.

When Calderón took office, at the end of 2006, the Harvard grad said he planned to wage war on the cartels. If he did, Washington's Mérida Initiative would send Mexico $1.5 billion in crime-fighting aid. It wasn't much next to the approximately $50 billion a year in tax-free business (about 5 percent of Mexican GDP) that drug users did with the cartels. But it was enough to buy a war. Calderón launched his ill-fated effort to purge Mexico of the cartels.

In Mexico, the cartels quickly saw the difficulty of fighting each other *and* Calderón's government. In 2007, Chapo Guzmán met Heriberto Lazcano at a hotel in Valle Hermoso. They agreed to divide the country. The meeting ended with a party and enemies coming together over whiskey and cocaine. But, like most promises in the cartel world, the Valle Hermoso Pact was short-lived.

Far from ending the conflict, it marked the beginning of its most bloody phase. The cartels fought the government, rival cartels, and even fought among themselves. Catorce—the original Zeta who co-led the organization with Lazcano and ran the Company's business in Veracruz—was shot dead at a Veracruz horse race, possibly on orders from Miguel. After Catorce's death, Miguel killed Catorce's loyalists in the Company, and plotted his rise.

The Mexican Drug War had begun.

GABRIEL CARDONA NEVER GOT HIS shot at La Barbie. But Gabriel and the other Wolf Boys served their masters well. By the end of 2006, the Zetas and the Gulf Cartel had repelled the Sinaloans and maintained the Company's grip on the Gulf Coast and the Laredo crossing.

La Barbie scrambled. He separated from his first wife, his high school sweetheart, and married Priscilla, the teenage daughter of a Laredo trafficking associate. But La Barbie was losing friends and money fast. Via his attorney, he contacted the DEA office in Laredo. DEA wanted an informant to help capture Arturo Beltrán-Leyva (ABL), the Sinaloan associate who was La Barbie's boss, as well as Chapo, the Sinaloan head. La Barbie told DEA that he would surrender only under certain conditions. From an internal DEA memo:

(1) VALDEZ-Villareal will provide information and intelligence on top corrupt Mexican Gov't officials, whom DEA and other federal agencies in Mexico work with;

(2) will not provide information on [cartel leaders] discussed in the first negotiation;

(3) if and when arrested, VALDEZ-Villareal wants to immediately be extradited to the U.S.;

(4) wants immunity from prosecution for himself and two of his cousins;

(5) does not want to testify against any person who he provides information on.

"Legal considerations still need to be reviewed by AUSA Angel Moreno," the memo said. "The terms agreed upon by the District Office and the McAllen District Office are listed below."

(1) VALDEZ-Villareal must agree to meet with Agents of the DEA in a neutral country in order to fully debrief;

(2) VALDEZ-Villareal must provide information which will result in the arrest of one of three [cartel leaders] (BELTRAN-Leyva, GUZMAN-Loera, or ZAMBADA-Garcia);

(3) VALDEZ-Villareal will not be granted full immunity from prosecution (possibly consider minimum jail time);

(4) VALDEZ-Villareal will turn himself in to U.S. authorities at a U.S. port of entry or a country where extradition is possible; and

(5) VALDEZ-Villareal will surrender an amount equal to the amount he wants to bring into the U.S. (VALDEZ-Villareal has expressed his desire to bring $5 million into the U.S.)

La Barbie offered to help nab ABL *or* Chapo, but not both. Laredo agents were eager to strike a deal, but their boss in Houston quashed the negotiations: "He's a fucking doper; if he doesn't want to cooperate, screw him."

At the time, the American government was talking to one of its biggest cartel cooperators. Osiel Cárdenas, the Gulf Cartel leader from whose mind the Zetas sprung a decade earlier, was extradited to the States in 2007, and sentenced in 2010. Eligible for a life sentence, Osiel was scheduled for release in 2025. His plea agreement remained sealed. But Osiel, through his own informant, passed along information to U.S. authorities about drug loads and the whereabouts of Gulf Cartel and Zeta underbosses—the kind of meaningful, real-time intelligence that only a top capo could possess. There may have also been an exchange of money between Osiel and the U.S. government. In 2013, in a Zeta-related federal trial in Washington, D.C., a former Zeta lieutenant would testify that the Company sent $60 million for Osiel "to use in the United States to lower his sentence."*

The kingpin strategy—in which American and Mexican authorities sought to dismantle cartels by going after their top leaders—was not just a fallacy (extradited leaders cut great deals for short sentences, while lackeys tended to get much heavier sentences) but a catastrophe: When a capo was captured, the ensuing power vacuums only ignited more violence. As one scholar observed, President Calderón's effort to clean up his country locked Mexico into "a self-reinforcing equilibrium of instability."

It wasn't all Calderón's fault. He may have lost Mexico to the savages, just like Presidents Fox, Zedillo, and Salinas before him . . . all the way back to Benito Juárez, Mexico's twenty-sixth president, from 1858 to 1872, who ran off the French and Spanish occupiers but established a too-weak central government of his own. Like the lord

---

* The government excluded this testimony from the public record, and denied the author's request pursuant to the Freedom of Information Act. The transcript, provided to the author by a confidential source, shows that the judge held a private meeting with the lawyers and said: "The witness implied that $60 million was sent here to help reduce [Osiel's] sentence. Are we going to let that stay just the way it is on the record?" The judge added: "It leaves a certain implication that one would like to have cleared up, if the $60 million was going to affect his sentence. I hope that wasn't the case. If it was $60 million to pay an attorney, maybe we could bring that out rather than making it sound like something different." The issue was never resolved and never raised again on the record.

of Culhuacán, ruler of the old empire when his Aztec mercenaries revolted, Calderón and Fox inherited a doomed kingdom. The paternalism of American drug policy—combined with the Great Father's clever trade agreements, geopolitical agendas, and tricky systems of debt—ensured that Mexico remained, as the intelligentsia put it, problematic.

30

The Messiest War

Ever since 1990, the old authoritarian PRI government that once managed a relatively peaceful drug industry in Mexico had been losing power in an average of eighty municipalities per year. Every electoral cycle, opposition parties claimed another 10 percent of Mexico's total local government. By 2012, a PRI president was in office again, but the party's dictatorial hold on Mexico was gone. A story that began, half a century earlier, with a centralized political system in which traffickers and politicians shared tables at wedding parties, ended with traffickers assassinating fifteen mayors and one gubernatorial candidate in 2010 alone.

In that year, Heriberto Lazcano, the Zeta leader, orchestrated a split from the Gulf Cartel, dividing the two entities that once comprised the Company, and turned the Zetas against their former masters. Lazcano appointed Miguel Treviño to be the Zetas' national commander.

Under Miguel's leadership, the Zetas appeared to pivot from a criminal business to a terror organization. When Miguel heard that the cartels allied against him were summoning reinforcements from the south, rumored to be arriving in northeast Mexico in low-profile public buses, he intercepted buses in San Fernando, a minor plaza between Veracruz and the border, and oversaw the slaughter of what appeared to be simple laborers. It was hard to tell what they'd been. When the burial pits were discovered, the bodies had been deformed by blunt-force trauma. "Who wants to live?" Miguel reportedly asked, before forcing the men into gladiatorial combat, with the losers beaten to death and the winners sent on missions against rivals.

Miguel also turned against his old Zeta co-commander, Iván Velásquez-Caballero, El Talivan, who split from the Zetas and recruited soldiers from a new cartel called the Knights Templar. In 2012, a *narcomanta*—a poster that cartels use, like a billboard, to spread intimidation—hung from a bridge in Tamaulipas, and was allegedly written by Miguel. The *narcomanta* provided insight into Miguel's thinking about the cartel landscape, as well as his take on the latest internecine battles:

> To all the Knights Templar and dumb asses that have left with the stupid fag and mediocre El Talivan, you can all suck my dick. You are a bunch of fags that run in packs. . . . You are a bunch of thieves, extortionists, and half-dead hungry fucks that don't know how to confront me. . . . You are traitors. . . . I am loyal to the Letter [Z] and to Comandante Lazcano. CDG [Cartel del Golfo, the Gulf Cartel] is done. . . . The ones that remain in CDG are thieves, snitches, and pussies. What is left is secondary and third-level guys. They're going to fuck each other up. That's what happens when there is no leader to control those pussies. The Knights Templar are a bunch of crystal meth addicts that are always charging avocado farmers quotas and even schools. . . .

When Lazcano tried to cool him off, Miguel turned on his boss and set him up. One month after the *narcomanta,* Lazcano was leaving a baseball game in Coahuila when Mexican security forces closed in. Lazcano and his companion sped away in a pickup truck as Lazcano shot rocket-propelled grenades from the back. The driver was hit first. Lazcano was shot dead three hundred yards from the vehicle. Masked men later stole his body from a funeral home.

As head of the Zetas, Miguel traveled from city to city, usually during the night, to check operations and deliver munitions to his *comandantes* and *soldados.* He would move with large groups of bodyguards, then disappear into a city by himself. Sometimes he hid out alone at ranches.

Through high-level informants, J. J. Gomez, now a veteran DEA agent, tracked Miguel's movements and coordinated with other U.S. and Mexican agencies. On July 15, 2013, Mexican authorities captured Miguel before dawn, without a shot fired, after he spent time with his newborn child at a house near the border. In his pickup truck, he had eight guns and two million dollars in cash. He assumed he could buy his way out of the arrest.

"Don't even ask any questions," he told his captors, "because I'm not answering any."

In his perp-walk photo, Miguel wore a black golf shirt and camouflage pants. Now in his forties, he'd put on weight. Bloat concealed his once-prominent cheekbones. Head back, chest out, he looked down his nose through irritated eyes, a commander interrupted during important work.

WEEKS AFTER MIGUEL'S ARREST IN Mexico, one of his older brothers, José Treviño, was convicted in the United States for laundering Company money through a quarter-horse outfit in Oklahoma.

Details about Miguel's horse business came out at trial: how races were fixed, how front men were used to buy horses, and how prominent members of the quarter-horse industry were co-opted.

It was good grist for local Texas newspapers. But to people like Robert Garcia, the horse trial was a case in point: massive resources poured into a years-long investigation that achieved, ultimately, nothing. In the overall scheme of cartel finances and money laundering, the horse business was minuscule. The real money-laundering cases never went to trial. Between 2004 and 2006, Wachovia, the American banking giant, helped cartels clean billions. The prosecutor said Wachovia disregarded banking laws and gave cartels "a virtual carte blanche to finance their operations." Wachovia's punishment was 2 percent of the bank's 2009 profits.

When Washington handed out the award for "Outstanding OC-DETF Investigation," the horse case, for all the press it received, was passed over. Instead, the award went to Operation El Chacal, a different Zeta case that yielded $22 million in cash, a half ton of coke, nearly a ton of marijuana, and 301 firearms. It also saved a kidnapping victim, and provided evidence to solve three Laredo homicides. In El Chacal, Robert was a lead investigator on the state side, handling the homicides and kidnappings, but it was hard to get too excited about the award.

On paper, OCDETF was a beautiful concept—a financing mechanism that facilitated interagency cooperation and focused resources on a single target. And top cartel guys did get captured. In 2013, Talivan was extradited to Laredo, where he pleaded guilty, was debriefed, and awaited sentencing. Omar Treviño, Miguel's brother, who liked to launder his money through the coal mining and construction industries, was captured in Matamoros in 2015.

Ten years earlier, this slate of arrests had been what Robert wanted: to bring down "the fuckers doing the violence." But these guys fell, and someone else stepped up. The southwest region could do fifty OCDETF investigations a year and see little impact. Removing the head of a cartel sent a message to criminals, but to what end? Without addressing the drug market on this side, it didn't matter how many capos you killed on the other.

LA BARBIE KEPT SHOPPING HIS intelligence around at federal agencies—CIA, ICE—and found a receptive party at FBI, which used his information (and used him to transfer a tracking device) to capture and kill Arturo Beltrán-Leyva in Mexico in 2009. "At that point, La Barbie would've loved to come to the States and get a big sentence reduction," said Art Fontes, an FBI agent who worked on the case. "But there was never an explicit agreement where we told him, 'Yes, we can help you.' It was complicated. Too many jurisdictions had charges on him. There'd also been some executions of police officers in Mexico."

So La Barbie was in the wind once again, hoping, in ABL's absence, to take control of the hefty cocaine business that came through the port at Zihuatanejo. But without affiliation, La Barbie didn't last long. He was captured by DEA, FBI, and Mexican authorities in 2010 at a house near Mexico City. Trotted before the cameras, smiling, he wore a green rugby jersey with a big Polo symbol on the chest. His legacy lived on in the fashion craze he created, "Narco Polo." After five years in a Mexican prison—a time during which his usefulness as an informant faded—La Barbie was extradited to Atlanta, where he pleaded guilty to one of the charges against him, and awaited sentencing.

Capo of capos, head of the Sinaloa Cartel, Chapo Guzmán, the most wily and enduring drug lord, was apprehended in 2014 and incarcerated in Puente Grande, one of Mexico's highest-security prisons. Underscoring the extent of Chapo's reach into the United States, American twin brothers from Chicago played a crucial role in his capture. Between 2001 and 2008, Pedro and Margarito Flores became the Midwest hub of the Sinaloa Cartel. The identical brothers were in their early twenties when they started, and smuggled at least seventy-one tons of cocaine and heroin to Chicago and beyond. They moved $700 million worth of drugs annually—about five times what's seized in Chicago during a typical year—and employed legions of henchmen.

After they were caught, the Flores twins became DEA informants and recorded conversations in Mexico with Chapo himself. At their 2015 sentencing, the Chicago federal judge called the twins the "most significant drug dealers" he'd ever seen, while praising their performance as snitches. The Flores twins got fourteen years; with six years already served, as informants, a time during which they secretly imported hundreds of pounds of heroin to Chicago, they'd be out of prison by their fortieth birthdays. Six months after the twins' sentencing, Chapo escaped from prison (again) through a tunnel, and six months later he was once again apprehended.

But in October 2015, while still on the lam, Chapo gave a rare interview to the American actor Sean Penn and the Mexican actress Kate del Castillo. Wearing a baseball cap and a button-down shirt of blue paisley, Chapo, located on what appeared to be some kind of farm, sat before a camera. While roosters crowed nearby, he answered questions for seventeen minutes.

Where he grew up, in the Sierra Madre mountains, there were no decent job opportunities, he told his interviewers. His family grew corn and beans. His mother made bread and he sold it, along with oranges, soft drinks, and candy. To survive, people also grew poppy and marijuana. Drug trafficking, Chapo explained, is part of a culture that originated with "the ancestors." But now there are more drugs, more people, more traffickers, and more ways of doing business. It's a reality that drugs destroy humanity, he confessed, but he's not responsible for the drugs in the world. The day he ceases to exist, drugs won't stop flowing. He also denied that his organization is a cartel. People who dedicate their lives "to this activity," he said, don't depend on him; drug trafficking doesn't depend on one person. As for the violence that goes with it, some people "grow up with problems, and there is some envy," he said, but he doesn't go looking for trouble. He only defends himself.

STATISTICS ABOUT HOMICIDE ARE HARD to prove, particularly in an underworld, and particularly in Mexico, where, scholars claim, only 25 percent (or less) of crimes are reported. Some say at least 60,000 people died between 2006 and 2012, the years Calderón held office. Others report that, during that same period, at least 150,000 died or went missing in Mexico. Neither of those estimates includes deaths from the pre-2006 era, nor the more than 800 people Miguel claimed to have killed by 2005. If the estimate of 150,000 dead or missing between 2006 and 2012 is based only on reported incidents, then multiply that number by four: The Mexican Drug War took more lives in those six years than all the American soldiers lost in World War I, World War II, and the Vietnam War combined. In Latin America, the murder rate for young males is the highest in the world.

Mainstream America's disinterest in the war is often attributed to a lack of spillover violence. But many in U.S. law enforcement see it differently: The war is pushing north to new contested areas. In 2005, the Department of Justice identified 100 American cities where cartels maintained distribution networks. By 2008, that number jumped to 230 cities—including Anchorage, Atlanta, Boston, and Billings. During that time, cartel-related violence occurred in Oregon, Minnesota, Illinois, Indiana, Michigan, Maryland, and New Jersey, among other northern states. After arresting fifteen members of the Sinaloa Cartel in North Carolina, the local sheriff said, "A few years ago, U.S. law enforcement didn't see this as a problem for somewhere other than the border. But what happens at the border doesn't stay at the border. It makes its way to my county pretty soon."

Back in Texas, the Department of Public Safety said six of Mexico's seven major cartels were actively recruiting Texas high school students to support drug, immigrant, currency, and weapon smuggling. Meanwhile, drug warriors in the DEA and elsewhere clung tighter to the war's righteousness. Spillover violence, they insisted, was justification for renewed efforts, not cause for reassessment of a policy.

War had become a huge industry at home, just as it had abroad. One of Laredo's many prosecutors-turned-defense-attorneys observed that Laredo, despite being on the border and mostly Hispanic, was similar to other big crime cities in America, insofar as approximately one-third of its legitimate economy depended on the drug war. Cops and agents, lawyers and judges, prisons and bail bondsmen—the list of beneficiaries went on.

The occasional victory made heroes out of agents. Jack Riley, the head of Chicago DEA, who helped turn the Flores twins against Chapo, said: "These days we operate as if Chicago is on the border." Riley's success was rewarded with a move to Washington and a promotion to number three overall in DEA. According to ABC's Chicago affiliate, Riley left "a city where heroin and crack cocaine are still sold like ice cream bars by street corner vendors."

31

No Angels

Operation Prophecy was a career case. It would be a shame for the work to go unknown to the public. Robert got his wish when a minor Wolf Boy on the Operation Prophecy indictment contested his association with the Company. There would be a trial after all, which would entail putting snitches on the stand to testify about their time in the Company.

For Angel Moreno, sitting a jury for these cases was not easy. Many prospective jurors were disqualified, either because they thought the government was the cause of Laredo's violence, and believed legalizing drugs was the solution; or because they were related to a detective who would testify in the case; or because they believed media sensationalized the cartels, since it was such a made-for-TV thing, and that much of what was reported wasn't true; or because a friend or brother or son or stepson or father or father-in-law or uncle or nephew had been imprisoned, and they couldn't be impartial; or because, as Juror 69 put it: "Drugs have been here for many years. It's only in the past five, ten, because of the trouble across, that we started speaking so much of it. But we were being ostriches. So what's the point? Where are we getting? Nowhere."

Richard Jasso agreed to cooperate with Moreno in order to get a deal for his wife: He'd serve time in state prison, for the Resendez double homicide, then join his father in the federal system for the double homicide of the American teens. Richard would be out in his fifties. In exchange for this deal, Richard agreed to testify against the obscure Wolf Boy on trial, a boy known as Cachetes, or "Cheeks."

Richard Jasso met his dad, briefly, in the Laredo prison where he stayed during the Prophecy trial. It was their first time meeting since his dad's 1999 incarceration on smuggling and murder charges. The conversation was awkward. His father, a member of the Mexican Mafia, didn't understand why Richard started killing people if he was doing well with smuggling. But Richard's main regret was the day he asked his wife to pick up Gabriel and Bart after they cooked Moises Garcia. Her imprisonment meant three years their kids went without parents. Otherwise, Richard expressed no remorse. He wondered whether, if he'd stayed at a certain level and lived comfortably with what he had, his life would've turned out differently. He'd never know. If he had the chance to do it over, he would, just better.

Richard barely knew the boy on trial; they worked together on the Resendez homicide. But this was a case about an enormous conspiracy, concerning low-level criminals who all worked, ultimately, for the same few criminals. And therefore it wasn't necessary that all witnesses knew the defendant, only necessary that they knew about the conspiracy alleged. Richard could also testify to his work with Gabriel. And Moreno could easily link Gabriel, through wiretaps, to the cartel leaders in Mexico.

Gabriel, even though he refused to testify, was brought down to Laredo from his state prison in North Texas and housed in the cell facing Richard for the several weeks the trial lasted. They didn't speak. Gabriel shut Richard out because Richard had cooperated with Moreno.

But in Richard's mind, everyone "threw mud at each other." Everyone ratted out everyone, because that's how the underworld works. Richard also believed the media attention blew up Gabriel's head. In addition to articles about him in the *New York Times, Esquire,* and *Details,* his case was all over South Texas media. Richard thought the attention locked Gabriel further into the image he'd always coveted: the stoic gangsta who accepted all responsibility and took what came. But Richard didn't believe it: Gabriel blamed everyone *but* himself for his situation. From childhood, Gabriel prided himself on his independence; in reality, he could never see a life for himself beyond affiliation. To Richard, this central contradiction defined much about his old hoodie, employee, and boss.

Sitting across the prison corridor from Richard, Gabriel thought, Let him take the stand if he wants. Good luck surviving as a snitch. Gabriel noticed Richard's new muscles. Richard knew he was going to the federal pen eventually. There was no "administrative segregation" over there. *All prison families roam free, and what awaits . . .*

Richard took the stand and performed well as a government witness. He spoke candidly, and believably. He described the March 2006 afternoon on which he, Gabriel, and another Wolf Boy went to the house of Laredo teen Poncho Aviles to find out who Poncho was recruiting for the Sinaloans.

"Did you see [Poncho] again?" Moreno asked Richard.

Yes, Richard said. One week later in Nuevo Laredo, Richard and two other Wolf Boys (not Gabriel) saw Poncho at Eclipse, the nightclub. Richard said that he and the other Wolf Boys spotted Poncho and followed him around the club. One of the Wolf Boys pulled out his pistol and hit Poncho over the head with the butt, then packed Poncho in the car. Richard said he called Gabriel, who was in Laredo at the time, and mentioned that they'd picked up Poncho. "Take him to the house," Gabriel allegedly said. At the Nuevo Laredo house, before Gabriel arrived, the Wolf Boys undressed Poncho and began to interrogate and beat him. They asked Poncho who he worked with, what he knew about the contras, and what he was doing in Nuevo Laredo. Poncho confessed that he was at the Eclipse nightclub with another boy, Inez Villareal. So Richard returned to Eclipse and kidnapped fourteen-year-old Inez. When Richard returned to the house with Inez, Gabriel had arrived and was on the phone with Meme Flores. At that point, Richard testified, Gabriel took the detainees to another house, and Richard returned to Eclipse to party.

"Do you know what happened to Poncho and Inez?" Moreno asked Richard.

"They were killed," Richard said.

"How did you find out they were killed?"

"The following day Gabriel told me."

"Did he tell you what they did with the bodies?"

"Just that they were dead at dawn, and that they had thrown them into *el guiso*."

"What's *el guiso*?"

"When they're thrown into barrels. They pour gasoline on them and burn them until they're powder."

Angel Moreno convinced several other Wolf Boys to cooperate and testify as well—including Bart and Wences. None of them seemed to have much information about the obscure Wolf Boy on trial, but they all had plenty of stories about being in the Company.

When cross-examining these witnesses, the defense attorney argued that this trial was about nothing more than a bunch of murderers taking the stand and saying whatever the government wanted them to say. In his cross-examinations, the defense attorney—as the defense does in such cases—focused on denigrating the character of the cooperating witnesses in an attempt to erode their credibility with the jury.

The defense attorney asked Bart, "You told Detective [Robert] Garcia that you thought you were 'Superman and shit,' right?"

"Yes, sir."

"And you would commit murders whether somebody paid you or not?"

"That was toward the end," Bart clarified.

"Is it true that you have participated in over thirty murders?"

"I can't really explain that," Bart said.

"And isn't it true that you told Detective Garcia about chasing people down and 'blowing the bitch's top off'?"

Wences followed Bart on the witness stand.

After fleeing to Mexico following the June 2005 murder of Bruno Orozco, Wences never returned to the States. His cartel career ended, however, a few days after Gabriel's. In April 2006, after Operation Prophecy raided the safe house on Orange Blossom Loop, Wences was driving drunk in Mexico, trying to roll a joint while steering with his knees, when he flipped his Avalanche and severed his spinal cord. Miguel drove to the accident, pulled Wences from the wreck, brought him to the Company hospital, remained at his bedside for three days, and then sent him to Cuba to be treated by specialists. Wences regained use of his upper body, and his sexual function, but he would be in a wheelchair forever. When he returned to Mexico, Miguel gave him a Dodge Charger and $10,000, told him that he didn't have to work anymore, and paid him $1,000 every two weeks. He stayed in Mexico for four years, managing pain with tequila and pot, until the American legal system tracked him through cell phone communications.

When it was the defense attorney's turn to cross-examine

Wences, the attorney asked him, "Why did you decide to cooperate with the government?"

"I think it's the right thing for my country," Wences said.

"And you're hoping to get something less than thirty years, correct?

"Yes."

"And you want that because being in a wheelchair in prison isn't easy?"

"No. No it's not easy."

It wasn't easy. At the medical unit in Butner, North Carolina, the same federal prison complex that houses Ponzi schemer Bernie Madoff, Wences was surrounded by the dying—men who were too fat or too old or too diseased for the regular pen. He fell asleep at night to the sounds of moaning. His kids visited, but Wences didn't like that. "Why are you here, Daddy?" they asked. "Because I played with guns," he said. "Don't play with guns." In prison, Wences became hooked on opioids, the cheapest way to maintain a cripple. Still, he was thankful "to have a date." Wences got a few years off his sentence for the murder of Bruno Orozco, a charge that turned federal (and more serious) because he and Gabriel crossed the border to commit a violent crime—Interstate Travel in Aid of Racketeering (ITAR)—and because Wences used a silencer on an assault weapon. He'd be out of prison when he was fifty.

Only Gabriel declined to testify, which made it easier for the government to position him as the crucial link between the Wolf Boys and Zeta brass. When asked, every snitch—Bart, Wences, Richard, and others—confirmed that Gabriel was their leader in Laredo.

When Rocky, the DEA informant, took the stand, the defense attorney tallied the DEA's payments to him, which, by 2008, came to $212,000—less than Robert Garcia's total Laredo PD salary for the same three-year period. The defense attorney asked Rocky, "Would you agree that in December of 2005 you were arrested for assaulting your wife? And that in March of 2006 your wife brought to the attention of DEA the fact that you had gone on a cocaine binge for three days and were again extremely violent to her?"

"Yes, sir," Rocky said.

"And you would agree that violence toward your wife could be a criminal act that would violate your agreement with DEA?"

"True, sir. Yes, sir."

Accustomed to this defense strategy, Angel Moreno addressed it in his closing argument. The defense, Moreno told the jury, was correct. You didn't want to trust these witnesses with your kids. You didn't want to trust them to sell you a car. You certainly didn't want to trust them to give you surgery. But that's not why they were testifying. They were there to explain how the Company works, how drug trafficking works, how assassinations work—and, in those operations, they were experts. "I'm sure the defendant wishes this would've happened in the Vatican," Moreno concluded, "and that every witness was a priest or a nun. Folks, you can't have angels as witnesses for crimes committed in hell."

The minor Wolf Boy's first trial resulted in a hung jury. He lost the retrial and got life in prison.

32

Hypocritical Bastards

In prison, lots of reporters visited Bart: the History Channel, Investigation Discovery, Fox, the *New York Times*.

His story suited a smorgasbord of prerogatives. The Fox correspondent, the sole female to interview Bart, became emotional. Another journalist compared Bart to child soldiers in Africa, and referenced Ishmael Beah, who, as a teenager, slaughtered villagers during Sierra Leone's civil war. After living in a rehabilitation camp, Beah flew to New York, addressed the United Nations, attended college in the States, and became a bestselling memoirist. Bart wondered if he could produce a similar literary work—something that fell between Beah's *A Long Way Gone* and *A House in the Sky,* the harrowing memoir by Canadian journalist Amanda Lindhout about her captivity in Somalia. He even had a title picked out: *Memoirs of a Teenage Assassin*.

Bart had an uncanny way of intuiting what his questioners wanted. In some interviews, he acted callous and proud. Even though the Zetas wanted to kill him for taking his case to trial, he remained in awe of Miguel, the general who led by example. In moments of cold bravado ("Too bad for them," referring to his victims), Bart's voice remained soft and melodic even when his words were menacing, noted the *Times*. The *Times* reporter observed how Bart's "countenance shifted back and forth, from the deadpan of a street tough with emotionless eyes to the oddly innocent laugh and smile of a boy for whom everything is a lark." In other interviews, Bart described atrocities with an air of reluctance, haltingly, as if wrestling with trauma and trying to make sense of repressed memories. In this mode—which, he learned, was a hit with his public—he expressed glassy-eyed regret and portrayed himself as a victim of "that world."

In 2011, Bart found new inspiration. He began exchanging letters with a mother of two in Massachusetts. Ten years Bart's senior, Eryca cried after watching the documentaries about him. She liked the devilish flames he tattooed around his eyes. She wanted some kind of relationship.

It seemed to Bart that her intentions were pure, but how could he be sure? He had a lot of time to do. He didn't want to start something that wouldn't be finished. He asked Eryca never to lie to him. A friendship, he wrote to her, should be based on trust, and earned, not just summoned upon request. He opened up. He explained that he was more of a lovey-dovey type. He said he never got tired of listening to R&B, but he also liked "instrumental music" such as Mozart. In school, which he attended till sixth grade, he was good in biology and biochemistry. He had always wanted to be a medical examiner who performed postmortem examinations. But shit, he wrote, he didn't want her to think he was a sicko. He certainly wasn't the monster they portrayed him as; in his circle, it was important to remember, it was either kill or be killed. But Bart never killed an innocent person, he said. It was a job. They were all just price tags with different prices on them. But yes, it was true. Where he was from, "Bart" was a feared name. When Eryca had problems with her ex, Bart told her she needed to buy herself a gun and blow his brains out. They fell in love and agreed to get married.

Eryca told Bart that she obtained something called "a proxy marriage," in which her sister stood in for Bart at the ceremony. But she never produced documentation when Bart asked for it. She wrote that she was looking at options for in vitro fertilization, and researched whether Bart could send his semen through the mail.

In one of Bart's TV segments, with the Center for Investigative Reporting, Eryca told the camera, "He became close with Miguel Treviño, he became real close with the big boss. He gave Rosalio the big jobs. . . . Miguel Treviño, he was a monster. The stuff he forced Rosalio to do should never have been forced on anybody." On Twitter, Eryca reveled in her new status as a "cartel wife." But when the Center for Investigative Reporting aired her videotaped interview without concealing her identity, she sued for $500,000 in damages. Since the 2013 broadcast, her complaint stated, "Ms. Almeciga has endured public humiliation . . . as well as the overwhelming fear that Los Zetas cartel at any moment may take retribution against her. . . . She has developed paranoia and has been treated for depression and Post Traumatic Stress Disorder ('PTSD'), specifically, symptoms which contributed to extreme anxiety, lack of sleep, constant nightmares, and so forth." A federal judge said Eryca "is not a remotely credible witness" and dismissed the case.

More reporters came, and Bart grew irritated with them. They were only interested in his past. No one asked about his future, his plans to appeal and move out of the Texas prison system to a state where the Mexican Mafia wouldn't bother him. (He'd been stabbed in prison as retaliation for the Moises Garcia hit.) But the journalists did give Bart an idea. What if he used an interview to make people see how he'd changed? That could help get his case reopened. He needed "a world-wide publicity." He wondered if a major media outlet might even pay for the interview. Then, to demonstrate his benevolence, he could donate the money to the families of his victims.

He connected with CNN's Ed Lavandera, who made time for Bart in 2013, after Miguel Treviño's capture in Mexico. Bart prepared extensively. But when the CNN piece aired on *Anderson Cooper 360,* he wasn't happy. Describing what he claimed was his first hit for Miguel, Bart told Lavandera: "I had to do it. What other options do I have? If I don't do it, I know what's gonna happen to me." He continued: "The first day I had to take someone's life—that's a day I'm never gonna forget. 'Cause after that I didn't have no life."

"But you kept on killing after that first time," Lavandera pointed out.

"I had to," Bart replied. "That's what a lot of people don't understand."

In voice-over, Lavandera said: "That's what Reta says now. But in this police interrogation video [with Robert Garcia] the young killer relished the deadly power he wielded. . . ."

The editing trick that Lavandera pulled, Bart felt, was "a bitch move." Why, after Bart talked about being coerced into executing a helpless man, did Lavandera have to play the interview of the Superman bullshit, then mention the "facial markings" even after Bart told "that hypocritical bastard" that the tattoos had nothing to do with the cartel lifestyle?

By contrast, Gabriel's frankness with Lavandera—"I guess I was trying to put an image out there"—didn't help Bart's cause.

As Bart's options closed, and media interest faded, advice arrived from the female Fox reporter who interviewed him.

She didn't pretend to understand how lonely and depressed Bart felt, and wished there was something she could say or do to make it better. No one was worthless, she wrote. Everyone possessed the ability to contribute to society. If Bart looked a bit harder, she had no doubt that he, too, would find a way. The sooner he moved away from the old world he lived in, the more freedom he'd have. That world gave him a false sense of power and belonging. Now he was going through withdrawal. But he'd rebuild his life, of that she was sure. It might take time, but he'd get there.

LIKE BART, GABRIEL WAS CLASSIFIED as a security threat and a high-profile inmate, and housed in a segregated unit where he saw other inmates infrequently. His days began at six o'clock, when an officer knocked on his cell and screamed, "Get your ass up!"

At eleven, he went outside for an hour of recreation in one of six fenced-in boxes. In his first state prison, he was housed on the same segregated tier as his old rap idol, South Park Mexican. They played a form of basketball, tipping the ball back and forth over the fence. SPM reinforced what Gabriel always believed—that the star was fooled by female fans who dressed up to appear older than they were. In fact, SPM got forty-five years for sneaking into his daughter's bedroom and performing oral sex on her nine-year-old friend.

Gabriel was caught between the image for which he had sacrificed everything and the better person he believed existed beneath it. To embrace the latter, he needed to disown the former. He could start by enrolling in a prison course called GRAD, Gang Renunciation and Disassociation. But it wasn't so easy. He was in a prison gang called HPL. Zetas were not well received in prison, and Gabriel was loath to relinquish the protection HPL provided. Besides, the old image was useful.

Since he didn't talk much, people often mistook him as weak. Others were tattooed from head to toe and rarely got disrespected. Aside from four tattoos of Santa Muerte on his back, arm, and legs, he didn't have many visible tattoos, except for "Christina" on his wrist and a second pair of eyes on his eyelids. People often tried to "throw game" on him. The worst were the Latinos from up north; they'd rather associate with the blacks than with "straight-up Mexicans" from South Texas, never minding that their parents all came from the same places: El Salvador, Honduras, Mexico. When Gabriel got moved to a new unit, he looked for the "gossip guy, the girl" and talked with him about "the cartel stuff." Then Gabriel sent articles, and the gossip spread.

That fool a killa for real!

That fool square bidness!

In his cell he did push-ups and sit-ups. He read magazines and legal texts. Random people wrote to him, mainly women and journalists. But they tended to disappear after a letter or two. One correspondent kept at it.

33

Another Media Guy

I t would be a stretch to say I was lured into a Mexican drug cartel by a poor economy and the decline of my legitimate business. But there is a connection. At thirty-one, I'd cycled through two careers, first abandoning law for journalism, then landing at the *Wall Street Journal,* where I covered legal stories. Following the paper's acquisition by Rupert Murdoch, I, along with two dozen other reporters and editors, lost my job—laid off, we were told, for non-performance-related reasons. I filed for unemployment insurance and stopped my *Journal* subscription. Which is why I was at home on a June morning in 2009 to fetch the *New York Times* from the stoop of my apartment building.

The paper's national section contained an article, by James C. McKinley Jr., headlined MEXICAN CARTELS LURE AMERICAN TEENS AS KILL-ERS. It was a story about two teenage thugs from Laredo, Texas, childhood friends who worked as assassins for the Zetas—a vicious drug cartel shaped by a man who, I would later be convinced, was among the most brutal warlords in modern history.

I read the article several times, absorbing its details as my imagination filled in the gaps. I was fascinated and horrified. I understood that children—Mexican children—regularly died fighting each other for the right to supply the American drug habit. I'd traveled to Sinaloa, and visited the "cartel cemetery," Jardines del Humaya, where many of the bodies entombed are boys, their hammy mausoleums decorated with cartoons and imagery from the movies they enjoyed as kids. But when it came to child soldiers, didn't the river divide the godforsaken land of cartels and corruption from the law and order of a drug-free America?

I read every book I could find on the history of drugs and Latin American cartels, starting with earlier books such as *Desperados* (1988), *Drug Lord* (1990), and *Killing Pablo* (2001).

Many of these books focused on the exploits of notorious smugglers and cartel leaders, those psychotic billionaires, like Chapo Guzmán, who landed on the pages of *Forbes*. Their exotic images made them obvious media curios, the new Pablo Escobars of Latin America; and, just like Escobar, who also made *Forbes* and whose grave site is one of Colombia's top tourist attractions, their glamour, audacity, and wealth sugarcoated their legacies and the atrocities that elevated them. They dug air-conditioned tunnels beneath the border and evaded capture via plastic surgery. They were rarely seen, yet their myths outlived them. America fetishized cartel mayhem but ignored its roots and consequences.

What about the young foot soldiers who pass unnoticed through American malls, I wondered. Who were *they*?

I set the *Times* article aside, along with several boxes of secondary research, and wrote a different book, about the online-dating business and how it affected modern romance. I would spend the next two years writing about love, not war.

But the cartel refused to leave me alone. I couldn't stop thinking about Gabriel and Bart.

In 2013, the young men popped up in the news again when Miguel was apprehended. I chose this time to reach out to the *lobos,* hoping their former boss's incarceration would make them willing to open up about their pasts. I introduced myself as a journalist who wanted to write a book about them. I apologized for not being more specific. I wasn't sure what direction the project would take.

I WASN'T INTERESTED IN CHRONICLING the history of cartels. The Zetas, with their roots in one of Mexico's elite combat units, stood for something new about the escalating drug war. But no particular cartel seemed to matter all that much more than another. I didn't care about the sociology of crime, the manhunts, or the toxic tangle of geopolitics that nourishes drug war violence on both sides of the border. Outrage over Mexico's endemic corruption, and the hypocrisy and willful ignorance of U.S. lawmakers—these, too, were well lodged in the literature.

The object of my inquiry was narrower: What is it like to be an employee of a global drug-trafficking organization? How do you apply for the job? What passes for entry-level training? How do you climb the ladder? What is the psychology of a young operative who kills daily? Are they all psychopaths? (Would that make sense, statistically?) How is he paid? How does he spend it? What kinds of women date him? How does he relate to friends? How does he know who his friends are? Why is the cartel life sending teenage boys and young men to their deaths at a faster rate than anywhere else in the world?

I wondered if Gabriel and Bart could lead me through this territory, to places I could never go, and bring the war home, contextualizing it not in shifting gangs and warring drug lords but in the unglamorous human terms of delinquency and delusion. If Gabriel and Bart were harbingers of the drug war's looming threat, I wanted to know what culture shaped these teenage serial killers, and what happened when the American justice system confronted the home-grown cartel operative. I suspected their stories contained some clue about where our country is heading, the evolving nature of the border, and how things got this bad.

I BEGAN EXCHANGING LETTERS WITH the two young men, who by then were in their mid-twenties. Bart initially declined my overture. "My life story is priceless to me," he wrote. "People will only taint it by telling it their own way, not the way things actually transpired. People use people, Mr. Slater. I have been used by medias only to fulfill their own personal needs." I visited Bart in prison. We spoke for eight hours. He told me stories. He said Miguel Treviño never did drugs and lived mostly on water and yogurt. Bart was thoughtful, inquisitive, and manipulative. He asked what I would do if Treviño were standing next to me. We laughed at my answer. He warmed to the idea of telling me about his past. I went home. We wrote for three months, until Bart transferred to Laredo for another debriefing by the U.S. attorneys. When he returned to the state prison system, he was alternately unwilling and unable to recall his life with any clarity. Our correspondence fizzled out.

My experience with Gabriel was different. After I visited him in prison, he wrote: "I do not mind sharing my life story, Dan. See, I don't pretend to be someone I'm not. But some media people have approached me with lies." He didn't like how reporters told him one thing and wrote another. They'd say, for example, that they were going to send a message to kids about the consequences of the cartel lifestyle, then write only about the sensational aspects. Nor did he appreciate how TV stations baited him with offers to tell his side of the story, then portrayed him only as a monster. "You come across as honest and are a likable guy. We'll see where it leads on your project."

Over the next two and a half years we covered every phase of his life from childhood through incarceration. The doomed narrative of his crew, corroborated by others, traversed a vast landscape of amazing characters and astonishing scenes. This wasn't Jeffrey Dahmer. Nor was it some marginal Brooklyn underworld of goodfellas and wiseguys. This was life in a narco-state, the underworld enveloping the overworld in Mexico and America. It was the normalization of murder and mayhem as business as usual, and it was chilling.

Gabriel and I exchanged more than eight hundred pages of writing. It was clear, from the first sentences, that his ninth-grade education belied a natural intelligence burnished by prison reading. His writing style was a high-low blend: From riffing on scripture, history, and current events, he'd transition to a detailed description of how to hold down a plaza, raid a house, knife an opponent to death, or incinerate a body with maximum efficiency. His letters drew me in.

Eight years in a cell, with life to go, had brought the young man perspective. He wrote about the "irrational pride" of men from his community, about the "devouring ego" that disguises low self-esteem, and about how the need to be the Man drives an entire region of men to such destructive ends. In one letter expressing remorse over the pain he inflicted on his mother, who sometimes wishes Gabriel were dead, he signed off, "da' self-forsaken disowned G-man!"

There was a limit to his insight. He was a killer; and, for whatever authentic remorse he felt, his correspondence contained its share of dissembling. He insisted the Zetas had a rule about sparing the families of their victims. The details of his own crimes revealed this claim as delusion. "I know I'll get hammered for this, but MT is a good man," he wrote, referring to Miguel. "Serious. Stoic. Never degrades anyone. Looks out for the people. Loyal and trustworthy to friends. Enemy to enemies."

Absurd as his misplaced respect could be, it was, in a way, what I had sought out: the allure of cartel logic. In Gabriel's willingness to correspond—in his candor and wry perspective, as well as his evasions and lies—lay an opportunity, finally, to learn what I'd always wanted to know: What is the life as lived?

For the first year, a cordial but intimate tone marked our letters. Inside jokes developed between us. Christina, whom he referred to, ironically, as "the love of my life," was known as "LOML." Bart, who angered the Zetas by taking his case to trial, was "persona non grada," or "the PNG," or sometimes just "the Midget." Of the books I sent him, his favorite was *Undaunted Courage,* about the Lewis & Clark expedition, and *The Lucifer Effect: Understanding How Good People Turn Evil.* My favorite book of 2014—*The Short and Tragic Life of Robert Peace*—bored him. He spent his life around blacks in the prison system, and knew their struggle well. What was the big deal about a black guy from poverty who went to Yale and died selling drugs?

Like any long-distance relationship, the temperature of our back-and-forth fluctuated. We persevered through misunderstandings, spats, and reconciliations. As I tried to reconstruct the elaborate criminal existence he led in just nineteen years, and understand how his life intersected the war raging around him, many inevitable inquiries provoked tension between us. After a string of letters posing questions about what he'd told law enforcement, about why he said this or that, or implicated associates, and about details of indicted crimes, he grew suspicious of my motivations and wondered if I wasn't just "another media guy" with an agenda, another writer looking to profit off the sensational narrative generated by "your colleagues."

Our relationship got worse before it got better. When I stumbled on evidence of a murder uncharged, we were at odds again. "I was not involved in any way and have no knowledge of that incident," he wrote. "Questions within that context are irrelevant to me." A curt and unproductive correspondence swallowed several months.

"Respect my gangsta" was a phrase he sprinkled throughout one letter. His real concern, it turned out, was his adherence to the code. When he was arrested for the final time, he refused to testify, or do "the pigs' homework." He walked out of meetings with U.S. attorneys who could've lessened his sentence while his crew curried favor by helping the government make its case. There were federal trials going on, and other snitches testifying, including several of his superiors in the Company. When Zeta leaders were extradited and given sweet deals in exchange for intelligence on fellow capos and drug lords, Gabriel remained mum. He was a man of principle, a son of God. He was no snitch. "Respect my gangsta."

Our work resumed. But by then my research had expanded far beyond him.

MAYBE IT WAS A GNAWING sense of the writing life having yielded little more than a better understanding of my native communities—Wall Street, the courts, their associated provinces. Maybe it was the acute discomfort with my comfort: newly married and settled in rural New England, with farmers' markets, fuel-efficient vehicles, and a flexible freelance schedule. Or maybe it was something more specific, such as my own past as a casual pot smoker since the age of seventeen, someone whose serious mistakes rarely earned serious consequence. I felt a pull. I heard a voice telling me to go before caution set in for good.

I began traveling back and forth to Laredo. I interviewed Gabriel's family, friends, and girlfriends. I visited and corresponded with several of his childhood friends who became his Zeta associates and are also in prison—including Richard Jasso, Wences Tovar, and other Wolf Boys who do not appear in *Wolf Boys*. (I excluded a significant Wolf Boy, Jesse Gonzales, from the narrative, because Jesse couldn't be interviewed; he was killed in a Nuevo Laredo jail in 2009.) I spoke with one of Gabriel's rivals. I exchanged a year of letters with one of Miguel Treviño's bodyguards. Most of them, like Gabriel, were engaging guys; smart, funny, and genuinely dangerous.

I drew on interrogations; wiretaps; more than fifteen thousand pages of court testimony across ten trials; and stacks of informant interviews and confidential reports detailing Company operations, personalities, and the conflict with the Sinaloa Cartel—the battle that started the war, set the stomach-churning standard for violence, and defined the lives of Gabriel Cardona and Robert Garcia.

I spent much time with Robert, his family, and his law enforcement colleagues. From illegal immigrant to migrant worker to military engineer to one of the border's top investigators, Robert was a fascinating counterpoint to the Wolf Boys. The Mexican immigrant who became the American cop busted the natural-born Americans who became the cartel crooks. Robert's arc of lost innocence, from fervent drug warrior to disillusioned critic, seemed to contain the entire story of American drug prohibition.

When Robert returned to the street, as a sergeant, in 2014, I rode along on patrol, usually during the night shift. We monitored crime reports and went where we wanted. A woman totaled her Mercedes coming around a corner drunk, then walked home before passing out. A disturbance at a rent-by-the-week motel revealed strange happenings between a man, wife, and their adult son. A gang kidnapped a rival gang member. When a lime truck was taken to Customs and dismantled, it turned out to be a legit conveyor of produce. Every night was different. No car insurance. Drug possession. An infant rolled off the couch and dislocated her shoulder. At a junior high party of cigarette smokers and curfew violators, one underage drinker looked at my jeans and T-shirt and asked, "Are you CIA?"

At 4:30 a.m., after a breakfast of *chilaquiles* and coffee with the other sergeants at Danny's, I would fade into the bucket seat, the city moving by in slow motion like a dream. Up and down Clark, Calton, and Del Mar, round and round the Bob Bullock Loop. Spindly signs sparking neon lights flashed by like wildfire, Whataburger W's stacked orange streaks. Predawn peace.

I traveled to Matamoros, Mexico City, and Veracruz with a retired DEA agent; for two days, we sat in the old Veracruz café, La Parroquia, drinking *lechero* and interviewing reporters about how media corruption works along the Gulf Coast. Back in Laredo, I tagged along with officers who patrolled specific ghettos. In the Heights—north and east of Lazteca—where TAMIU president Ray Keck once lived as a boy, during the 1950s, when the neighborhood was middle-class suburban, we patrolled what is now a refuge of heroin addicts and prostitutes. We pulled over ladies of the night. We called in female cops to conduct cavity searches on women like the white trick from Mississippi whose powdered face failed to conceal the effects of a bad heroin batch. I rode with detectives from other divisions, such as Chuckie Adan, Robert's old homicide partner, who now ran Laredo PD's undercover drug unit. I interviewed potential informants, raided a stash house in Saint Baby, searched for drugs in statues of Santa Muerte, and watched shirtless boys carted off. I went to Laredo nightclubs with Gabriel's brothers. I shadowed Robert's son, Eric, while he worked his second job as a bouncer at one of those clubs. I attended barbecues at the homes of agents from DEA and Border Patrol. I would hang out with hoodrats one night, drink with prosecutors the next. Angel Moreno often asked, incredulous, "How are you vetting what these guys in prison are telling you?" I bought beer from Mami Chula's Drive-Thru, and spoke with the underage girls serving six-packs in French maid outfits. I attended a Sunday cruise, hung out at Martin High, and watched a football game on Friday night.

One night, I drove into the Heights with Luis, Gabriel's older brother, purchased an eight-ball, went back to my hotel, and tried cocaine for the second time in my life.

Luis served most of his twenties in prison for two marijuana smuggling cases. Out of prison for a year when I met him for the first time, in the fall of 2014, he was living with La Gaby's extended family in San Antonio, and frying chicken at Popeye's while finishing an associate's degree in information technology. In the hotel, Luis and I mingled lines of coke with bottles of Heineken.

We talked about the cycle of domestic violence; about La Gaby's good intentions and how she was overwhelmed raising four boys. We talked about Laredo politicians, and how easy it was to steal from uneducated people. We talked about the intoxicating effect of power on a poor kid; and about how Gabriel mistook fear for respect. On the third beer, Luis became emotional, enumerating the steps he thinks he could've taken to rescue his volatile brother from fate. Such as that time La Gaby kicked Gabriel out of the house after finding his Mini-14 in the closet and Gabriel responded by taking a baseball bat to the Malibu she bought to repair and flip. "I should've done something," Luis said. "My mom favored me because I was the oldest. For my fifteenth birthday, she gave me a gold necklace and a hundred bucks. When Gabriel turned fifteen, he didn't get anything. He said, 'Hey, so you're not going to give me anything?' And then . . ." Luis broke down before he could finish the story.

BOOKS BEGIN WITH AN IMPULSE, then take off, like firecrackers, in unpredictable ways. I set out to investigate the cartel experience and observe the effects of the drug war on American life, but found other notions, too. As the 2016 election approached, and a raucous presidential hopeful made his own theater on Laredo's political stage, the struggles of Laredo seemed to resonate with a growing segment of this nation—an America that existed beyond the op-ed pages' daily concerns of college admissions and corporate scandals. An America of fatherless families and unintegrated families and sprawling immigrant families all trying to survive, in this case, on the sinking edge of an empire that's built and maintained off their backs yet wants to keep them out.

What, I wondered, were *their* attitudes toward this country? Here, in one of the largest commercial ports in the world, with thousands of trucks zipping by each day like so much lost opportunity, what did people hold on to as they watched their dreams slip away? What did they believe had happened to their America? Or had it always been a mirage?

If I found answers to these questions, it wasn't because Laredo was a border town, but because it was an American one. In the end, I wasn't drawn to Gabriel and the Wolf Boys because they were accomplished criminals (they weren't), or because they worked for one cartel or drug lord versus another. They were attractive subjects, rather, because they could've been any kids living at the juncture of American opulence and the dismal poverty required to preserve it.

If the Wolf Boys weren't unique, what were they? The ungoverned boys who turn on one another in *Lord of the Flies*? In the abstract, yes. The cartel virus indicated troubling things about evil as a natural product of human consciousness. But it also underlined our own capacity as Americans to sustain obliviousness, to ignore the disease even as it spread.

Back in 2009, when Gabriel was being sentenced on his federal charges, his lawyer, arguing for something less than a life sentence, told the judge, "I don't know what's in my client's mind. I'm not Freud. I'm sure Freud would have a field day. I don't know what the motivation was. We don't know what makes him tick. No one seems to really care."

EPILOGUE

E arly on a Saturday in 2015, the main international bridge connecting Laredo and Nuevo Laredo is shut down and cleared for a couple of hours as it is every year. February is a month of celebration in Laredo, with carnivals, parades, beauty pageants, car shows, cocktail hours, and fireworks—all in honor of George Washington's birthday. No one seems to know why one of the most marginalized cities in America puts on the biggest George Washington celebration in the country, only that it's long been a tradition.

The month of partying concludes on this morning with the Abrazo Ceremony. Two American children from Laredo, dressed in colonial-era costumes, walk across the international bridge beneath a military-style canopy of salutes, swords, and flags; halfway across, they embrace two children from Nuevo Laredo who wear the Mexican equivalent of period dress. Dignitaries, patrons, and politicians from both countries align on their respective ends of the bridge, like a cross-border showdown of love.

A highly ranked U.S. federal official is in attendance. Gil Kerlikowske walks toward the makeshift stage in the middle of the bridge. Ruddy-nosed and square-jawed, with narrow eyes and thin lips that turn down at the corners, Kerlikowske looks like a caricature of officialdom, a Fred Willard–type comedian playing a serious bureaucrat. After a policing career in Florida, New York, and Washington State, he accepted Barack Obama's request, in 2009, to become the director of the Office of National Drug Control Policy. As drug czar, Kerlikowske fought the legalization movement, argued that marijuana was dangerous, and that Nancy Reagan's "Just Say No" campaign was one of the great successes of the war on drugs. In 2014, the U.S. Senate confirmed Kerlikowske as commissioner of U.S. Customs and Border Protection, the second-highest revenue-earning agency in the country behind the IRS.

Kerlikowske hasn't been to the Abrazo Ceremony since 2000, when air force jets blessed the event with a flyover. Walking toward the stage, he laments that the jets have been replaced with buzzing drones that will film this year's hug from on high. In his keynote address, he says the goodwill exchanged between the sister cities of Laredo and Nuevo Laredo reinforces a strong bond, rich with patriotism. He calls the two-thousand-mile border between Mexico and America the greatest international neighborhood in the world.

The children hug.

As they retreat, a volley of gunfire in Nuevo Laredo's middle distance shatters the ceremonial silence. On the bridge, the disturbance is largely ignored. The reverence of spectators tightens. Robert Garcia, one of several hundred law enforcement employees making overtime to cover the event, smothers a smile.

These days, Robert drives around in a red Chevy Avalanche, a blue Suburban, a silver BMW—"seizure cars," originally acquired by drug dealers. Not discreet. But they send the right message.

It's been a decade since Operation Prophecy, and Robert has

parted with the photos of Gabriel Cardona that long adorned his office. His own boys turned out all right. Trey is an army gunner who defuses bombs in the Middle East. Eric is one of the top Harley-Davidson mechanics in the Rio Grande Valley.

Robert speaks at conferences around the country, explaining to law enforcement colleagues what he's gotten from his intelligence gathering and what's being done at the border to combat the cartels. For years he believed that the information gleaned from watching the kids in the safe house mattered. "We got to see how these guys operate in their environment," he would say ambiguously, but then at some point he stopped believing it. He hopes the Treviño brothers will be extradited so they can make deals with Angel Moreno, or someone like him. They'll give up information about long-established smuggling routes, and variations on familiar corruption.

"We must like the cartels," he now says. "We must in some way want them, or need them. It's crazy. It's like we need the evil to determine the good. The yin and the yang."

In Robert's world, it's sometimes hard to tell the difference. In 2007, his former boss, Laredo police chief Agustin Dovalina, pleaded guilty to federal corruption charges related to the kickbacks he took from the Mexican Mafia in return for looking the other way on the gang's money-laundering activities at its slot casinos. Indicted with Dovalina were the cops who brought him the kickback scheme: the lieutenant from the stolen-property division; and the sergeant from narcotics—a cop who lived on Lincoln Street, a block away from the Cardonas.

In 2008, Robert attended the National Forensic Academy in Nashville, Tennessee, known as the Body Farm. For ten weeks he studied chemicals, photography, bombs, and the art of restoring serial numbers. When he returned to Laredo he taught his own crime-scene processing curriculum at the police academy, but discovered he hated teaching. He didn't have the patience to sit back and let students make their own mistakes. In 2012, after eight years in homicide, he requested a transfer. The cartel had returned to its old ways, hiring more seasoned gangsters in Laredo to carry out executions. But overall, there was a lull in murders, and Robert got bored with the mom-and-pop killings, where wife kills husband and there's no investigation to put together. When he started using the phrase "good murders" to describe desirable cases, he figured it was time to quit.

Now, after twenty-five years, he feels done with Laredo. Too hot, not green enough. All he knows is cops, crooks, and lawyers. He has $25,000 left to pay off on the house, plus payments on the new SUV for his parents, and the college funds for three grandchildren. On the side, he makes $800 per day for speaking appearances, and $40 an hour handling nighttime security at construction sites. On Saturday nights, from midnight to six, he sits in a car, reads books about astronomy, and does homework for online classes in criminology.

He rides the circuit as often as he can, driving 140 miles northwest along the border to see his parents in Eagle Pass, then north to Ronnie's parents, who moved from Arizona to Kerrville, Texas, where they bought eleven acres on rolling green hills. Despite considerable wealth accumulated in the bar business, they live modestly in a three-bedroom mobile. From the moment he steps out of the car in Kerrville to the moment he leaves, Robert fixes things, mows, and clears land for the retirement home he wants to build for him and Ronnie. Watching Robert absorb himself in labor, his father-in-law thinks that whatever he does for a living must be boring, or involve too much desk work. Where else would that energy come from?

As head of PD's intelligence unit, he pursues Laredo's largest drug-dealing family, the Melendez clan. They own a square block of houses in South Laredo—Saint Baby. Robert's break comes when the Melendez patriarch stiffs the carpenter who built custom fireplaces, outdoor bars, and stash compartments. Bereft, the carpenter decides to collect an informant's fee from Laredo PD instead. It isn't Operation Prophecy, but the Melendez case will put more hides on the wall for Angel Moreno. What does the case mean for Robert?

A Melendez son recently purchased a yellow Corvette.

"MY TWENTIES HAVE COME AND gone," Gabriel writes. "I pray every day for the people I've hurt and the lives I can never repair or return. I've had a lot of time to wonder about where my violent streak came from. Dr. Freud would surely identify some trauma in childhood from which I built up *coraje* that begged for release. But I feel no anger toward my parents, not even my father. I believe my parents are good people and I believe I am a good person. I speak as honestly as I can. I share with others and respect their opinions."

In Laredo, Christina works as a receptionist at a medical office and raises her girl, the daughter she had with an old boyfriend who is also now in prison. Gabriel makes a Valentine's Day card for Christina's daughter: "Be good little princess and always listen to your mother." Christina's brother urges her to throw away Gabriel's letters. Since Gabriel prayed to Santa Muerte, her brother says, demons lurk in the drawer where she keeps the letters. The letters, he says, are why her life isn't going so great.

Life in Lazteca remains unchanged. La Gaby is caught bringing $25,000 in illegal proceeds to Mexico. Her third husband is sentenced to a year in prison for smuggling a ton of marijuana. Her brother, Uncle Raul, succumbs to fate; when his nephew's name no longer ensures impunity, Raul is killed by the Zetas during a barroom spat in Boystown.

Luis, nearing the end of that associate's degree, says he plans to apply for college in San Antonio, until he breaks parole by crossing into Mexico to see a young woman for whom he's fallen. He pays for her to be smuggled across, but by the time she arrives in Laredo, pregnant with Luis's third child, Luis is back inside for six months on the parole violation and looking at a possible charge for conspiracy to distribute meth. If Luis gets career-offender status, he could be looking at heavy time.

Gabriel's younger brother narrowly avoids a felony murder charge after driving to a home invasion that ends with his own guy dead. Police expect him to go missing eventually. At twenty-four he'll leave six children born to three women.

That all of this is standard for the hood doesn't make it easier for Gabriel to watch: the disintegration of the family for whom he took so much pride in providing.

But the most painful piece is perhaps also the most predictable: Uncle Raul's only child, Raulito, the sweet-faced boy whom Gabriel knew only as an infant. Raulito is now ten and lives with his grandmother in San Antonio. She wants him to be successful. But he talks about bazookas, guns, killing people. He doesn't get straightened in school. He kicks the teachers. He kicked a little girl. School administrators placed him in a room alone until his grandmother came to get him. But he wouldn't go with her. So the police handcuffed him and took him home. Gabriel wonders: What will become of Raulito?

They take the boy to see a shrink. *Well, gee. How do you think Raulito's mind is functioning right now?* The boy knows his dad is gone. Knows his mom left. He writes his mom letters. They go unanswered. He talks to the whore only when she calls to ask for money from the grandmother. *Do you think Raulito feels rejected?*

In prison, Gabriel reads history, mythology, psychology. His knowledge of the world expands. Study sharpens his mind while isolation dulls his senses. In some ways he grows. The arrogant boy becomes self-aware, pokes fun at his own pretensions, jokes about having been used by Miguel and the Company. He translates entire

Mexican books into English, sending them off chapter by chapter to the Jewish journalist—"Slaterooni," or "Slaquiao"—who wants to know everything, whom Gabriel addresses as "Daniel" when he has a serious point to make, scolds for having "bad habits" when the journalist does airhead things like send letters without confirming receipt of Gabriel's previous letter.

He also studies law, and mails filings to government offices. He works hard at it. But there are gaps in his understanding. "There wasn't even a restraint," he argues regarding the aggravated kidnapping of Bruno Orozco. "The acts occurred in broad daylight. A struggle took place. The victim refused to get restrained. His death was his restraint."

Gabriel's prison sentences are unfair, he believes. If, as the judge said, the G-man has no remorse, then why, knowing he's going to spend the rest of his life in prison—a place full of envy, anger, frustration, oppression, and selfishness—would he take Bible study classes? The Bible gives peace, makes you a better man. The Bible changes people. It teaches you to love others. It teaches you the history of how the world was before, and how it was after. It's a wisdom book. *He don't need to bow down to no bitch-ass judge to get forgiveness from God.*

But if you don't believe he's changed, just ask Mr. Tenorio, the counselor in the Laredo federal prison that housed Gabriel in the aftermath of Orange Blossom. Tenorio walked by their tank every day, took Gabriel to his office. They had great conversations. Tenorio said he didn't believe Gabriel deserved life. Gabriel is reminded of Tenorio when he reads *The Lucifer Effect* . . . circumstances, conformity, blind obedience to authority. A boy became his environment. *He got placed in Lara Academy, which was full of shit. No options. No means to get money. Slang and bang.* Put any kid in that environment. Give him a couple nicks and dimes to sell. He loves the easy money.

Give him a gun to protect himself. He wants to feel the rush of firing it. Get him shot. He retaliates. And when he's immersed in that world, where he's done it once, he wants to advance in responsibility and power.

"Out there I wore the clown gown of poverty," Gabriel writes, "wasting $2,000 a week on fashion alone. I was the aggressive guy who'd get the job done *a todo a costa*. Only retrospectively do I see the insecure kid. Back then I thought of myself as a businessman. I could justify any act considered normal within that business. It's a culture of men who lack self-restraint, and who let little things that affect their pride get in the way of a calm life."

One thing he does *not* want is glorification—to give youngsters the sense that what happened with the Wolf Boys is cool. He hears about these school shootings. The copycat shit that happens when the criminal world gets sensationalized. If anything, he wants youngsters to see how stupid it is to try to fit in, to try to be someone you're not. *A fucking follower. A gangster wannabe.* It's not a good life. It's not worth it. You let a lot of people down, people who look up to you. He personally let a lot of people down. His football team. His classmates. His beloved grandfather, who, on his deathbed, told Gabriel and Luis to tuck in their shirts, keep going straight, and always listen to their mother. In the months after their grandfather passed, Luis did straighten out. He made it to senior year and only needed two credits to graduate when Gabriel and the Lazteca homies pulled him back in and he dropped out.

Of all things, Gabriel is broken because of his little cousin Raulito. Their grandmother takes Raulito to see Gabriel. Raulito asks why Gabriel is in prison. Gabriel says he misbehaved at school. Raulito smiles. "I already know about everything from the Internet."

Dinner comes at three. He listens to the radio. ESPN. Fox. *Dateline. Marshal Law: Texas.*

The showers don't come on until nine, which is late for him.

So he hangs his white jumper over the door and turns on the sink. He puts a plastic pen tube under the faucet, kneels next to the sink, and redirects water to the side. He scrubs down, then lets his body air-dry as he pushes the water toward the drain. He stays kneeling—frozen in time but hoping to evolve beyond what he's been—and begs for forgiveness.

EDITOR . . . . . . Ben Loehnen

PUBLISHER . . . . . . Jon Karp

AGENT . . . . . . Farley Chase

SPANISH EDITOR . . . . . . Sam Slick

A NOTE ON SOURCES

I based *Wolf Boys* on interviews, letters, law enforcement reports, and trial testimony. But for context and history I relied heavily on the work of others.

Smuggler Nation: How Illicit Trade Made America (2013), by Brown University's Peter Andreas, is a landmark. Andreas writes: "Political appeals to 'regain control' of the nation's borders are afflicted by an extreme case of historical amnesia, nostalgically implying there was once a time when our borders were actually 'under control.' This is pure myth; there never was a golden age of secure borders." *Smuggler Nation* helped me understand the scope of the book I was writing, and served as a gateway to other important books, such as William E. Unrau's *White Man's Wicked Water: The Alcohol Trade and Prohibition in Indian Country, 1802–1892* (1996), and John J. Adams Jr.'s *Conflict and Commerce on the Rio Grande: Laredo, 1755–1955* (2008). Andreas's first book, *Border Games:*

A NOTE ON SOURCES

Policing the U.S.-Mexico Divide (2009), helped me put Robert Garcia's DEA experience in context.

For Mexico's democratic transition, the impact of NAFTA, and the infamous oligarch banquet of 1993 (described in Chapter 8), I couldn't have asked for a better guide than Andrés Oppenheimer's *Bordering on Chaos: Guerrillas, Stockbrokers, Politicians, and Mexico's Road to Prosperity* (1996). The Harvard PhD dissertation by Viridiana Rios Contreras, "How Government Structure Encourages Criminal Violence: The Causes of Mexico's Drug War" (2012), drew a convincing link between political liberalization and underworld expansion.

What I know of the early Mexican drug trade comes largely from Elaine Shannon's *Desperados: Latin Drug Lords, U.S. Lawmen, and the War America Can't Win* (1988), and Terrence Poppa's *Drug Lord: The Life and Death of a Mexican Kingpin* (1990). Were it not for a fleeting mention, on page 92 of George T. Díaz's *Border Contraband: A History of Smuggling Across the Rio Grande* (2015), I never would've discovered Colonel Esteban Cantú, the first Mexican vice lord, nor the journal articles detailing Cantú's reign over Mexicali: James A. Sandos's "Northern Separatism During the Mexican Revolution: An Inquiry into the Role of Drug Trafficking, 1919–1920," *Americas* 41, no. 2 (October 1984); and Eric Michael Schantz's "All Night at the Owl: The Social and Political Relations of Mexicali's Red-Light District, 1913–1925," *Journal of the Southwest* 43, no. 1 (Winter 2001). As far as rabbit holes go, the Cantú research sent me down a great one.

"Yes, I would say Cantú is the first vice lord," Díaz confirmed in an email to me. "The only earlier parallel I can think of is Santiago Vidaurri, who aided the Confederate cotton trade. Still, Vidaurri was nothing like Cantú, who profited from opium, gambling, and prostitution."

My section epigraphs, all drawn from Inga Clendinnen's *Aztecs* (1991), suggest the indispensability of that book. A Meso-American historian of equal stature is T. R. Fehrenbach; I regularly consulted the second edition of Fehrenbach's Mexico history, *Fire & Blood* (1995).

Elijah Wald's *Narcocorrido: A Journey into the Music of Drugs, Guns, and Guerrillas* (2001) is a singular work. For an update on the *narcocorrido,* I turned to Shaul Schwarz's documentary, *Narco Cultura* (2013).

The short life of Tupac Shakur inspired many books; Randall Sullivan's *LAbyrinth* (2002), the book Gabriel read in county, offers the most clearheaded and nonpoliticized account of Tupac's life, and posits the most likely version of what happened on that Las Vegas evening in 1996.

Concerning hip-hop idols, it was interesting to compare Gabriel's idealized impression of Carlos Coy, aka South Park Mexican, to the brazen pedophile profiled in John Nova Lomax's 2002 article for the *Houston Press,* "South Park Monster."

I've worked for a university, a literary agency, a law firm, a TV production company, magazines, newspapers, restaurants, a ranch, and a can-recycling company. In addition to my vast—and vastly unsuccessful—personal experience with office politics, Robert Jackall's masterpiece of corporate sociology, *Moral Mazes: The World of Corporate Managers* (1988), helped me articulate the social environment of the Company that Gabriel and other Wolf Boys described.

I am indebted to the staffs of the *Laredo Morning Times* and the *San Antonio Express-News,* as well as to the journalists whose reporting about the Wolf Boys—as well as about Chapo, La Barbie, and the cartels—provided loads of insight and factoids: Julián Aguilar, Randal C. Archibold, Malcolm Beith, Charles Bowden, Jason Buch, Damien Cave, Mary Cuddehe, Samuel Dillon, Luke Dittrich, William Finnegan, George Grayson, Vanessa Grigoriadis, Ioan Grillo, Anabel Hernández, Jesse Hyde, Marc Lacey, Samuel Logan, Patrick Radden Keefe, Elisabeth Malkin, James C. McKinley Jr., Julia

A NOTE ON SOURCES

Preston, Ricardo Ravelo, Sebastian Rotella, Ginger Thompson, and Ed Vuillamy. In *The Beast: Riding the Rails and Dodging Narcos on the Migrant Trail* (2014), Óscar Martínez took me on a ride-along through what the Zetas eventually became: roving tyrants.

In his pitch-black memoir—*Midnight in Mexico: A Reporter's Journey Through a Country's Descent into Darkness* (2013)—the swashbuckling Alfredo Corchado reports the agreement between the Zetas and *El Mañana* and chronicles his own role in publishing "The Barbie Execution Video" (2005). I make specific reference to Corchado's interview with the "drug czar" and prosecutor alleged in the video to have taken money from the Company. "Why don't you focus on tourism stories?" the prosecutor asked. "They're safer." I salute Corchado—sad grandstander though he may be—for declining to follow the prosecutor's instruction.

I owe this book to the people of Laredo, so many of whom I met during my seven trips to the city. As a reporter, I am often paranoid by the sense my presence gives, that of a person who is way too eager to spin your life into a story for his own profit. I kept expecting someone to say, loud enough for me to hear, *What kind of asshole just hangs around asking all these questions about our lives?* I couldn't have been more wrong, of course. It's easy to make friends in Laredo, and I made many. The people are open and gracious, a warm bunch, on the south side and the north.